Studies in Economic Reform and Social Justice

Social Provisioning, Embeddedness, and Modeling the Economy

Edited by
Frederic S. Lee

WILEY-BLACKWELL

Studies in Economic Reform and Social Justice

Social Provisioning, Embeddedness, and Modeling the Economy

Edited by

Frederic S. Lee

WILEY-BLACKWELL

This edition first published 2011

Registered Office
John Wiley & Sons Ltd, The Atrium, Southern Gate, Chichester, West Sussex, PO19 8SQ, United Kingdom

Editorial Offices
350 Main Street, Malden, MA 02148-5020, USA
9600 Garsington Road, Oxford, OX4 2DQ, UK
The Atrium, Southern Gate, Chichester, West Sussex, PO19 8SQ, UK

For details of our global editorial offices, for customer services, and for information about how to apply for permission to reuse the copyright material in this book, please see our website at www.wiley.com/wiley-blackwell.

Library of Congress Cataloging-in-Publication Data

Social provisioning, embeddedness, and modeling the economy / Frederic S. Lee, editor-in-chief.
p. cm.
Originally published as v. 70, no. 5 (Nov. 2011) of: The American journal of economics and sociology.
ISBN 978-1-118-24519-4 (casebound)—ISBN 978-1-118-24520-0 (pbk.)
1. Economics. 2. Economics—Sociological aspects. I. Lee, Frederic S., 1949– II. American journal of economics and sociology.
HB171.S677 2011
330—dc23

2011041672

A catalogue record for this book is available from the Library of Congress.

Set in 10 on 13pt Garamond Light by Toppan Best-set Premedia Limited
Printed in Singapore by Markono Print Media Pte Ltd.

01—2011

Contents

Editor's Introduction

By FREDERIC S. LEE*

While economics is a social science, it often gets presented in textbooks as a science with little connection to the social. Moreover, models, arguments, and agents are articulated by mainstream and heterodox economists alike that are exemplars of non-social theorizing about what are clearly social activities. Hence, it is not any wonder that there exists the long running social embeddedness debate that permeates the interstices between economics and sociology, that is, economic sociology. There is, however, work done by economists that does bring the social into economic theorizing; but it is done by adopting a different view of economics as explaining the social provisioning process. That is, the conventional economists' view of economics is one of the allocation of scarce resources among competing ends given unlimited wants of individuals that are in themselves asocial; and the objective of the individuals is to increase their own self-centered utility. From this perspective, the economic activities that are engaged in to achieve an increase in utility lie outside society or are at least not embedded in social relationships that affect the self-centered utility objective of the individual. On the other hand, economics defined in terms of the social provisioning process is concerned with explaining and with proposing and advocating changes in the historical process of producing the social surplus that provides the flow of goods and services required by society to meet the reoccurring needs and promote the well-being of those who participate in its activities. So to do work from this perspective means doing social (as opposed to asocial) economics utilizing a theoretical framework in which the economy and its various activities are theoretically conceived and modeled in a way that they are socially enveloped.

*University of Missouri–Kansas City, Department of Economics, 211 Haag Hall, University of Missouri–Kansas City, 5100 Rockhill Road, Kansas City, Missouri 64110, United States, E-mail: eefs@umkc.edu

American Journal of Economics and Sociology, Vol. 70, No. 5 (November, 2011).

Economists working from the social provisioning perspective have examined what social provisioning means, discussed the relevance of the social embeddedness of economic activity for economics, and articulated different ways to examine and model the economy as a whole such as the social surplus approach, social fabric matrix approach (SFM-A), input-output modeling, social accounting matrix (SAM), social structures of accumulation, system dynamics, and stock-flow consistent modeling. However, they have done their work largely independent of each other, resulting in an underdeveloped socially-encased model of the economy as a whole; and without a better framework qua model of the social economy, further developments in the social provisioning perspective are uncertain. This concern prompted me to hold an *AJES*-sponsored workshop at the University of Missouri–Kansas City on 24–26 September 2010 to deal with the themes of social provisioning, embeddedness, and modeling the economy as a whole in an integrative fashion. The charge to the participants was to present papers that engaged with one or more of the themes and take on board the comments made at the workshop—that is, the point of the workshop was to bring scholars together and learn from each other. Twelve papers were presented at the workshop, of which eight are included in this issue of the *AJES.*

Tae-Hee Jo begins the issue with a first-of-its-kind discussion of what the social provisioning process means and its implications for modeling the economy. In particular, he finds that it resonates very well with various approaches in heterodox economics and that it is compatible to a greater or lesser extent with different kinds of socio-economic modeling: the social surplus approach, SFM-A, and systems dynamics. The next three articles by Scott Carter, Gary Mongiovi, and Erik Olsen deal with the social surplus approach. Scott starts with a discussion of what the social surplus means (such as whether it includes wage goods or not), tracing its development from the Physiocrates and Quesney to Marx and finally to Sraffa. The historical excursion ends with the decided conclusion that the social surplus includes wage goods. With this in hand, he proceeds to develop a social surplus model to examine income distribution and economic growth. The conclusion Scott reaches from this exercise is that the social surplus approach is robust in that it allows for two conceptions of causality to "close" the system based on equating wages and profits with the production of the social surplus—the one from the income (wages and profits) side deals with the determination of prices and distribution of income, and the keep from the quantity side (social surplus qua effective demand) deals with the determination of output or the total social product. Gary begins his article with a historical discussion of the concept of social provisioning as used by classical and neoclassical economists and then articulates a surplus model along classical-Keynesian lines. In particular, he delineates a dual price-output Sraffa-Leontief-type model, but focuses on the quantity side. The fundamental property of the quantity model is that the decisions driving the social surplus (which consists of consumption and investment goods) drives total output and employment. Gary proceeds to develop interesting arguments about what determines consumption and investment demand in light of the fact that it cannot be in any systematic, deterministic manner related to prices, interest rates, and the rate of profit. Finally, in his article, Erik introduces SAM into the social surplus approach from a Marxian perspective. That is, the social surplus is the same as the final demand in national income and product accounts (NIPA). However, because the calculation of final demand and the incomes to purchase it does not take into account the Marxian notions of unproductive and productive labor, the NIPA does not represent the surplus, wages, and profits that are consistent with Marxian theory. What Erik does is use SAM to develop an algorithm that transforms NIPA into its Marxian counterparts. Once in place, it is possible to use Marxian theory to explain the production and distribution of the social surplus in capitalist economies.

What is missing from the previous three articles is historical contextualization (beyond just capitalism) and clear lines that connect cultural values, norms, and societal institutions to the decisions by the state, business enterprises, and households that drive the price-output models and through them the provisioning process. Greg Hayden deals with the latter omission with his social fabric matrix approach. He delineates how SFM-A connects the social as well as the technological and ecological to decisions affecting production, distribution, and eventually social provisioning. Greg goes further and argues quite at length that much is to be gained from integrating SFM-A with the SAM approach. However, he admits that SFM-A is too general because it is too under-historically contextualized. This is where Terry McDonough and his article on the social structures of accumulation step in. He argues that capitalism is not a historically unchanging entity, but varies over time—that is, there are stages to capitalism. Thus, the social structures of accumulation approach provide the historical context for the social fabric, which in turn affects production and social provisioning. This of course means that the provisioning process is a historically changing process that cannot be adequately understood via ahistorical analysis and modeling.

To anyone familiar with the SFM-A, input-output modeling, and SAM, their integrative compatibility seems obvious as well as their application to real world issues. Andrew Trigg and Jonquil Lowe illustrate the applied theme with an analysis of defined-benefits and defined-contributions pensions using a circular flow of income model. The foundations of the model include circular production with a surplus, financial structure of the economy, and a social accounting matrix. Thus, their future research will involve modeling the social provisioning of pensions using a social accounting approach.

The final article of the issue is the editor's attempt to bring the different workshop themes together. Starting from the position that economics is about explaining the social provisioning process, the objective of the article is to model the economy as a whole in a way that it is socially encased, enveloped. That is, the model of the provisioning process is bracketed at one end by cultural values, norms, and societal institutions and at the other end by household social activities and government services. Thus, the beginning and end point of social provisioning is encased by the SFM-A historically contextualized by the stages of capitalism drawn from the social structures of accumulation approach. The model of the provisioning process itself is an integration of the social surplus approach, input-output and stock-flow consistent modeling, and SAM with a structure-agency methodology.

The message of the workshop and the articles in this issue of the *AJES* is that the fruitful study of the social provisioning process requires a particular conceptualization or model of the economy as a whole. This has two implications. First, using macroeconomic models in which there is a single asocial representative agent, no produced means of production, and no state and state money, for example, for economic analysis and policy recommendations concerning social provisioning is something akin to academic dishonesty, since such models have no real world, theoretical sensibility. Without it, the models are not any different from social disinformation myths that are promulgated to defend the status quo. Secondly, modeling is important, and it is important to construct the right kind of models. But this requires the use of mathematical equations and symbols, representable matrices, and complex graphs and diagrams. Hence many of the articles in this issue have many equations (and quasi-equations) and thus embrace a degree of mathematical formalism (that is empirically grounded). The aim of this issue of the *AJES* is to develop the right kind of model of the economy as a whole utilizing the right degree of formalism; and being the right kind of model, it is also the only kind that can be used to study the social provisioning process. A bold conclusion for a bold issue of the *AJES*.

FSL

Social Provisioning Process and Socio-Economic Modeling

By TAE-HEE JO*

ABSTRACT. The radical difference between orthodox and heterodox economics emanates from the different views of the capitalist socio-economic system. Economics as the science of social provisioning felicitously describes the heterodox view that the economy is part of the evolving social order; social agency is embedded in the social and cultural context; a socio-economic change is driven by technical and cultural changes; and the provisioning process is open-ended. Such a perspective on the economy offers ample methodological and theoretical implications for modeling the capitalist economy in a realistic manner. It lends itself especially to the micro-macro synthetic approach. Thus the objective of this article is twofold: 1) to examine how the concept of the social provisioning process can be clarified and expanded by virtue of recent development in heterodox methodology and 2) to discuss how methodological development would nourish the heterodox modeling and theorizing of the capitalist social provisioning process.

Introduction

Ever-changing society is never stable because of conscious actions and interactions of social agency. A historical change in socio-economic structures is unpredictable but is always controlled by the dominant social agency of the time. Capitalist markets are formed and governed by social agency being vested with social-economic-political power. The vested interests are protected in the process of the provisioning of goods and services. To do so, resources are made

*Tae-Hee Jo is Assistant Professor in the Economics and Finance Department at SUNY Buffalo State College, 1300 Elmwood Ave., Buffalo, New York 14222, USA. Email: taeheejo@gmail.com. He is also Co-Editor of the *Heterodox Economics Newsletter*. The author is grateful to John F. Henry, Frederic S. Lee, and two anonymous referees for most helpful comments and suggestions.

American Journal of Economics and Sociology, Vol. 70, No. 5 (November, 2011).

available by the command of the dominant agency. While consumption is dependent upon those who make production decisions, production is dependent upon the expectation of profits. The provisioning of goods and services is thus a social process rather than an isolated rational decision-making process. Such a story is not told or adequately theorized by neoclassical economists who rely exclusively on the isolated optimizing behavior given scarce means. No institution in its broadest sense presents itself in neoclassical economics. Nor do embedded individuals and embedded economy.

The significance of the view that economics is the study of the social provisioning process lies in its relevance to the account of ever-evolving economy. With the social provisioning process as a method of inquiry into social reality, a theory assisted by an adequate model would provide deeper understanding of how provisioning of goods and services of a society is organized in accordance with existing values and social structures—including, but not limited to, class, gender, culture, power, politics, and environment. It is also well acknowledged now by many heterodox economists that, given the contested disciplinary landscape, the concept of social provisioning is a useful guidepost for the development of heterodox economics. Institutionalists, Post Keynesians, Marxians, social economists, feminists, ecological economists, among others, have made valuable contributions to the advancement of heterodox economics with the view of the social provisioning process (Gruchy 1987; Stevenson 1987; Dugger 1996; Lee 2008; Lawson 2003, 2006; Davis 2006; Power 2004).[1]

An important implication follows. The concept of social provisioning offers a way to promote much-needed cross-communication of ideas within various heterodox economics traditions as well as with other like-minded social scientists who are free of neoclassical values and methods. This can be the case since the social provisioning perspective is a worldview, as described in the opening paragraph and further detailed below, that reflects the concern of the historical development of human beings and society. In other words, the social provisioning perspective is the social ontology that looks into the foundations of socio-economic evolution.

The objective of this article is to conceptually elaborate the social provisioning process with close reference to the core principles common to various heterodox economic traditions. This effort will render heterodox modeling distinctive from and alternative to orthodox-neoclassical modeling. To this end, this article is organized in the following order. The second section discusses the meaning of the social provisioning process and finds implications for modeling the socio-economic system. In the following section, selected heterodox models—the social fabric matrix, system dynamics, and the social surplus approach—are compared and contrasted from a social provisioning perspective. The final section concludes the article.

Social Provisioning Process

Conceptualizing the Social Provisioning Process

Almost all economists, either heterodox or otherwise, believe that they are explaining the real world. But it is well known that the level of inquiry and the way of making a theory are radically dissimilar. Orthodox economics of our time is primarily concerned with building a model qua theory based upon axiomatic assumptions such as scarce resources, hedonistic-rational *homo economicus*, the isolated decision-making process, and disembedded economy. A good model is then expected to yield a higher degree of predictability by ascertaining the empirical regularity between quantitative variables. A century-old tradition of model construction in a formal-mathematical fashion has led orthodox economics to the high state that only trained economists fully understand what the model explains. The reality is obscured rather than explained; or it is the manufactured reality that is explained by refined models.

Take an evolutionary game model as an example. It is designed to address a strategic decision-making process by incorporating bounded rationality, mutative behavior, path-dependence, and the interactive influence between agents over time. These are not considered in the static game model (McKenzie 2009). With the help of the development in computational technology like simulation, it becomes easier to show the complex evolutionary process that leads to an evolutionary stationary solution. But still fundamental problems of a game model remain untouched. One of the critical problems is that the initial model setting can be manufactured so as to obtain a particular outcome. In addition, an evolutionary game model does not question how a set of agents' strategies, a payoff function, and the rule of the game are constructed and changing because it begins with the "elimination of society, relationships therein, and historical movements thereof" (Henry 2009). Consequently, the model world is too limited to explain the changes in real history and thereby the "evolutionary approach loses all its analytical power the moment it allows humans to do what they have been doing throughout history" (Varoufakis 2008: 87).

On the contrary, heterodox economists have not been bothered much by the mathematical model. In its place, the emphasis is put on social reality (of the model). It is the quantitative rigor that is to be sacrificed, if either the rigor or the reality is to be chosen. This is due largely to the fact that the reality that heterodox economists—Post Keynesians, Marxians, and Institutionalists, in particular—perceive is much deeper than what orthodoxy does. That is, social reality is layered and open. The structure of society is open in historical time because of conscious social agency and the persistent causal mechanisms that are not always observable. For the sake of explaining ever-changing society, therefore, both "intensive" (causal-substantive) and "extensive" (positive-empirical) investigations are required. Such a methodological position further implies that social transformation (or elaboration at a lesser degree) can be made not through the manipulation of empirical variables but through the changes in structures driven by agency (Polanyi 1968; Archer 1995: ch. 10; Danermark et al. 1997: 10, 165; Park 2001; Dow 2005: 388).

We find such a realistic reasoning in a variety of heterodox traditions. Consider Marx:

> In the social production of their existence, men inevitably enter into definite relations, which are independent of their will, namely relations of production appropriate to a given state of the development of their material forces of production. The totality of these relations of production constitutes the economic structure of society, the real foundation, on which arises a legal and political superstructure and to which correspond definite forms of social consciousness. The mode of production of material life conditions the general process of social, political and intellectual life. (Marx 1970: 20–21)

Consider now Veblen:

> The economic life history of any community is its life history in so far as it is shaped by men's interest in the material means of life. This economic interest has counted for much in shaping the cultural growth of all communities. Primarily and most obviously, it has guided the formation, the cumulative growth, of that range of conventionalities and methods of life that are currently recognized as economic institutions; but the same interest has also pervaded the community's life and its cultural growth at points where the resulting structural features are not chiefly and most immediately of an economic bearing. The economic interest goes with men through life, and it goes with the race throughout its process of cultural development. It affects the cultural structure at all points, so that all institutions may be said to be in some measure economic institutions. (Veblen 1961: 76–77)

Therefore, the complex and evolving social reality requires that

> [h]e [an "ideal" political economist] must reach a high standard in several different directions and must combine talents not often found together. He must be mathematician, historian, statesman, philosopher—to some degree. He must understand symbols and speak in words. He must contemplate the particular in terms of the general, and touch abstract and concrete in the same flight of thought. He must study the present in the light of the past for the purpose of the future. No part of man's nature or his institutions must lie outside his regard. He must be purposeful and disinterested in a simultaneous mood; as aloof and incorruptible as an artist, yet sometimes as near the earth as a politician. (Keynes 1972: 173–174).

Despite the well-known theoretical differences between Marx, Veblen, and Keynes, there is a common theme that unites these "worldly philosophers" and that sharply distinguishes heterodox economics from orthodox economics. They offer causal explanations of the social provisioning process. This is in radical contrast to the currently dominant orthodox view that "Economics is the science which studies human behavior as a relationship between ends and scarce means which have alternative uses" (Robbins 1932: 15).[2]

Then what do we mean by the social provisioning process? In brief (further discussion follows below), it means that all the economic activities are occurring in a social context—cultural values, class/power relations, norms, ideologies, and ecological system. With this theme, a serious inquiry into economic matters requires the deeper understanding and thicker explanations of the foundations of society. Marx, for example, explains how the capitalist mode of production controlled by a minority ruling class gives rise to social ills (alienation and exploitation), disorder (crisis), and irrationality (commodity-money fetishism). Veblen intensively explicates how a social evolution is conditioned by underlying dichotomous forces—business principles and social principles—and how the ruling class maintains its vested interests. Keynes furthers these ideas by advancing the theory of monetary production and the principle of effective demand to the extent that the production of surplus goods and services as a material basis of society is determined by the demand decisions made by the business enterprises and the capitalist state (Henry 2009, 2011; Howard and King 1992: ch. 5; Bortis 1997: ch. 3; Lee and Jo 2011).

It was Allan Gruchy who popularized the concept of the social provisioning process. He defines that

> economics is the study of the on-going economic process that provides the flow of goods and services required by society to meet the needs of those who participate in its activities . . . [Economics is] the science of social provisioning. (Gruchy 1987: 21)

Gruchy (1987: 21–23) continues that the social provisioning process is cultural, historical, technological, open and thereby economics is to be interdisciplinary and pluralistic so as to explain potential material abundance as a basis of social progress. That is, as many heterodox economists have long recognized, human society is organized by both market and non-market activities; economic activities take place, and thus have meanings, in a social context. Polanyi (1968) addresses this point very clearly.

> [The economy is] an instituted process of interaction between man and his environment, which results in a continuous supply of want-satisfying material means . . . The human economy, then, is embedded and enmeshed in institutions, economic and noneconomic. The inclusion of the noneconomic is vital. For religion or government may be as important for the structure and functioning of the economy as monetary institutions or the availability of tools and machines themselves that lighten the toil of labor. (Polanyi 1968: 145, 148)

Therefore, as Veblen maintains, both "speculative" (mathematical) and "scientific" (causal analysis) analyses are necessary. The former is a logical exercise that is distant from real life experience (hence ceremonial and institutional), and the latter is workmanlike knowledge closely associated with material exigency (hence, technical and instrumental). Mathematical/statistical formulations reflect, continues Veblen, no more than observed "idle quantitative concomitance" of the reality, while cumulative causation "is a fact of imputation, not of observation, and so cannot be included in data" (Veblen 1961: 32–35).[3]

Not surprisingly many other heterodox economists find social provisioning germane to heterodox economics. For example,

> "Social provisioning" is a phrase that draws attention away from images of pecuniary pursuits and individual competition, and towards notions of sustenance, cooperation, and support. Rather than be naturalized or taken as given, capitalist institutions and dynamics become subjects to be examined and critiqued. (Power 2004: 6)

And Frederic Lee defines heterodox economics explicitly from the social provisioning perspective:

> [H]eterodox economists extend their theory to examining issues associated with the process of social provisioning, such as racism, gender and ideologies and myths. Because their economics involves issues of ethical values and social philosophy and the historical aspects of human existence, heterodox economists make ethically based economic policy recommendations to improve human dignity, that is, recommending ameliorative and/or radical, social and economic policies to improve the social provisioning and hence well-being for all members of society and especially the disadvantaged members. (Lee 2008: para. 7)

Implications for Modeling

Then one would ask: Why is the concept of the social provisioning process important for heterodox economics? We find that there are at least four implications that are relevant to the present purpose—that is, linking the social provisioning process and socio-economic modeling.

Firstly, heterodox economists can do away with impersonal market fundamentalism. Placing social provisioning at the center of an inquiry, one starts a study with a purview of the capitalist socio-economic system that includes social agency, socio-economic structures, and causal mechanisms. Then economic activities, both market and non-market activities, such as self-interested and cooperative behaviors, control and resistance, accumulation of capital, and provisioning of welfare can be explained in a comprehensive manner. That is, market provisioning is a subset of social provisioning (Dugger 1996; Power 2004). The material basis of social provisioning is the structure of production, technology, and natural environment, the social basis is socio-economic classes, and the cultural basis is the society-specific value system (including a set of norms and beliefs) (Hayden 1982; Stevenson 1987; Lee and Jo 2011). These bases qua structures are made open by social agents through causal mechanisms.

To illustrate this point, the production of surplus goods is determined by the capitalist agency given technical conditions (which determine the use of various inputs), its capitalist value (the business principle—efficiency and profitability rather than serviceability). In turn investment, employment, financing decisions follow. In the society where absentee ownership and its vested interests are dominant, the provisioning of goods is coordinated in favor of the vested interests of the capitalist agency. In another society where social cohesion and environmental concern are emphasized over the business principle, the production and distribution of surplus goods are coordinated following a different causal mechanism. Consequently, the social surplus consists of the goods and services determined by the values and forces that create the social activities that the provisioning process underwrites (Adams 1991; Clark 1992). Therefore, the social provisioning perspective, when it is dealt with carefully, enables us to understand the fundamentals of the socio-economic system and their consequences on human agency and the ecological system, while neoclassicism, as defined by Robbins (1932) does not allow one to go wider than market exchanges.[4]

Secondly, both methodological individualism and methodological holism become irrelevant to the explanation of the social provisioning process. In other words, rather than the pseudo-interaction between individuals and commodities (as in individualism and neoclassicism in general) or between structures (as in pure structuralism), it is the genuine interaction between social agency and structures that is to be understood and explained. In the course of such an interaction, there emerge institutions—for example, rules, values, norms, and conventions—that constitute and transform the structure of society. Therefore, the qualitative linkage "between the 'social' and 'systemic' " or "between 'action' and its 'environment' " is to be the primary subject of heterodox economics (Archer 1995: 11). And Veblen (1909: 629) makes this point clearly that the evolutionary process is the result of interactions between active social agency and evolving institutions.

Thirdly, it follows from the above discussion that the conventional micro-macro dichotomy is a limited analytical apparatus. The account of social provisioning requires heterodox microfoundations of macroeconomic outcomes that offer more than the fallacious neoclassical microfoundations. That is, heterodox microfoundations begin with the active human agency embedded in the social provisioning process. And the theoretical focus is the in-depth analysis of the historical or evolutionary process. As a result, real social agency and emergent institutions are taken into account as the driving force of social provisioning. That is to say, in the complex and open social provisioning process, the free transition between micro and macro—aggregation or disaggregation, in other words—is not possible (Jo 2007; Lee 2010).

Lastly, when it comes to the "capitalist" social provisioning process, the understanding of class, dominance, power, control, and regulation becomes important. Unlike the market provisioning process in which vendible goods and services are exchanged through the price mechanism, the analysis of social provisioning calls for explanations on how the social product is generated, how the social surplus is created, how agents gain access to and engagement in the social provisioning process, and how social institutions including market institutions are organized and controlled so as to ensure the class interests, the reproduction and stability of the capitalist system. Indeed, these issues have long been discussed by many heterodox economists. The social provisioning perspective would induce further development.

To summarize, heterodox economics distinguishes itself from orthodox economics by taking social provisioning as its methodological core. Consequently, with social provisioning a heterodox theory or model provides us with a more realistic and comprehensive account of the issue in hand. This is the starting point of the following section in which selected heterodox socio-economic models such as the social fabric matrix, system dynamics, and the social surplus approach are discussed from the social provisioning perspective.

Socio-Economic Modeling

Models in Heterodox Economics

Orthodox economists are nearly in total agreement on using formal models.[5] Heterodox economists are, however, divided in their position on formal models. Some argue that heterodox economists should make more use of formal methods such as game theoretic models and econometric tools with more realistic assumptions. They believe that developing heterodox theory in a formal manner would render heterodox economics more popular so that there will be productive scholarly communications between the heterodoxy and the orthodoxy (Colander 2003; Colander, Holt, and Rosser 2004; Radzicki 2003).

Many other heterodox economists are skeptical about developing heterodox theory in a formal way since the formal method is a fundamentally limited way of analyzing social reality that is historical, complex, and open (Baran and Sweezy 1965; Eaton 1965; Georgescu-Roegen 1979; Rima 1994; Sugden 2001; Lawson 2003; Varoufakis 2008). Perhaps the strongest rejection to mathematical formalism is explicated by Tony Lawson. He argues that neoclassical economics relying exclusively on the formalistic, deductive, closed-system method is destined to fail to grasp constantly changing, interconnected, and structured social reality. An overt example is the failure of neoclassical economics in the account, *ex ante* and *ex post*, of the financial crisis of 2008 (Lawson 2006, 2009).[6]

In short, it is clear in skeptics' view that the fundamental difference between orthodoxy and heterodoxy is the view of social reality that leads to distinctive theories and methods. From the heterodox point of view, society is peopled, structured, and organized so that the real world is more complex than the model world established by the best available mathematical tool. Indeed, the quantitative method is serviceable to the extent that it is properly used to capture *ex post* reality or demi-regularity (Lee 2002: 795–796; Lawson 2003: 105–106). Therefore, whether using analytical-historical narratives or quantitative models, what is important for conducting heterodox analysis is to provide causal explanations of the social provisioning process in which active human agency is fully operational. If a theory or a model is taken for granted without recourse to social reality, "then man is not a 'prime mover.' Rather, humans, and society as a whole, merely respond to extra-societal laws and forces over which they exert no control" (Henry 1986: 382).

Consequently, a constructive strategy for the development in heterodox economics would be to better explain the social provisioning process without losing social agency, emergent social institutions, underlying structures and cultures, and the instability and/or reproduction of the system as whole. To this end, various models can be utilized as a means of inquiry. That is to say, models are to be designed to provide "actual explanation" rather than "conceptual exploration" (Sugden 2002: 117).

As discussed in the following section, heterodox models are, more or less, built with the emphasis on actual-historical explanation. Examples of such models are the social fabric matrix, system dynamics, and the social surplus approach. A caveat is in order here. In this special issue of the *Journal*, a list of heterodox models, if not exhaustive, is investigated and integrated one way or another. Therefore, the present article does not mean to deal with all those heterodox models. Instead, three selected models are examined from the social provisioning perspective for the sake of finding constructive implications for developing heterodox models.

Social Fabric Matrix

The social fabric matrix (SFM, hereafter) is an Institutionalist analytical tool designed to "assist in describing the system and providing the data base for evaluation, planning, especially for a complex technological society" (Hayden 1982: 653). To this end, the socioeconomic system is divided into five fabrics—values, beliefs, institutions, technology, and environment—that are linked (in the sense of "delivering" to and "receiving" from one another) through three organizing principles—reciprocity, redistribution, and exchange. This is the general SFM framework and of course some components can be temporarily left mute when they do not play a significant role in the matrix of a society in question. For example, Hayden (2009b) illustrates the SFM of Nebraska state aid for a local K–12 public school system. In this case study, the defining components of SFM are social beliefs, authority institutions, and processing institutions. That is, SFM is flexible such that it can be built for different levels of inquiry.

As developed from the Institutionalist perspective (in particular, Thorstein Veblen, John Commons, Clarence Ayres, Karl Polanyi, and Allan Gruchy), SFM is firmly grounded in the process of social provisioning. This methodological ground makes SFM comprehensive and realistic to the extent that the real social domain as well as the economic domain are organically integrated into SFM. In particular, the input-output matrix and analytical techniques associated with it can be readily integrated into SFM. This fact further implies that economic activities are embedded in and interdependent with the surrounding social domain that is composed of institutions (including, but not limited to, rules),[7] culture (values and beliefs), environment, and technology.

Another notable advantage of SFM is its capacity to illustrate the inextricable linkage between the micro and the macro in the social provisioning process. As Hayden puts it:

> The matrix is meant to capture the characteristics of the parts, as well as the process of the whole. This is accomplished by a nonequilibrium, noncommon denominator process matrix . . . there is no final demand, absolute requirement, or end to the process. (Hayden 2009a: 645)

In a nutshell, a SFM (like an input-output table) is a structure that mirrors the correlations among various elements in a society. To explicate causal relations, the identification of social agency and causal mechanisms is of necessity. Once it is successfully done, the SFM become an open-system; it provides insightful causal explanations on how such a socio-economic system is organized, changing, and transformed by agency.

SFM is a realistic and sophisticated model in describing internal structures and complicated internal interrelationships (dependence and feedbacks) of the socio-economic system. But it is not without weakness and difficulty. One difficulty is that SFM can be a very large matrix, if it tends to be more comprehensible. A model builder's reasonable judgment call and justification is thus necessary to make a SFM manageable. Related to the point just made, one weakness can be addressed. How is the instability of the socio-economic system as a whole explained? Or how does a radical change in the system happen as we experience in the real history? To answer these questions concerned most by heterodox economists, the SFM requires incorporating dynamic aspects of socio-economic domains as well as causal explanations of interactions between agents—in particular, between those who are controlling the process of social provisioning and those who are ruled.

System Dynamics

Another heterodox model of interest from the author's point of view is system dynamics (SD, hereafter). This model shares many components and principles with other heterodox models, in particular with SFM. It is, however, argued here that SD is often inconsistent with the social provisioning perspective delineated above due mainly to some elements borrowed from orthodox economics.

According to Radizicki, "[s]ystem dynamics is a computer modeling technique originally developed by Jay W. Forrester . . . for the purpose of simulating socioeconomic systems in a realistic manner" (Radzicki 2010: 3). He points out the essential properties of SD:

> It is dynamic, disequilibrium approach to modeling complex systems that portrays human behavior and micro-level decision making as it actually is (bounded or procedural rational goal seeking) rather than it might be in an idealized state . . . The system dynamics modeling process is aimed at creating of a decision maker's mental model (consistent with any available numerical data or written information) so that it is made precise and its underlying assumptions are stated and open to inspection by others. In addition, since a system dynamics model can be simulated on a computer, the modeling process enables the dynamic behavior inherent in a decision maker's mental model to be accurately revealed. (Radzicki 2003: 138, 151)

A SD model is composed of three parts (or phases): a set of assumptions, descriptive relations (stocks, flows, feedbacks, and limiting factors), and simulations (projected changes over time). Consider a SD model of three firms competing for a greater market share (Radzicki 2003). It begins with a set of assumptions—three virtual manufacturing firms with equal initial market share, identical products, price competition, price change by increasing either quantity or efficiency. At the second phase of the model, the behavior of each firm is described by the changes in stocks of production and knowledge through the learning-by-doing process. The third phase is the simulation of the market share for each firm. Consequently, Radzicki finds the implications of the model as follows:

> What is clear from the simulations . . . is that the behavior of the model is emergent and path dependent. The time path each firm will take during any simulation run is not knowable from inspection of their microstructure, and the dominant firm can be different from run to run. The model does a nice job of illustrating the importance of efficient production, learning by doing, learning from rivals, and protecting proprietary production methods. (Radzicki 2003: 163–164)

Indeed, as far as the above SD model is concerned, it is useful to the extent that the model results correspond to the reality in question. And the model clearly manifests that both microstructure and the system as a whole are to be considered in order to fully understand the interdependent evolutionary process over time (Radzicki 2010: 6). The model results, however, are not novel. Strategic and path dependent decision-making process under uncertainty, importance of knowledge and legal institutions, and the like are well articulated by many heterodox economists. For the sake of constructive discussion, additional problems in the SD model can be pointed out.

Firstly, it may be necessary to tame the real world to find systematic causes and effects related to an issue in hand. However, assumptions made in the SD model are very unrealistic. It is hardly possible to represent actual business activities as in the above SD model. In other words, "system dynamics work is usually completed with made-up components, relationships, and data that are not based on real-world findings" (Hayden 2009a: 1062).

Secondly, the notion of (dis)equilibrium is problematic. SD requires the equilibrium state (and thereby the system be closed) at the initial stage in order to generate the dynamics of the system. Otherwise, it is hardly possible to find meaningful outcomes concerning a shock–responses–change process (Radzicki 2010: 20, fn 12). The genuine social provisioning process, however, has nothing to do with an equilibrium or disequilibrium (see Robinson 1980; Henry 1984–1985).[8]

Lastly, a good SD model is the one that "[makes] sure that the model's structure and behavior correspond as closely as possible to those of the real-world system experiencing the problem. As more tests are passed, more confidence is generated in the model's results" (Radzicki 2010: 7). This statement rings a bell. Robert Lucas, one of the leading neoclassical economists of our time, notes that:

> A "theory" is not a collection of assertions about the behavior of the actual economy but rather an explicit set of instructions for building a parallel or analogue system—a mechanical, imitation economy. A "good" model, from this point of view, will not be exactly more "real" than a poor one, but will provide better imitations. (Lucas 1980: 697)

At a more fundamental level, one may wonder how SD explains a qualitative or radical change in the system itself, and how the system behavior is different from agents' real behavior and from the real historical change. SD is limited in these respects that are essential for the causal explanation of the social provisioning process.

Social Surplus Approach

The social surplus approach has a long history. The social surplus as a net product (or final goods and services) was first conceptualized by François Quesnay's *tableau économique*. Classical political economists, especially Ricardo and Marx, articulated the production and distribution of the social surplus. In so doing a set of "givens" are assumed: (1) the production technology, (2) the level and composition of social product, and (3) real wage rates determined by the size of the industrial reserve army (in Marx) or at the subsistence level (in Ricardo). Later, Sraffians reconstructed the classical surplus approach concentrating on the determination of price of distribution. The social surplus approach sheds much light on the fact that the social surplus is the material basis of the capitalist economy, that the production of the social surplus depends directly on the social process of production, and the distribution of the social surplus depends upon the structure of social classes and the power relation therein. However, due to the second assumption above, the determination and composition of the social surplus is not dealt with in either the classical or Sraffian surplus approach (Bortis 1997: 91–95; Lee and Jo 2011).

With the social provisioning process as the methodological foundation, the conventional social surplus approach can be altered without losing its key insights. The process of social provisioning consists of social agency, social structures, and causal mechanisms. It is embedded social agency who makes decisions. More specifically, it is the agency of the capitalist class (for example, the business enterprise) and the capitalist state that make the decisions on the production of social surplus so as to maintain them and expand their socio-economic privileges. In this regard, given production technology embodied in the input-output matrix of the economy, the total social product is determined by agent-based expenditure decisions and economic activities are organized and directed toward the creation of the surplus. That is to say, the social product is not given but determined by the expenditure decisions through the Keynesian-Kaleckian effective demand. Hence, the social surplus is not a residual (Lee and Jo 2011).

The social surplus approach coupled with the social provisioning process offers the following theoretical implications. First, the decisions to produce the social surplus coordinate economic activities by requiring the various basic industries to produce the goods and services for the production of the social surplus. Second, the level and composition of the social surplus are determined by the class-oriented values that direct the social provisioning process. That is, the objective of the production of the social surplus is to provide for the social provisioning process. Thirdly, unlike the conventional social surplus approach, the "heterodox" social surplus approach delineated here requires both micro and macro accounts since agents' strategic decisions (real micro behaviors) are made with a view to overall and future economic conditions (real macro conditions). Finally, a model of the social surplus is an open system in two senses; one being that social agency makes real decisions that reproduce the system, the other being it can be incorporated into a more general model of an economy (like SFM) insofar as the latter is open and is consistent with the social provisioning process.[9]

Conclusions

Heterodox economists have advanced their theories in a markedly different manner from the orthodoxy. The difference is in the first place the view of social reality captured by the social provisioning process; all the economic activities are occurring in a social context—cultural values, class/power relations, norms, ideologies, and ecological system. With this view, a serious inquiry into economic matters requires the deeper understanding and thicker explanations of the foundations of society. Further implications that are relevant to the model building from the social provisioning perspective can be summarized as follows:

(1) Impersonal market fundamentalism supported by orthodox economics is readily rejected. Instead, market provisioning is treated as a subset of social provisioning whose material basis is the structure of production, technology, and natural environment, whose social basis is socio-economic classes, and whose cultural basis is the society-specific value system.
(2) With the social provisioning process as a means of inquiry, both methodological individualism and methodological holism become irrelevant. That is, rather than the pseudo-interaction between individuals and commodities or between structure, it is the genuine interaction between social agency and structures that are be understood and explained.
(3) The conventional micro-macro dichotomy is to be rejected. The account of social provisioning requires microfoundations of macroeconomics beyond fallacious neoclassical microfoundations by focusing on embedded behaviors and on the in-depth analysis of the historical provisioning process.
(4) A model grounded in the social provisioning process would aptly deal with issues such as how the social product and the social surplus is generated, how agents gain access to and

engagement in the social provisioning process, and how social institutions including market institutions are organized and controlled so as to ensure the class interests, and the reproduction and stability of the capitalist system.

From the social provisioning perspective articulated here, we evaluated three selected heterodox models—the social fabric matrix, system dynamics, and the social surplus approach. One of findings is that the social fabric matrix and the social surplus approach have great potential to provide casual explanation of social reality since they are firmly grounded in the social provisioning process. System dynamics, however, contains some crucial problems that need to be resolved if it is to offer the causal explanation of real historical changes over time.

Notes

1. Heterodox economics refers to historically grounded theories of the social provisioning process and the community of economists who produce such theories. Heterodox economics is in its nature pluralistic rather than monistic, social rather than individualistic, open rather than closed, procedural rather than equilibrial, value-directed rather than value-neutral, retroductive rather than deductive, dynamic-evolutionary-historical rather than static-optimal-ideal (O'Hara 1992; Dugger 1996; Lawson 2006; Power 2004; Lee 2008).

2. The Robbins definition of economics was not widely accepted among neoclassical economists until the end of 1960s. Its popularity came along with the mathematization of economics (for example, solving constrained maximization problems). Consequently, not only are "social" behaviors analyzed by mathematical-axiomatic methods, but also historical, philosophical, ethical, cultural, and institutional issues are left outside the domain of mainstream economics (see Backhouse and Medema 2009).

3. Veblen's, Polany's, and Gruchy's vision of economy and economics is shared and elaborated by many later Institutionalists. To summarize, institutional economics is (to be) cultural, complex, historical, realistic, emergent (or anti-reductionist), open-ended, path-dependent, dynamic, phylogenetic, and evolutionary (Dugger 1996; Tilman 1996; Mayhew 1998; Mearman 2002; Hodgson 2004).

4. Another notable example that reveals the sharp difference between "two views" is development economics. From the orthodox point of view, the foremost obstacle to development of an economy is the scarcity of resources.

To promote economic growth and development, they suggest the mobilization of resources (including labor force), the liberalization of domestic markets to attract foreign capital, and the like. However, from the heterodox perspective, it is not necessarily the lack of resources that hinders an economy from developing. The major obstacle to development is the lack of technical progress defined in its widest sense (including organizational techniques, knowledge and learning process, and institutional set-ups) that would increase the capacity of agency and hence facilitate social provisioning within the economy (see Kregel 2004).

5. Even the difference between a model and a theory is hardly discerned in orthodox economics (Leijonhufvud 1997). Consider the Solow growth model (Solow 1956). It is a simple and abstract model with a set of strict assumptions—a closed economy without the state, the CRS aggregate production function, saving determines investment, and investment determines capital accumulation. The model generates the steady state of an economy that depends mainly upon the rate of technical growth. This is the neoclassical growth theory. This theory does not go beyond the idealized model world, even though some of the strict assumptions are relaxed by later neoclassical economists. Heterodox economists, however, believe that a theory is to explain the real social provisioning process and it can be assisted by an abstract *and* realistic model (Fleetwood 2011: 23). That is, orthodox economists idealize social reality so as to gain predictability through a formal model, whereas heterodox economists object to idealization and instead opt for abstraction in order to grasp the reality.

6. We may add here that if the cause of the problem lies at the methodological core of orthodox economics, an alternative or more complex formal model would not be the solution to this failure.

7. It is worthwhile to note that neo-Schumpeterians tend to equate rules to institutions in the evolutionary process, following the Schumpeterian tradition rather than the Veblenian tradition. So it becomes the matter of making or innovating rules by independent-capable individuals (that is, entrepreneurs) (Dopfer, Foster, and Potts 2004; Dopfer and Potts 2004). Hayden (2009b) and Elsner (2007) argue that such a viewpoint is problematic since agents without power, value, beliefs, and social relations do not exist. As the social provisioning process maintains, an agent is not an isolated and passive individual. Social agency makes not only rules but also structures.

8. Some would argue that disequilibrium is not different from nonequilibrium. In order to have a disequilibrium, however, one must assume that there exists an equilibrium and *vice versa*. Otherwise, disequilibrium has no meaning (as in the genuine historical process).

9. For this matter, see Frederic Lee's article appearing in the present issue of the *Journal*.

References

Adams, J. (1991). "Surplus, Surplus, Who's Got the Surplus? The Subtractivist Fallacy in Orthodox Economics." *Journal of Economics Issues* 25(1): 187–197.

Archer, M. S. (1995). *Realist Social Theory: The Morphogenetic Approach*. Cambridge, UK: Cambridge University Press.

Backhouse, R. E., and S. G. Medema. (2009). "On the Definition of Economics." *Journal of Economic Perspectives* 23(1): 221–233.

Baran, P. A., and P. M. Sweezy. (1965). "Economics of Two Worlds." In *On Political Economy and Econometrics: Essays in Honour of Oskar Lange*. Ed. Oskar Lange, pp. 5–29. Oxford: Pergamon Press.

Bortis, H. (1997). *Institutions, Behaviour and Economic Theory*. Cambridge, UK: Cambridge University Press.

Clark, C. M. A. (1992). "An Institutionalist Critique of Sraffian Economics." *Journal of Economic Issues* 26(2): 457–468.

Colander, D. (2003). "Are Institutionalists an Endangered Species?" *Journal of Economic Issues* 37(1): 111–122.

Colander, D., R. P. F. Holt, and J. B. Rosser. (2004). "The Changing Face of Mainstream Economics." *Review of Political Economy* 16(4): 485–499.

Danermark, B., M. Ekstrom, L. Jakobsen, and J. C. Karlsson. (1997). *Explaining Society: Critical Realism in the Social Science*. London: Routledge.

Davis, J. B. (2006). "The Nature of Heterodox Economics." *Post-Autistic Economics Review* 40: 23–30.

Dopfer, K., and J. Potts. (2004). "Evolutionary Realism: A New Ontology for Economics." *Journal of Economic Methodology* 11(2): 195–212.

Dopfer, K., J. Foster, and J. Potts. (2004). "Micro-Meso-Macro." *Journal of Evolutionary Economics* 14(3): 263–279.

Dow, S. C. (2005). "Axioms and Babylonian Thought: A Reply." *Journal of Post Keynesian Economics* 27(3): 385–391.

Dugger, W. M. (1996). "Redefining Economics: From Market Allocation to Social Provisioning." In *Political Economy for the 21st Century*. Ed. Charles J. Whalen, pp. 31–43. Armonk, NY: M.E. Sharpe.

Eaton, J. (1965). "Some Thoughts About Mathematical Models in Relation to Economic Theory." In *On Political Economy and Econometrics: Essays in Honour of Oskar Lange*. Ed. Oskar Lange, pp. 97–103. Oxford: Pergamon Press.

Elsner, W. (2007). "Why Meso? On 'Aggregation' and 'Emergence' and Why and How the Meso Level is Essential in Social Economics." *Forum for Social Economics* 36(1): 1–16.

Fleetwood, S. (2011). "Sketching a Socio-Economic Model of Labour Markets." *Cambridge Journal of Economics* 35: 15–38.

Georgescu-Roegen, N. (1979). "Methods in Economic Science." *Journal of Economic Issues* 13(2): 317–329.

Gruchy, A. G. (1987). *The Reconstruction of Economics: An Analysis of the Fundamentals of Institutional Economics.* New York: Greenwood Press.

Hayden, F. G. (1982). "Social Fabric Matrix: From Perspective to Analytical Tool." *Journal of Economic Issues* 16(3): 637–662.

——. (2009a). "Rejoinder to Response by Michael J. Radzicki and Linwood Tauheed." *Journal of Economic Issues* 43(4): 1062–1065.

——. (2009b). "Utilization of the Social Fabric Matrix to Articulate a State System of Financial Aid." In *Institutional Analysis and Praxis: The Social Fabric Matrix Approach.* Eds. T. Natarajan, W. Elsner, and S. Fullwiler, pp. 209–235. New York: Springer.

Henry, J. F. (1984–1985). "On Equilibrium." *Journal of Post Keynesian Economics* 6(2): 214–229.

——. (1986). "On Economic Theory and the Question of Solvability." *Journal of Post Keynesian Economics* 8(3): 371–386.

——. (2009). "The Illusion of the Epoch: Neoclassical Economics as a Case Study." *Studi e Note di Economia* 1.

——. (2011). "Sismondi, Marx, and Veblen: Precursors of Keynes." In *Heterodox Analysis of Financial Crisis and Reform.* Eds. Joëlle J. Leclaire, Tae-Hee Jo, and Jane E. Knodell, pp. 72–83. Cheltenham, UK: Edward Elgar.

Hodgson, G. M. (2004). *The Evolution of Institutional Economics.* London: Routledge.

Howard, M. C., and J. E. King. (1992). *A History of Marxian Economics.* Volume II, 1929–1990. Princeton, NJ: Princeton University Press.

Jo, T.-H. (2007). "Microfoundations of Effective Demand." PhD thesis. University of Missouri–Kansas City, USA.

Keynes, J. M. (1972). *Essays in Biography.* London: Macmillan.

Kregel, J. A. (2004). "Two Views on the Obstacles to Development." *Social Research* 71(2): 293–307.

Lawson, T. (2003). *Reorienting Economics.* London: Routledge.

——. (2006). "The Nature of Heterodox Economics." *Cambridge Journal of Economics* 30(4): 483–505.

——. (2009). "The Current Economic Crisis: Its Nature and the Course of Academic Economics." *Cambridge Journal of Economics* 33: 759–777.

Lee, F. S. (2002). "Theory Creation and the Methodological Foundation of Post Keynesian Economics." *Cambridge Journal of Economics* 26: 789–804.

——. (2008). "Heterodox Economics." In *The New Palgrave Dictionary of Economics.* Eds. S. N. Durlauf and L. E. Blume. Second ed. London: Palgrave Macmillan. Available at: http://www.dictionaryofeconomics.com/article?id=pde2008_H000175 (accessed 15 March 2011).

——. (2010). "Alfred Eichner's Missing 'Complete Model': A Heterodox Micro-Macro Model of a Monetary Production Economy." In *Money and Macrodynamics: Alfred Eichner and Post-Keynesian Economics*. Eds. M. Lavoie, L.-P. Rochon, and M. Seccareccia, pp. 22–42. Armonk, NY: M.E. Sharpe.

Lee, F. S., and T.-H. Jo. (2011). "Social Surplus Approach and Heterodox Economics." *Journal of Economic Issues* 45(4): forthcoming.

Leijonhufvud, A. (1997). "Models and Theories." *Journal of Economic Methodology* 4(2): 193–198.

Lucas, R. E. (1980). "Methods and Problems in Business Cycle Theory." *Journal of Money, Credit and Banking* 12: 696–715.

Marx, K. (1970). *A Contribution to the Critique of Political Economy*. New York: International Publishers.

Mayhew, A. (1998). "On the Difficulty of Evolutionary Analysis." *Cambridge Journal of Economics* 22: 449–461.

McKenzie, A. J. (2009). "Evolutionary Game Theory." In *The Stanford Encyclopedia of Philosophy*. Ed. Edward N. Zalta. Fall 2009 ed. Available at: http://plato.stanford.edu/archives/fall2009/entries/game-evolutionary (accessed 15 March 2011).

Mearman, A. (2002). "To What Extent is Veblen an Open-Systems Theorist?" *Journal of Economic Issues* 36(2): 573–580.

O'Hara, P. (1992). "A Critical Analysis of the Reproduction of Institutions Within Capitalism: Integrating Macroinstitutional Themes from Marxist and Institutional Political Economy." PhD thesis. University of Newcastle, New South Wales, Australia.

Park, M.-S. (2001). "Critical Realism." In *Encyclopedia of International Political Economy*. Ed. R. Jones, pp. 270–271. London: Routledge.

Polanyi, K. (1968). "The Economy as Instituted Process." In *Primitive, Archaic and Modern Economies: Essays of Karl Polanyi*. Ed. George Dalton, pp. 139–174. Garden City, NY: A Doubleday Anchor Original.

Power, M. (2004). "Social Provisioning as a Starting Point for Feminist Economics." *Feminist Economics* 10(3): 3–19.

Radzicki, M. J. (2003). "Mr. Hamilton, Mr. Forrester, and a Foundation for Evolutionary Economics." *Journal of Economic Issues* 37(1): 133–173.

——. (2010). "Was Alfred Eichner a System Dynamicist?" In *Money and Macrodynamics*. Eds. M. Lavoie, L.-P. Rochon, and M. Seccareccia, pp. 3–21. Armonk, NY: M.E. Sharpe.

Rima, I. H. (1994). "The Role of Numeracy in the History of Economic Analysis." *Journal of the History of Economic Thought* 16: 188–201.

Robbins, L. (1932). *An Essay on the Nature and Significance of Economic Science*. London: Macmillan.

Robinson, J. V. (1980). "History Versus Equilibrium." In *Collected Economic Papers*. Vol. V, pp. 48–58. Cambridge, MA: MIT Press.

Solow, R. (1956). "A Contribution to the Theory of Economic Growth." *Quarterly Journal of Economics* 70(1): 65–94.

Stevenson, R. E. (1987). "Institutional Economics and the Theory of Production." *Journal of Economic Issues* 21(4): 1471–1493.

Sugden, R. (2001). "The Evolutionary Turn in Game Theory." *Journal of Economic Methodology* 8(1): 113–130.

——. (2002). "Credible Worlds: The Status of Theoretical Models." In *Fact and Fiction in Economics: Models, Realism, and Social Construction.* Ed. U. Mäki, pp. 107–136. Cambridge, UK: Cambridge University Press.

Tilman, R. (1996). *The Intellectual Legacy of Thorstein Veblen: Unsolved Issues.* London, UK: Greenwood Press.

Varoufakis, Y. (2008). "Capitalism According to Evolutionary Game Theory: The Impossibility of a Sufficiently Evolutionary Model of Historical Change." *Science & Society* 72(1): 63–94.

Veblen, T. B. (1909). "The Limitations of Marginal Utility." *Journal of Political Economy* 17(9): 620–636.

——. (1961). *The Place of Science in Modern Civilization and Other Essays.* New York: Russell & Russell.

A Simple Model of the Surplus Approach to Value, Distribution, and Growth

By SCOTT CARTER*,†

ABSTRACT. The surplus approach to value and distribution represents an older and in this author's opinion much more relevant way to model capitalistic socio-economic systems than the mainstream neo-classical approach. This essay develops the analytical structure of the surplus approach by tracing its origins to the groundbreaking work of the circular flow concept in the Physiocrats and Quesnay's *Tableau Economique*, the Classical economists, Marx, and Piero Sraffa. Original archival material from the Sraffa Papers at the Wren Library, Trinity College, University of Cambridge is also presented in support of the thesis advance. Finally, the surplus approach is developed in terms of the distribution and growth nexus.

The Social Surplus Defined

The "social surplus" is defined generally as a quantum of (new) wealth, value, and/or product over and above that necessary for a social system to reproduce itself. It can be conceived as the residual after the societal necessaries have been properly accounted for and deducted out of total end-of-period gross output. Letting A[1] stand for these societal necessaries at the beginning of the round of social reproduction (t_0) and Q stand for total gross output emergent at the end of this round, the surplus (Y) can be seen as the difference between Q and A. This simplistic interpretation is depicted in Figure 1.

*Assistant Professor, Department of Economics, The University of Tulsa, Tulsa, Oklahoma, 74104, (918) 631-2795, scott-carter@utulsa.edu

†The author would like to thank Fred Lee and the participants at the *AJES* Workshop on Social Provision, Embeddedness, and Modeling the Economy sponsored by the *AJES* and held in September 2010 at the University of Missouri, Kansas City. He would also like to thank Pierangelo Garegnani for permission to quote from the Sraffa Papers, Wren Library, Trinity College, University of Cambridge, UK. All errors are of course the author's own responsibility.

American Journal of Economics and Sociology, Vol. 70, No. 5 (November, 2011).

Figure 1

Societal reproduction and the social surplus as a residual

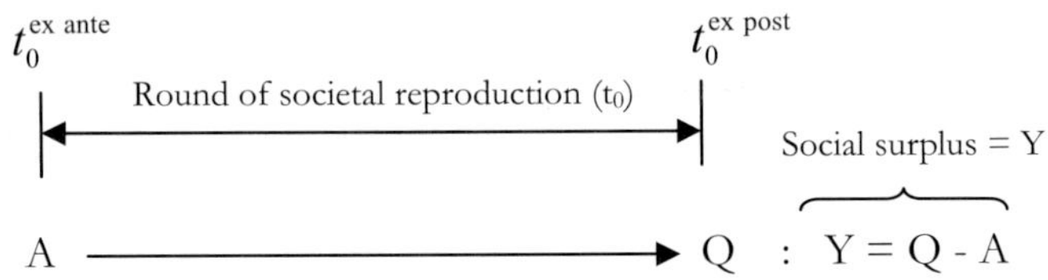

The surplus component has been alternatively termed the *net product, value added, gross profits,* and *shares of remunerated national income*. It has been defined in different contexts as both *excluding* as well as *including* wages. It has been conceived as the fund from which distributed revenues partake, and is also the source of capital accumulation and growth in subsequent rounds (t_{+1}; t_{+2}, . . .) of social reproduction.

The existence of surplus so defined is the hallmark of modern capitalist socio-economic systems; the net productivity associated with this mode of production is enormous. This is not to suggest that in earlier historical epochs a social surplus did not exist. From the moment when human civilization emerged out of the hunting and gathering stage the social surplus was the source of net wealth, it was what enabled the construction of Babylonian hanging gardens and Egyptian pyramids. However, what is indisputable is that the growth in net wealth—that is the *surplus*—became exponential in capitalistically-oriented systems of production and distribution, dwarfing the surpluses engendered in any previous socio-economic system. Economic theory aims, in part, to explain the phenomenal ability of capitalism to generate and accumulate large social surpluses.

We speak of two broad approaches to the social surplus in capitalistic and market oriented systems, each couched within one of two respective theoretical paradigms of value and distribution (see Garegnani 1984). The more recent or "modern" of the two is the marginalist or neoclassical approach to value and distribution. This approach remains the dominant one in economic theory. Net productivity here is recognized; however, it is *not* referred to as a "surplus";

"surplus" in this approach is conceived *not* in terms of net wealth creation, but rather in terms of "extra" satisfaction gained, seen in the concepts of consumer surplus and producer surplus—that is quanta of "satisfaction" that accrue to the respective individual "demanders" and "suppliers." The opposing forces of demand and supply especially of the "factors of production" seen to "naturally" (imperfections cast aside) come into equilibrium such that remuneration of each factor corresponds to its (marginal) productivity. Increases in social net wealth are due to the (marginal) productivity of each factor, especially that of capital (human, physical, or entrepreneurial). Wages accrue to labor and profits accrue to the owners of the various forms of capital. Euler's theorem ensures that, under perfect competition, each factor is paid according to its contribution to net-wealth creation. This theory conceives the market the societal expression of human nature, and as a fundamentally harmonious mechanism.

On the other hand, the surplus approach to value and distribution represents the older tradition in political economy the origins of which we can trace to the circular flow of the Francois Quesnay's famous *Tableau Economique*. Despite the feudal residue of its treatment of agriculture as the sole "productive" sector—as the only source of the surplus product—on a fundamental plane the *Tableau* contains insights that remain relevant. Modern developments to the surplus approach begin with the publication of Piero Sraffa's (1960) thin but quite terse and somewhat cryptic book *Production of Commodities by Means of Commodities: Prelude to a Critique of Economic Theory.* Eschewing completely the marginalist approach to value and distribution (one neoclassical reviewer laments that there is no literature in the book cited after 1914),[2] Sraffa lays the foundations for what Ronald Meek has coined the "rehabilitation" of the Classical approach to value and distribution.[3] It was Sraffa's student Pierangelo Garegnani who most precisely articulated certain characteristic features of the surplus approach, what he terms the "core" in the surplus theories. For Garegnani and subsequent theorists in this tradition, the "surplus" by definition consists of the non-wage portion of the share of national income:

> Besides the necessary replacement of the means of production [it] included the subsistence of the agricultural labourers . . . [t]he fact that the subsis-

> tence of workers was considered necessary for reproduction established a direct link between [the] analysis of social reproduction and that of the division of the product among the classes society is divided . . . [i]n principle [the] way of determining the non-wage incomes is simple. Three sets of circumstances are assumed to be known prior to this determination . . . (i) the real wage . . . ; (ii) the social product: that is the output of the commodities produced in the year; (iii) the technical conditions of the production. (Garegnani 1987: 560)

The question of whether or not wages should be included in the surplus is a major analytical point of debate within the surplus approach to which we return below.

The Physiocratic Basis of the Notion of "Surplus" in the Classical Economists, Marx, and Sraffa

We trace the origin of the classical surplus concept to the Physiocrats and the *Tableau*. The groundbreaking character of Physiocratic thought cannot be underestimated. Writing in pre-revolutionary France, Quesnay, his close disciple Mirabeau, and other adherents to the Physiocratic school developed the first formal economic model of an integrated economic system. At the heart of the Physiocratic doctrine was the concept of the *produit net*, or *net product*. As Ronald Meek (1962: 19) has put it, "the Physiocrats . . . endeavoured to discover some key variable . . . causing an expansion or contraction . . . in the general level of economic activity. The variable which they hit upon was the capacity of agriculture to yield a 'net product', a disposable surplus over necessary cost." The Physiocrats expressed the social surplus within the "feudal shell" of agricultural production. Only the agricultural sector was deemed "productive" in the sense that it alone was thought to yield the excess of product above cost, hence they deemed the social surplus the "gift of nature." The other two sectors in the Physiocratic framework were to be "sterile" in the sense that no new net product was created by this activity: (i) the manufacture sector was conceived as "sterile" in the sense that output was produced, the "value" of which was seen as the same magnitude as that of the inputs; and (ii) the landlords were not even "sterile" in the sense that they represent pure (unproductive) consumption without any equivalent exchange.

Moving to developments by economists on the British Isles, one of Adam Smith's many original contributions to the then-budding science of political economy was precisely the generalization of the Physiocratic "gift" from agricultural production to manufactured production proper. Rejecting the old mercantilist notion that national wealth consisted of hoarded precious metals and the necessity of favorable terms of trade manifest from protectionist trade prescriptions, for Smith the wealth of nations was instead expressed in the net productivity of a nation's industry and workforce. We may perhaps conceive this as the "gift of net productivity" that modern surplus producing society is able to enjoy.

The classical economists proper, specifically David Ricardo and Thomas Robert Malthus, also conceived of an economic system within a surplus approach paradigm. For his part Ricardo placed great emphasis not only on net productivity, but even more importantly on the distribution of this net productivity to the three original "classes of the community." Here we find the primal role given to the distribution of the "produce of the earth" as the remunerated revenues of wages to the class of laborers, rents to the class of landlords, and profits to the class of capitalists. Malthus too worked within the surplus approach paradigm, and the fundamental differences between him and Ricardo revolved not around the efficacy of the approach *as such* but rather on certain nuances within this approach such as the correct measure of value and the possibility and implications of overproduction/underconsumption (the debate on Say's law).

The developments by Karl Marx, although strictly speaking a *critique* of then-extant (bourgeois) political economy, also remain within the confines of the surplus approach paradigm. Marx's developments are actually less clear-cut, and it is here we find a different interpretation of the notion of "surplus." Whereas with the Physiocrats, Smith, Ricardo, and Malthus, the surplus is in the main conceived as surplus *product*—that is, a surplus quantum of output over and above the necessary conditions of social reproduction—in Marx we encounter quite explicitly the idea that this surplus product in fact is the material expression of *surplus value* explicitly conceived as *unpaid labor time*. This is to say, for Marx the idea of a "social surplus" lay squarely in the exploitative nature of a skewed class society. Here we can begin to distinguish the

Sraffian surplus from the Marxian surplus. The Sraffian surplus by definition encompasses the entire net product, both the wage portion as well as the profit portion. The Marxian surplus, by contrast, includes only the profit portion, the wage portion being relegated to the realm of necessaries. Sraffa himself struggled with this difference with Marx, as we shall see below, and was able finally to resolve this with the distinction between the subsistence vs. the surplus wage.[4]

Turning to Sraffa, the surplus approach to value and distribution in its modern version can be traced to the interpretation of the Italian Cambridge economist. When one considers the peculiar mode of exposition that Sraffa ultimately chose for his book, as expressed in the first five chapters, we find that Sraffa adopts a "physicalist" approach to the transition to capitalist commodity production. The term "physicalist" refers to the development of the model using the physical structure of inputs and outputs measured in given quantities of use-values, and the surplus-producing model is differentiated only by the quantum of "extra" output at the end of the production round.[5] Sraffa first posits an "ideal type" system of simple commodity production found in Chapter I's production for subsistence model where no surplus product emerges. This represents the physicalist analogue of Adam Smith's "early and rude state"[6] such that the labor requirements are not made explicit and instead are regulated as analogous to fodder for animals and hence included within the means of production requirements.[7] Sraffa gives no mention to the implicit unitary wage share of this system; we are only told that this "simple society . . . produces just enough to maintain itself," and to illustrate Sraffa gives us a simple numeric example that shows the summed economy-wide inputs "necessary" for production are exactly equal to the quantity of resulting outputs. The model for capitalist commodity production is presented in Chapter II's production with a surplus model. The surplus production conceived here is the case where for at least one commodity more output is produced than is "necessary" as inputs for systemic production. Here the surplus is conceived as surplus *product*, resulting in "extra" output left over after the conditions of production have been replaced. The numeric example in the two chapters highlighting this "physicalist" aspect is seen quite clearly when placed side-by-side as seen in Table 1.

Table 1

Production for subsistence and production with a surplus numeric examples in Sraffa (1960)

Production for Subsistence (Sraffa 1960, Ch. I, p. 3)	Production with a Surplus (Sraffa 1960, Ch. II, p. 7)
$\begin{pmatrix} 280 \text{ qr. wheat} : 12 \text{ t. iron} \rightarrow 400 \text{ qr. wheat} \\ 120 \text{ qr. wheat} : 8 \text{ t. iron} \rightarrow 20 \text{ t. iron} \end{pmatrix}$	$\begin{pmatrix} 280 \text{ qr. wheat} : 12 \text{ t. iron} \rightarrow 575 \text{ qr. wheat} \\ 120 \text{ qr. wheat} : 8 \text{ t. iron} \rightarrow 20 \text{ t. iron} \end{pmatrix}$
$\sum = (400 \text{ qr. wheat} : 20 \text{ t. iron})$	$\sum = (400 \text{ qr. wheat} : 20 \text{ t. iron})$

The summed means of production requirements for each system is shown in the penultimate row. The physical structure of production on the input-side is exactly the same, the only difference being that in surplus-producing society we now have the addition of an extra quantum of output, here to the tune of 175 quarters of wheat. Because Sraffa explicitly adopts the notion of the "subsistence wage," this "extra" quantity of wheat is available for distribution *as profit.* Here Sraffa directly identifies the surplus product with *profit.* The distribution of this surplus-qua-profit to the owners of the means of production is strictly along the capitalistic lines of a uniform rate of return on the capital advanced in each industry. It is in this way that the owners of the capital in the iron industry, although they produce no physical surplus,[8] nonetheless share in the gains "produced" by the wheat industry in that the exchange values of both wheat *and* iron will include the general rate of profit (r*).

Surplus as the Value-Added and the Choice of the Wage

Both Sraffa's and Marx's conceptions of the surplus conceive of the surplus as the residual remaining once the so-called "necessaries" have been deducted out of the total gross product. But Sraffa in archival notes himself questions exactly what constitutes "necessary," such that the very definition of the "surplus" turns on this definition. As early as 1928 we find Sraffa deeply concerned with this issue. In a five-page document entitled "Surplus Product," Sraffa remarks that

> The study of the "surplus product" is the true object of economics: the great difficulty of the matter is that this object either vanishes or remains unexplained. It is a typical problem to be handled dialectically. This notion is connected with that of "necessity", and "necessity" has only a definite meaning from a given point of view, which must be explicitly stated and adhered to consistently. The surplus product goes to expenses which are not "necessary" for producing a given commodity. (D3/12/6/161: 1)[9]

The crux of this matter revolves around the conceptions of the wage, since there is no ambiguity about the "necessary" character of the means of production requirements. Sraffa in somewhat of a fudge introduces two distinct notions of the wage, the "subsistence" portion plus the "surplus portion." Taken literally, this idea of the wage is expressed in the following equation:

$$\text{Total wage to workers} = \text{subsistence portion of wage} + \text{surplus portion of wage}$$

Sraffa himself treats the subsistence portion of the wage as part of the means of production, which are in a sense "augmented" by the subsistence portion of the wage. Sraffa speaks of this "double character of the wage" (Sraffa 1960: 9–10), but in the end refrains from employing it and instead opts to treat "the whole wage as variable" (Sraffa 1960: 10). It is our contention that Sraffa's abstraction from the subsistence portion of the wage was done so not so much for convenience but rather because of the analytical difficulties associated with the subsistence wage concept. Adoption of the share approach certainly is articulated in the important Majorca Draft of March 1955, which was Sraffa's first attempt to pen a working draft of the first part of his book on single product industries while holed-up in the luxurious Palma Hotel on the island of Majorca in early 1955.[10] From that document we read that:

> Hitherto we have regarded wages as being composed of the necessary subsistence for the workers and thereby being on the same footing as the fuel for the engines or fodder for the working animals. Wages however partake of a double nature and while always containing the element of subsistence they may, in certain social conditions, contain secure also a share of the surplus product. And it is indeed the stress and strain arising from this possibility that has given economic theory its shape. (Sraffa Papers, D3/12/52/6)

Notice the importance that Sraffa gives to the so-called "surplus component" of the wage—namely, that it is the "stress and strain" associated with the struggle of workers to secure a portion of the surplus product as opposed to capital "that has given economic theory its shape." And it is here that we follow Sraffa and conceive of the "surplus product" as the magnitude of product and/or value over and above the necessary means of production requirements, in other words, the net product, the division of which falls into wage versus profit revenues. This surplus represents the newly created wealth of a productive economic system, and following the Classical and Marxian tradition, the source of this newly created wealth lies solely in the productive power of living labor. In Carter (2011a) we have termed the notion that living labor is the source of newly created (net) wealth the *fundamental economic normalization*. This certainly is made quite explicit in Sraffa (1960) in terms of the setting of the total value of living labor in paragraph 10 to the value of the net product in paragraph 12, both of which are normalized as unity (see Bellofiore 2008, 2010). As early as December 1942, Sraffa remarked that "the net product as a whole is always produced by L" (D3/12/29/18). And in both the Majorca Draft and in *Production of Commodities*, Sraffa eschews the bundle "subsistence" approach in favor of the share "surplus" approach to the wage, and in doing so sets the stage for setting both the total value of living labor and the value of the net product equal to unity. This is to say, the formal model that Sraffa develops in his economic system is one where the surplus product itself is associated with the explicit inclusion of the requirements of living labor. In the Majorca Draft, immediately following the above quote regarding the "stress and strain," we read the interesting passage that:

> It therefore becomes necessary to treat wages, like the rate of profits, as one of the variables in the system. We shall therefore have to represent explicitly the quantity of labour employed in each industry in the place of the quantities of subsistence we have hitherto rolled up with the raw material . . . We shall designate the wage per unit of labour as w, this is a price to be determined like all other prices in terms of the commodity which is chosen as a (standard). The unit of labour being the annual social labour, w[11] will at the same time represent the fraction of the national income that goes to wages (it will be the proportionate wage of Ricardo). (D3/12/52/6-7)

The parallel passage of this first draft appears precisely in the famous paragraph 10 in *Production of Commodities*. It is important to emphasize that for Sraffa the wage here represents the surplus wage, namely, the *fraction* of total national income or surplus product, the latter quantity being produced by the total annual social labor. This essentially involves the adoption of the share approach to the wage because here the wage rate, w, can be directly assessed to the quantum of living labor, as opposed to representing a "given" quantity of a subsistence bundle. On this latter point Sraffa continues:

> The double nature of wages, as means of production and as a share in the surplus, gives rise to the question whether the whole of wages should be included in the w; or only the "surplus" part of them, while the subsistence part is left in its previous shape as raw material . . . There is much to be said for either method. The latter of separation is in many ways more reasonable, for it represents by a constant the quantity that is unchanging and by a variable the quantity that can be more or less according to circumstances. It is the view of the classical economists, who did not regard wages as part of the national income, but as being advanced out of capital, although they did admit that in some cases they might succeed in getting part of the surplus. It has also the advantage of including the necessary wage in the year's advances which must be multiplied by the factor $1 + r$, while leaving outside the part which must come out of the product at the end of the year. (D3/12/53/7-8)

Sraffa, however, decides *against* this bundle *ex ante* approach to the subsistence wage:

> Much as there is to recommend it in theory this method would give rise to some difficulty in practical application, if such had ever to be attempted; for the segregation of the commodities composing the two parts of the wages while no doubt feasible in the early stages of society, would meet in modern conditions with "insurmountable obstacles"[12] (the attempt to overcome them by a division of the "value" of the wage would create more trouble than it overcomes). (D3/12/52/8)

Thus Sraffa settles on the share approach to the wage:

> The other [share] method has much less logic to recommend it; but it has the decided advantage of being in conformity with the current wage, in that *it treats the wage as a single unit*, and it includes the whole of it as part of the national income; and it is the distribution of this (rather than that of the less inclusive "National Net Revenue" of A. Smith) which we shall have to discuss. It implies also accepting the view that wages are paid entirely out of the annual product, instead of being advanced . . . In what follows we shall therefore include the whole wage under w. (D3/12/52/8, emphasis added)

Notice how in these latter two passages Sraffa explicitly introduces historical context: the "early stages of society"—we conjecture that this is in reference to Adam Smith's "early and rude state," that is, the no-surplus production model—are compatible with the wage conceived as a bundle; whereas in "modern conditions"—we conjecture the surplus production model—the wage conceived as a share becomes much more relevant. And it is very interesting to note why: because in "modern conditions" the wage is "treat[ed] as a single unit." Clearly, Sraffa is referring here to the *money* wage,[13] or at least to a wage that is paid to the worker as a single unit of *numeraire* per hour, which in the system of equations is multiplied only by the quantum of living labor added, *L*. Hence by conceiving the wage as a share of the annual product, Sraffa was able to avoid in general the "troubles" of the composition of the basket of worker consumption goods that arise when workers do not purchase with their wage the required quantities of such goods. The share approach to the wage also avoids the thorny issue of the organic composition of the wage-good sector.[14] The juxtaposition of the bundle vs. the share approach to the wage in the context of Sraffa was first brought to light by John Eatwell in two important articles written in the mid-1970s (Eatwell 1974, 1975), where we read that "necessary labor time could be defined in two ways: (A) as the value of 'the sum of money v expended upon labor-power', in effect as the *share* of wages in the value of the output, and (B) as 'the value of (the) means of subsistence', that is, as the value of the commodities comprising the real wage" (Eatwell 1974: 299, emphasis in original, and inserted quotation from *Capital*, Volume I). Although revisiting the character of this debate is beyond the scope of our present task, that Eatwell faced vehement criticism by both and Marxist and Sraffian alike is beyond dispute, and we think quite misplaced.[15]

Hence we have come into marked distinction between the development of the surplus approach to value and distribution advanced in the present essay versus that development by Professor Garegnani. For Professor Garegnani (1984: 311), one of the "characteristic premises" of the surplus approach is that the "the real wage and the social product are given when determining the rate of profit and relative prices." Hence the "surplus" here is exclusively that of the non-wage portion of the value-added. By contrast, the approach adopted here conceives of the "surplus" as the entire value-added, from which wages *as well as* profits are remunerated to respective owners of "factors" of production. We have attempted to show through archival evidence that our approach is completely compatible with Sraffa's own thinking, and in this capacity can in at least a small degree vindicate Eatwell's (1974, 1975) original framing of the question related to this issue.

The "Value Theory of Labour"

Under these assumptions we can now begin to formalize our model of single product industries.[16] We begin first with a system of surplus production that has abstracted from the particular distribution of the surplus-*qua-* value-added between wage versus profit revenue. In archival notes, Sraffa refers to this as the "value theory of labour":

> 21.2.1955
>
> In the dust raised by the controversies on the Labour Theory of Value, a valuable interesting aspect has been overlooked, or what be called the Value theory of Labour . . . For, whatever disputes there may be about the determination of value by the quantity of labour, there can be no doubt (nobody doubts so far as I know) that the value of a commodity (its price for r = 0) determines (measures) the quantity of labour which directly or indirectly has entered into its production. (Sraffa Papers D3/12/44/3)

This is an economic system conceived when the rate of profit is zero and all net productis distributed to workers in the form of what Pasinetti (1977: 122) calls the "complete wage rate" (see also Carter 2011a). In terms of a simple two-commodity model of single product industries, Sraffa's "value theory of labour" can be expressed as the following system of equations:

$$\begin{aligned} A_{11}p_1^0 + A_{21}p_2^0 + L_1w^0 &= Q_1p_1^0 \\ A_{12}p_1^0 + A_{22}p_2^0 + L_2w^0 &= Q_2p_2^0 \end{aligned} \qquad (1)$$

The physical structure of production represents known quantities, represented by the ith commodity input requirement for the jth industry (A_{ij}) as well as the jth industry's direct labor requirement (L_j) necessary for the jth industry's output (Q_j). This represents a system of two equations in three unknowns, the respective prices of each commodity (p_1^0, p_2^0) and the "complete" wage (w^0). To close this system we make the assumption of an "unassisted" commodity-money sector, which we call "gold," the physical measure of which is directly in terms of currency units ("$"):

$$L_{gold} w^0 = Q_{gold} p^0_{gold}$$
$$p^0_{gold} = 1 \qquad (2)^{17}$$

where Y_{np_i} represents the physical net output of the ith industry.

All price variables have been superscripted with zeroes to indicate that they represent what in the Marxian literature is referred to as direct prices (see, for example, Shaikh 1977), that is prices proportional to values.

The concept of the "complete" wage figures heavily in the following analysis and thus requires some further comment. Pasinetti (1977: 122) coins the particular term in the context of the introduction of a no-distribution "ideal" system: of production:

> An "ideal" system of prices, as understood, for example, by the "Ricardian socialists" (who had claimed at the beginning of the 19th century that the whole net product of an economic system ought to go to the workers), might be $pA + wa_n = p$.[18] This is a linear system of $(n-1)$ equations. It determines $(n-2)$ relative prices and a wage rate *which absorbs the entire net product of the system*. This [is] regarded as the "maximum" wage rate . . . since it corresponds to a profit rate of zero. We may call it the "ideal" wage rate here, or, from a different point of view, the "complete" wage rate." (emphasis added)

In our interpretation, the "complete" wage rate is not merely one of "complete" distribution of the net product to workers; more importantly in it represents the relation of the *net productivity of labor*—that is, it is a relation not only of "complete" remuneration but also net productivity (see Carter 2011a).

In this system, a net surplus product is assumed to be produced in the sense that the sum of the commodity input requirements for each industry are of a lesser quantity that the resulting gross output of that industry, that is, $\sum_{i=1}^{2} A_{ij} < Q_j$. We assume that this is the case for each industry, hence both industries are fertile, but the only requirement for a surplus producing system is that at least one industry is fertile, with the other possibly being sterile.[19] Accordingly, in terms of sheer physical use-values, the total gross product of each industry can be broken down into the following commodity structure:

$$\text{Industry 1} = \text{Wheat: } A_{11} + A_{12} + Y_{np_1} = Q_1$$

$$\text{Industry 2} = \text{Iron: } A_{21} + A_{22} + Y_{np_1} = Q_2$$

We have already seen that Sraffa with the adoption of the pure surplus wage model necessarily links the total value added by living labor to the value of the net product. Hence for a two-commodity surplus-producing system of basic goods, the commodity and industry structures are related as in Figure 2.

Figure 2

Integrated structure of two-commodity basic system

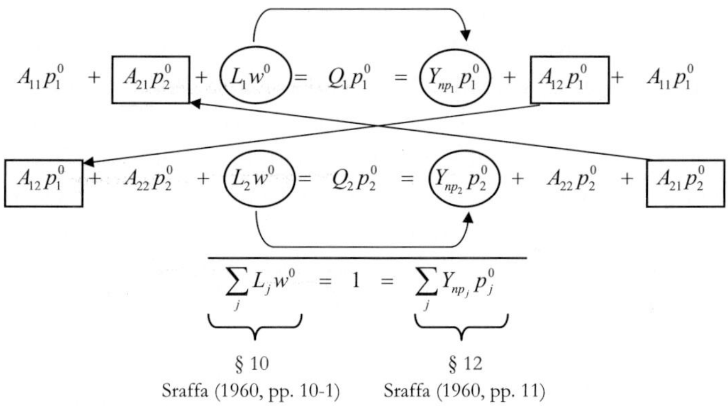

In this figure the surplus product is represented by the total value of the net product $\left(\sum Y_{np_j} p_j^0\right)$, which in the price structure is related directly to the value-added by workers whose labor is assessed at the "complete" wage rate. At the level of the industry the value-added by workers is in general not equal to the value of the net product; this would only be the case when equal organic compositions of capital prevail throughout. However, as Sraffa does in paragraphs 10 and 12 of his book, the system is so normalized such that in the aggregate these respective values do coincide.

Pasinietti's "complete" wage rate is very much like the monetary expression of labor-time (MELT) concept developed independently in the early 1980s by Gerard Duménil (1983–1984) and Duncan Foley (1982) that appears in the New Interpretation literature.[20] The major difference between Sraffa's normalization and that of the DF framework is that the latter do not explicitly set each quanta equal to unity. The MELT represents the "unit money-price" at which living labor is net-productive, and is measured in "dollars" per unit labor. As with the Dumenil-Foley interpretation, this is simply the inverse of the "value of money" concept (and vice versa) found in Marx:

$$w^0 = \frac{\$}{unit_L} = \frac{\$}{HR} = \left(\lambda_{\$}^{-1}\right) \approx MELT$$
$$\lambda_{\$} = \frac{unit_L}{\$} = \frac{HR}{\$} = \left(w^0\right)^{-1} \tag{3}$$

The net productivity of the surplus-producing system is constituted by the system's net product, which under our assumption normalizes the value of living labor's productivity to the value of the newly created product, conceived here as the fruits of the productive laborers.

Consider now the analogue of the capital-labor ratio that Sraffa (1960) employs, which we term the labor to means of production ratio (LMP). Taken right out of Sraffa (1960: Chapter III), the LMP ratio is defined as the value of the living labor added divided by the value of the means of production requirements:

$$\text{Labor to Means of Production Ratio} = LMP = \frac{w^0 L}{pA} = \frac{pY_{np}}{pA} = R = \text{maximum rate of profit} \tag{4}$$

It is also equal to the value of the net product divided by the value of the means of production, both of which come to coincide with the maximum rate of profits (R). The normalization consistent with the New Interpretation such that the value-added by living labor is set equal to the value of the net product is retained in what follows.

Functional Income Distribution and Growth: Further Development of the Surplus Component

Having posited the fundamental economic normalization such that the value-added by living labor is equal to the value of the net product, both of which are under our assumption equal to the surplus produced in the economic system, we now turn to the question of how this surplus is distributed as revenue and to what ends the distributed revenue is utilized. One of the most developed expositions of the relationship between functional income distribution and economic growth from the perspective of the surplus approach to value and distribution appears in Duncan Foley and Thomas R. Michl's (1999) *Growth and Distribution*, and what follows in the present essay is greatly informed by this exposition. There the accounting relationship between the surplus conceived as forms of distributed revenues (national income) is juxtaposed against the surplus conceived as forms of aggregate expenditures. This gives rise to the surplus-product accounting T-table where the value-added by productive living labor (Y) is expressed in terms of the income account of aggregate income divided into wage and profit distributive revenues and the output account of aggregate expenditures divided into consumption and investment.

Table 2

Surplus Product T-Table of Income and Output Accounts

Income Account (Distributed Aggregate Revenues)	Output Account (Aggregate Expenditure)
Surplus product = Y = W + Z	Surplus product = Y = C + I

Table 2 shows the two different aspects of the social surplus = value added = newly created wealth. On the income account side of the ledger, this newly created wealth is divided into wage (W) and profit (Z) revenues. The aggregate levels of wage and profit revenue can be conceived as the respective income shares (ω = wage share and π = $(1 - \omega)$ = profit share) multiplied by the value-added by productive labor:

$$W = \omega Y \tag{5}$$

$$Z = \pi Y = (1 - \omega) Y$$

The determination of the respective income shares is—as in Sraffa (1960)—for the present purposes left open. The system can be closed on the wage side or the profit side of the income ledger and what follows still remains equally valid. What is clear is that irrespective of the mechanisms of closure of the distribution parameter, at the level of abstraction considered here the ratio of distributive shares can be construed as an index of the Marxian rate of exploitation. The idea of the rate of exploitation as a ratio of distributive shares is the approach taken by Joan Robinson, who despite her rejection of the labor theory of value, in the Preface to the Second Edition of *An Essay on Marxian Economics* locates "the theory of exploitation" with "the theory of the distribution of the net product of industry between wages and profits" (Robinson 1966: *vii*).

Each distributive share is in inverse relation to the other and both are upper-bounded by unity and lower-bounded by zero. In terms of the ratio of distributive shares, which we chose to call the rate of exploitation (e_j; where j = value of wage share), the lower limit is zero and corresponds to a wage share of unity ($\omega = 1$) and a profit share of zero ($\pi = 0$) whereas the upper limit is infinite and corresponds to a wage share of zero ($\omega = 0$) and a profit share of unity ($\pi = 1$):

$$\begin{aligned} e_{\omega=1} &= \frac{\pi_{\omega=1}}{\omega_{\omega=1}} = \frac{0}{1} = 0 \\ e_{\omega=0} &= \frac{\pi_{\omega=0}}{\omega_{\omega=0}} = \frac{1}{0} = \infty \end{aligned} \tag{5}$$

We can depict this in Figure 3.

When the rate of exploitation is greater than zero, the net product of industry or surplus is divided between wage and profit revenue, each of which is expressed as the respective distributive share multiplied by the value created by productive living labor. Making explicit the means of production requirements (A), the rate of profit (r) emerges defined as the ratio of profits to the value of the capital advanced. Abstracting from depreciation, the rate of profit is given by:

$$r_j = \frac{Z_j}{pA} \tag{6}$$

Figure 3

Rate of exploitation as the ratio of distributive income shares

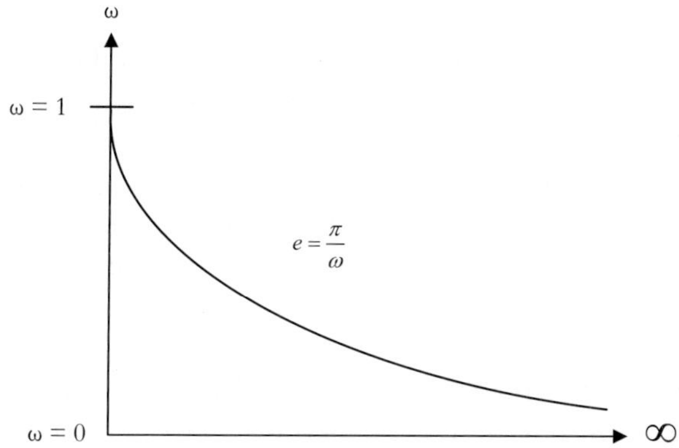

Given the static nature of inquiry, within each technology the rate of profit will vary with changes in the wage share (ω = j) such that when the latter is unity, the rate of profit is zero, and when the latter is zero, the rate of profit is at its maximum value R. It is important to note that the maximum rate of profit is associated with a rate of exploitation that is undefined—that is, is infinity. Here the entire value-added is unpaid and is remunerated to the owners of capital as pure profits.

The question now turns on the relationship between the distributive revenues, wage revenue and profit revenue, and the subsequent uses of each of these revenue forms. In order to keep the analysis as simple as possible, we introduce the standard assumption in many theories of growth that workers' aggregate revenues are completely consumed; that is to say, workers do not save. Hence all savings revenues subsequently mapped to investment will in this simple model come wholly out of profit revenues.

The rate of exploitation defined above, the determination of which is left open for the present purposes, allows for the division of net (surplus) productivity into the distributive revenues wages (W) and profits (Z), each of which will be equal to the respective income share multiplied by net (surplus) product (Y):

$$W = \omega Y = \text{aggregate wages} = \$$$

$$Z = (1 - \omega)\, Y = \pi Y = \text{aggregate profits} = \$$$

By definition the sum of wages and profits equals the aggregate net (surplus) product, and the identity showing this equality is referred to as the *income account* (Foley and Michl 1999: Chapter 2) and is seen in the first column of Table 2 above. Distributive wage and profit revenues must be mapped to the *output account* (Foley and Michl 1999: Chapter 2) that shows the expenditures associated with each revenue form. In this simple model developed here, the easiest way to conceive this mapping between aggregate accounts is to assume a constant propensity to save, denoted β. In general, the propensity to save will be a pure number between zero and one; when $\beta = 0$ the propensity to save is zero and all revenues are consumed as expenditure. When $\beta = 1$ the propensity to save is unity and all revenues are saved for subsequent net investment. The propensity to consume is equal to one minus the propensity to save. Savings on the income account of the ledger will be mapped to investment expenditures on the output side of the ledger; alternatively, consumption revenues on the income side will be mapped to consumption expenditures on the output side. This mapping of the surplus product between the different accounts can be expressed in terms of the simple diagrammatic depiction[21] of Figure 4.

The relationship between the different expressions of the surplus product, that is the income account expression as compared to the output account expression, can be formalized in the simple mathematical distribution-growth model as inspired by Foley and Michl (1999)[22] (recall we are assumming that depreciation is 100 percent):

$$\begin{aligned} &\text{Income Account:} \quad W = Y - (r)\, pA \\ &\text{Output Account:} \quad C = Y - (g_A)\, pA \end{aligned} \tag{7}$$

Note that g_A is the rate of growth of the means of production, or *accumulation rate of capital*, which we return to below. The income account and the output account so conceived can be drawn in output-profit rate space such that each account is expressed by the same schedule, referred to as the *growth-distribution schedule* (Foley

Figure 4

Diagrammatic Depiction of Mapping of Surplus Product

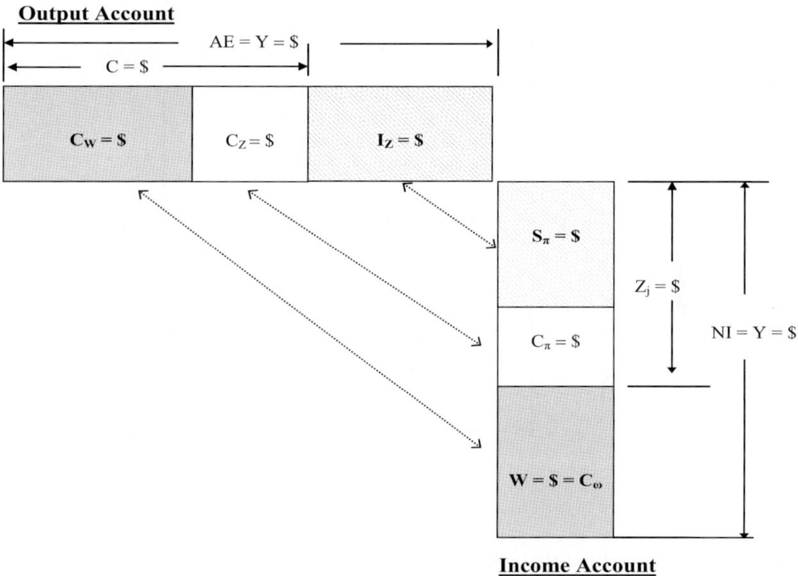

and Michl 1999: 29–31). The vertical axis of this schedule will show the net (surplus) product as distributed on both the income account side (W + Z) and the output account side (C + I) of the ledger. The horizontal axis will show the rates of profit (r) and growth (g_A) and will intersect at the maximum rate of profit (R) associated with a zero wage-share. This is shown in Figure 5.

The growth rate of the means of production, or accumulation rate of capital (g_A), is in this simple framework equal to the profit portion of surplus product saved as revenues for investment expenditures (I) divided by the original value of the means of production (**pA**):

$$g_A = \frac{I}{pA} \tag{8}$$

Recall from the mapping between the different aggregate accounts that the level of investment is equal to the propensity to save out of

Figure 5

Growth-distribution schedule

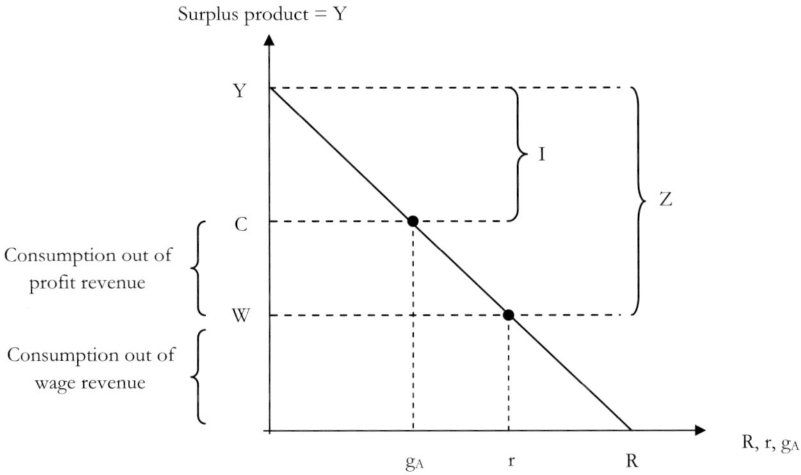

profits multiplied by the profit revenue (Z); hence the growth rate can be alternatively expressed as:

$$g_A = \frac{\beta_\pi Z}{pA} = \beta_\pi r_j \Leftrightarrow r_j = \frac{g_A}{\beta_\pi} \Leftrightarrow \beta_\pi = \frac{g_A}{r_j} \tag{9}$$

This equation states simply that the growth rate is equal to the savings propensity out of profit revenue multiplied by the rate of profit, and the profit rate is equal to the growth rate divided by this same propensity to save. This is nothing more than the simplest expression of the Cambridge Equation, an equation originating with Pasinetti (1962) that expresses the functional relation between profitability and growth.[23] When the propensity to save out of profit revenue is unity, all profits are saved for investment and the rate of growth is equal to rate of profit: that is, $(g_A)_{\beta=1} = r$. Alternatively, when the savings propensity is zero, profit earners invest nothing and consume wholesale their revenue. This case corresponds to Marx's model of simple reproduction. When the wage share is zero, the profit rate is at its maximum value R, and if the savings propensity out of profits is equal to unity, then the growth rate too is at its maximum value corresponding to R. This maximum rate of growth has been called the "Golden Rule," and here profit earners are purely parsimonious and accordingly throw all of their revenue towards growth of the system.

Depicting the growth rate-profit rate Cambridge Equation nexus in Quadrant IV and combining it with the growth-distribution schedule,

Figure 6

Growth-distribution schedule and the savings propensity out of profit revenue

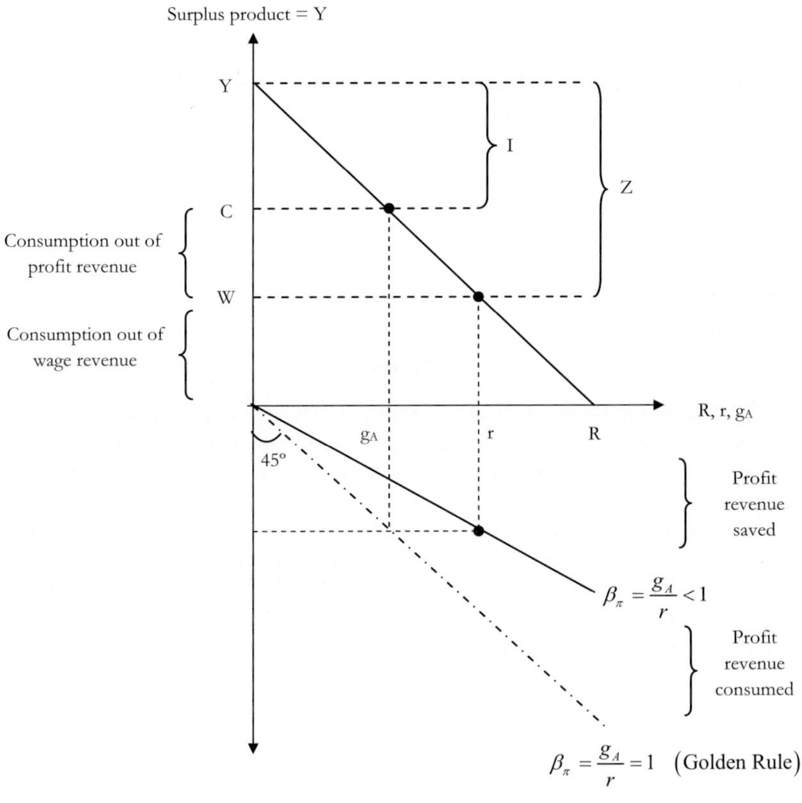

we can provide a more complete picture of a surplus-producing economy expressed in terms of the income and output relations as in Figure 6 (a similar graph appears in Kurz and Salvadori 2005: 48).

Conclusion

The surplus approach to value and distribution represents an alternative manner to the orthodox neoclassical modeling of modern capitalistic economic systems. The framework is robust and allows for income account relations and output account relations to be put into relation with each other such that a holistic interpretation of the economy can be expounded and developed. The robustness of the framework allows for different conceptions of causality to be advanced; hence both Classical closure emanating from the income account side of the socio-economic ledger as well as Post Keynesian closure emanating from the output account of the ledger can equally be advanced and developed. The openness and robustness of the framework allows for the different theoretical traditions within heterodox economics to be put to the test vis-à-vis empirics, with the end result that the development of the laws of motion of modern capitalistic socio-economic systems can at last be understood and progressive policies aimed at addressing the exploitive and oppressive nature of these systems can be articulated and developed.

Notes

1. This essay deals exclusively with circulating capital models in which the means of production requirements are completely exhausted in the single round of production and the rate of depreciation is assumed to be 100 percent.

2. The review in question is by Melvin Reder (1961) writing for the *American Economic Review*, and the reference is Phillip Wicksteed (1914), whom Sraffa refers to as the "purist of marginal theory" (Sraffa 1960: v).

3. In his 1961 review of Sraffa's book for the *Scottish Journal of Political Economy*, Meek remarks that:

> Mr. Sraffa's important book . . . can be looked at from various points of view. It can be regarded . . . simply as an unorthodox theoretical model of a particular type of economy, designed to solve the traditional problem of value in a new way. It can be regarded as an implicit attack on modern

marginal analysis . . . [o]r finally it can be regarded as a sort of magnificent rehabilitation of the Classical (and up to a point Marxian) approach to certain crucial problems relating to value and distribution. (Meek 1967: 161)

4. I would like to thank Erik Olsen of the University of Missouri, Kansas City for making this distinction clear at the Workshop where the initial version of the present paper was presented.

5. This is in marked distinction to the approach Sraffa adopted in Chapter VI of his book on the reduction to dated labor, where the analytics of the first five chapters that use the "physicalist" method are reproduced via the reduction methodology in this single chapter. In fact, Sraffa heavily utilized the reduction framework in the 1940s prior to the arrival of the Standard system (see D3/12/21 Notes on Industrial Schemes of September 1942, D3/12/2 and D3/12/24 Notes "Reduction" of October-December 1942; it was not until February 1944 that Sraffa finally discovers the properties of the Standard system and formally develops the *q*-system of quantity—read physicalist—multipliers; the relevant folder is archived D3/12/36 and is simply entitled "Notes"; see Carter 2010). See Kurz and Salvadori (2008) for an account of Sraffa's forays of this time in the reduction methodology.

6. This is actually a very significant point. Classical political economy, from Smith to Marx, has consistently utilized a comparative approach to the analysis of market-dominated economies through the juxtaposition of an "ideal" society of direct producer-owners who command the entirety of the net product resultant from their productivity. Smith (1976) referred to this as the "early and rude state" (Book I, Ch. iv); Ricardo and Malthus too discussed and debated this idea to the extent that both agreed that "labour commanded" coincided with "labour bestowed" in the "early and rude" society; Marx refers calls this simple or petty commodity production, and spends tremendous intellectual energy in the first three chapters of *Capital*, Volume I on the value form in this socio-economic system; and lastly Sraffa develops this through the physicalist analogue of the production for subsistence model in Chapter I of his book and expresses this socio-economic structure in value terms with the development in his unpublished notes of the "value theory of labour" (see below). What is beyond contention is that in this socio-economic system the labor theory of value holds. See Carter (2011a) for further analysis of this important point.

7. Pasinetti (1977: 126–127) develops a formal model inclusive of the subsistence wage in terms of the "augmented A-matrix," the means of production matrix " 'augmented' by the consumption coefficients needed for the maintenance of the workers."

8. Matthew Forstater pointed out to me in 2009 that Sraffa's surplus production model is precisely analogous to the model in Quesnay's *Tableau* in the sense that it consists of "fertile" wheat production and "sterile" iron production.

9. Sraffa continues:

> What is necessary are the given circumstances, the known ones (whether natural of social) of a given subject . . . Therefore, according to what an economist selects as the "subject" of his economy (usually identifying himself with it), the "surplus" will be different. The standpoint of capitalist society itself is that of the ruling class and therefore the surplus is composed of rent, interest and profit: Marx is the only economist who takes explicitly and consistently this point of view—and also Ricardo (specifically in Notes to Malthus) but not consistently. Marshall, who tries to take a classless human standpoint, regards all men as responsible subjects, and therefore all human consumption (he includes savings; this question of the inclusion of savings in income is also a question of who is "subject") wages, interest, and rent as part of the surplus (which he calls the national dividend). Keynes, who takes the standpoint of the company director, regards only the "entrepreneur" (who is "responsible for production") [as the subject, and] specifically defined "profits" as surplus, all the factors having to be induced or paid according to contract (he goes as far as to regard past contracts as part of the given circumstances). Finally if one attempts to take an entirely objective point of view, the very conception of a surplus melts away. For if we take this natural science point of view, we must start by assuming that for every effect there must be a cause, that the causes are identical with the effects, and that there can be nothing in the effect which was not in the cause: in our case, there can be no product for which there has not been an equivalent cost, and all cost (= expenses) must be necessary to produce it. (D3/12/7/161 : 2–3)

10. The importance of the Majorca Draft of 1955 has yet to be properly accounted for in the nascent literature on the Sraffa Papers (the same holds for Sraffa's archival activity in the 1950s generally speaking). The document itself, archived as D3/12/52, is a fascinating 31-page handwritten first draft of Part I of his book (single product industries).

11. The underlined "$\underline{w}$" represents the proportionate wage, or wage share, in the notation used in Sraffa's archival material.

12. The reference to "insurmountable obstacle" is actually a reference to the term coined in a different context by Wicksell (1934, Volume II: 221). Sraffa employs this term repeatedly throughout his archival notes mostly in terms of the "value theory of labour" (see below).

13. In the present essay we do not enter into the thorny issue of the determination of the money form of value and simply make the assumption that it can be determined, say by the simple assumption of commodity money the product of which is the result of "unassisted labour" that results from "silver picked up on the sea-shore in a day" (Sraffa and Dobb 1951, Vol. XI: 94). The latter was a significant point of debate between Ricardo and Malthus

(see Sraffa and Dobb 1951, Vol. II: 81; see also Carter 2011b). A major limitation of this assumption is the implicit neutrality of "money" in the present framework; hence "money" here serves simply as a measure of generalized exchange and the "universal" numeraire.

14. The issue of the organic composition of the wage good sector has plagued Marxian economics since its inception, especially around the problem of Marx's transformation. This was brought to light by Wilhelm Lexis in a review of *Capital*, Volume III, that was published in the *Quarterly Journal of Economics* in 1895 (Lexis 1895) Sraffa mentions Lexis on several occasions in his papers, speaking when addressing the wage good sector of the "'Lexis' consideration" in the Majorca Draft (D3/12/52/5). See Howard and King (1989: 47) for a discussion on Lexis regarding this very point. Garegnani (1984: 313–320) develops some of the analytics of this with the construction of the "vertically-integrated wage-good sector," conceived as an abstract subsystem within a larger economic system of both basics and non-basics around which the rate of profit for the entire system is determined. In essence he constructs a vertically-integrated "corn model," where Ricardo's "corn" is replaced by Garegnani's wage good sector (he admits as much on page 313, note 39). He then juxtaposes this treatment to Sraffa's own construct of the Standard commodity and highlights the resonance between both approaches (see Section VII).

15. The Marxist critique is found in de Brunhoff (1974–1975) and Laibman (1974–1975), and Sraffian in Roncaglia (1978); Kurz and Salvadori (1987); Garegnani (1984); and Pasinetti (1977). Sinha (2000) also discusses Eatwell's approach with disapproval.

16. The analysis that follows is strictly conducted in terms of the aggregates of given quantities that Sraffa himself utilized in his book. Hence the equations express the physical levels of output, labor, and money-as-numeraire magnitudes, that is, they are *not* unit input-output coefficients that are divided by gross output. Hence no questions of returns to scale need apply (see Kurz and Salvadori 1995: 43).

17. The idea of gold as the product of "unassisted labour" was proposed by Malthus and strongly contested by Ricardo; see *Works and Correspondence of David Ricardo*,Volume II, *Notes on Malthus*, pp. 81–82, and Volume VI, *Letters 1819–1821*, pp. 233–234. For a full reference to Malthus's different measures of value see Volume XI, *General Index*, p. 107 (Sraffa and Dobb, 1951–1954). See also Carter (2011b).

18. Pasinetti's notation does reflect the more conventional inter-industry framework, with the matrix $\mathbf{A}$ equal to the inter-industry coefficients matrix, the (row) vector $\mathbf{a_n}$ equal to the direct labor requirements, the (row) vector $\mathbf{p}$ equal to the (no-distribution) set of prices, and the scalar value w the wage rate.

19. The extreme case of an economic system containing only one fertile industry is that of Ricardo's corn model, especially as Sraffa interprets the 1815

Essay on Profits. (see Sraffa's Introduction to *Works*, Sraffa and Dobb, 1951, Vol I: xxx–xxxvii).

20. On the resonance between the New Interpretation and Sraffa, see an important paper by Stefano Perri (2010).

21. Although in somewhat modified form, the present diagrammatic depiction between the income and output account is inspired by similar (though not exact) diagrams, of increasing complexity, in Shaihk and Tonak (1994).

22. The present distribution-growth model differs from Foley and Michl (1999) in that ours does not divide each account by the number of workers; that is, ours are "$" magnitudes whereas Foley and Michl's are "$^{\$}/_{wkr}$" magnitudes.

23. Foley and Michl (1999: Chapter 5) develop a more sophisticated model of consumption, savings, and investment through the utilization of an inter-temporal logarithmic discounted Cobb-Douglas utility function subject to the inter-temporal budget constraint of current consumption and next-period capital accumulation.

References

Bellofiore, R. (2008). "Sraffa After Marx: An Open Issue." In *Sraffa or Alternative Economics*. Eds. G. Chiodi and L. Ditta, pp. 68–92.

——. (2010). "The 'Tiresome Objector' and Old Moor: A Renewal of the Debate of Marx and Sraffa Based on the Unpublished Material at the Wren Library." Paper presented at Cambridge Journal of Economics Celebratory Session on Sraffa's 50th Anniversary of *Production of Commodities*: *New Perspectives on the Work of Piero Sraffa*, Queens College, Cambridge

Carter, S. (2010). "Sraffa and the 'Corrected' Organic Composition of Capital." Unpublished manuscript, University of Tulsa.

——. (2011a). "Sraffa on Income Distribution in a Capitalist System." Paper presented at Cambridge Journal of Economics Celebratory Session on Sraffa's 50th Anniversary of *Production of Commodities*: *New Perspectives on the Work of Piero Sraffa*, Queens College, Cambridge

——. (2011b). "Sraffa, Malthus, and the Measure of Value." Unpublished Manuscript, University of Tulsa.

De Brunhoff, S. (1974–1975). "Controversies in the Theory of Surplus Value: A Reply to John Eatwell." *Science and Society* 38(4): 478–482.

Duménil, G. (1983–1984). "Beyond the Transformation Riddle: A Labor Theory of Value." *Science and Society* 47(4): 427–450.

Eatwell, J. (1974). "Theories of Surplus Value: Old and New." *Science and Society* 38(3): 281–303.

——. (1975). "Mr. Sraffa's Standard Commodity and the Rate of Exploitation." *Quarterly Journal of Economics* 89(4): 543–555.

Foley, D. (1982). "The Value of Money, the Value pf Labor Power, and the Marxian Transformation Problem." *Review of Radical Political Economics* 14(2): 37–46.

Foley, D., and T. R. Michl. (1999). *Growth and Distribution.* Cambridge, MA: Harvard University Press.

Garegnani, P. (1984). "Value and Distribution in the Classical Economists and Marx." *Oxford Economic Papers* 36(2): 291–325.

——. (1987). "Surplus Approach to Value and Distribution." In *New Palgrave Dictionary of Economics.* Eds. J. Eatwell, M. Milgate, and P. Newman, pp. 560–574. London: Palgrave

Howard, M. C., and J. E. King. (1989). *A History of Marxian Economics, Volume I: 1883–1929.* Princeton: Princeton University Press.

Kurz, H., and N. Salvadori. (1987). "Burmeister on Sraffa and the Labor Theory of Value: A Comment." *Journal of Political Economy* 95: 870–881.

——. (2005). Theory of Production. A Long Period Analysis. Cambridge: Cambridge University Press.

——. (2008). "On the Collaboration Between Sraffa and Besicovitch: The 'Proof of Gradient'." In *Sraffa or Alternative Economics.* Eds. G. Chiodi and L. Ditta, pp. 260–274. London: Palgrave.

Laibman, D. (1974–1975). "Controversies in the Theory of Surplus Value: A Comment." *Science and Society* 38(4): 482–487.

Lexis, W. (1895). "The Concluding Volume of Marx's *Capital.*" *Quarterly Journal of Economics* 10(1): 1–33.

Meek, R. (1962). *The Economics of Physiocracy.* London: George Allen & Unwin, Ltd.

——. (1967). *Economics and Ideology and Other Essays: Studies in the Development of Economic Thought.* London: Chapman and Hall, Ltd.

Pasinetti, L. L. (1962). "Rate of Profit and Income Distribution in Relation to the Rate of Economic Growth." *Review of Economic Studies* 29: 267–279.

——. (1977). *Lectures on the Theory of Production.* New York: Columbia University Press.

Perri, S. (2010). "From 'Loaf of Bread' to 'Commodity Fetishism': A 'New Interpretation' of the Sraffa-Marx Connection." *History of Economic Ideas* 28(1): 33–59.

Reder, M. (1961). "Review of *Production of Commodities by Means of Commodities: Prelude to a Critique of Economic Theory.*" *American Economic Review* 51(4): 688–695.

Robinson, J. V. (1966). *An Essay on Marxian Economics, Second Edition.* London: St. Martin's Press.

Roncaglia, A. (1978). *Sraffa and the Theory of Prices.* New York: John Wiley and Sons.

Shaikh, A. (1977). "Marx's Theory of Value and the 'Transformation Problem'." In *The Subtle Anatomy of Capitalism.* Ed. J. Schwartz. Santa Monica: Goodyear.

Shaihk, A., and E. A. Tonak. (1994). *Measuring the Wealth of Nations: The Political Economy of National Accounts.* New York: Cambridge University Press.

Sinha, A. (2000). "Understanding the Transformation Problem: Is the Standard Commodity a Solution?" *Review of Radical Political Economics* 32(2): 265–281.

Smith, A. (1976). *An Inquiry into the Nature and Causes of the Wealth of Nations,* Glasgow Edition. Oxford: Oxford University Press.

Sraffa, P. (1960). *Production of Commodities by Means of Commodities: Prelude to a Critique of Economic Theory.* Cambridge: Cambridge University Press.

Sraffa, P., and M. Dobb. (1951). *The Works and Correspondence of David Ricardo,* Eleven Volumes. Cambridge: Cambridge University Press.

——. (1951–1954). *The Works and Correspondence of David Ricardo,* Volumes I–XI. Cambridge: Cambridge University Press.

Wicksell, K. (1934). *Lectures on Political Economy,* Volume II. London: George Routledge and Sons.

Wicksteed, P. (1914). "Political Economy in Light of Marginal Theory." *Economic Journal* 24: 18–20.

Demand, Structural Interdependence, and Economic Provisioning

By GARY MONGIOVI*

ABSTRACT. Industrial and post-industrial economies are characterized by a high degree of structural interdependence. Once an economy attains a level of economic development in which the technology enables a substantial portion of the population to enjoy a standard of living significantly above subsistence, "the material needs" of the system become difficult to define because they are interconnected with the relations of production in complex ways. In particular, demand comes to play a key role in the subsequent development of the system. This article presents an intersectoral model that integrates Keynesian and Kaleckian elements onto the classical surplus approach. The aim of the model is to provide a non-neoclassical framework that can be used to analyze how demand, income distribution, and production are interconnected.

Introduction

The function of an economic system is to enable the individuals who comprise it to meet their material needs. Different systems do this in different ways; some do the job "better" than others, according to various criteria (the rate of growth of per capita income; access to subsistence; distributive justice; and so forth). Owing to the division of labor, industrial and post-industrial economies are characterized by a high degree of structural interdependence: technical interdependence among productive sectors; interdependence between demand and employment; and interdependence between state and economy. Structural interdependence has been the subject of economic analysis since the emergence of classical political economy in the 17th century, notably in the *Tableau Économique*, in

*Professor of Economics, St. John's University, Jamaica, New York 11439 (USA), e-mail: mongiovg@stjohns.edu. The helpful comments of two anonymous referees are gratefully acknowledged.

American Journal of Economics and Sociology, Vol. 70, No. 5 (November, 2011).

Marx's schemes of reproduction, in the post-Marx writings on the trade cycle, in Input-Output economics and activity analysis, and in the Sraffa model.

This article reflects upon the role of demand in the context of such models of structural interdependence. Once an economy attains a level of economic development in which the technology enables a substantial portion of the population to enjoy a standard of living significantly above subsistence, "the material needs" of the system become difficult to define because they are interconnected with the relations of production in complex ways. In particular, demand comes to play a key role in the subsequent development of the system. Wages are no longer analogous to the fuel that is needed to power an engine, or the fodder that a team of oxen need to enable them to pull a plow. Aggregate demand drives growth, and the composition of demand regulates the allocation of resources. Under modern capitalism, the situation is complicated by the fact that the composition of demand is shaped in large part by the marketing activity and wage policies of powerful oligopolistic entities. This article examines these issues in the light of the class of structural models associated with Leontief, Pasinetti, Lowe, and Sraffa. These models avoid the pitfalls of the conventional treatment of demand in terms of price-elastic demand functions, but they have made only tentative progress in explaining the evolution of demand. The aim of the article is not to provide a theory of demand, but to assess how these structural models have treated demand and suggest how the theory of demand can be further developed within the broad framework of such models.

The Provisioning Process in the History of Economic Analysis

The first attempts, by the mercantilists in the 16th and 17th centuries, to describe how market economies work were necessarily primitive, and with few exceptions (for example, Mun 1664) barely scratched the surface of the problem. Focused as they were on commerce—on flows of goods and money—the mercantilists had little to say about how those goods get produced, allocated, and reproduced in such a way as to enable the economy to persist through time. On development and structural change they offered nothing at all. In the 17th century William Petty (1662) correctly identified production as the ultimate source of income, an insight that represented a significant advance on the misleading mercantilist view that trade is the basis of national prosperity. Petty also introduced the crucial idea that an economy is prosperous in so far as it is capable of producing a surplus over and above the wage goods and material inputs consumed in the production process. By the next century, even before the onset of industrialization in Britain, political economists had thoroughly internalized Petty's outlook.

Bernard Mandeville, less a political philosopher or social scientist than a mischievous wag who specialized in poking the eye of bourgeois complacency, recognized not only that production is what enables a society to thrive, but also that once the economy has advanced beyond a bare subsistence standard of living, production is to a large extent driven by demand. The metaphorical hive of Mandeville's *Fable of the Bees* (1724) is a sophisticated economic system exhibiting a fairly extensive division of labor. Until its conversion to virtuous austerity, the hive is an engine of self-reproduction. In its thriving phase, the hive undergoes no structural evolution, though Mandeville allows for changes in fashion. When the hive becomes virtuous, eschewing vain luxury, the resulting contraction in demand leads to economic and social collapse: without the stimulus of "avarice," industry withers.

To Petty's notion of surplus the physiocrats added an explicit recognition of the interconnectedness of production. Quesnay's *Tableau Économique* (1759) depicts the economy as a network of interconnected sectors and social classes. Economic activity is conceived as a circular process of production and consumption in which the outputs of the agricultural and manufacturing sectors serve as inputs into each other's production processes. Adam Smith (1776) made two significant advances on the rudimentary physiocratic model. First, he recognized that the manufacturing sector is as capable as agriculture of generating a surplus, and consequently plays an indispensable role in growth and development. Second, he sketched out the mechanism by which a market economy coordinates atomistic self-interested behavior to enable the material reproduction of the system. It is a remarkable feature of market economies that commodities are produced not in random quantities, but in amounts that roughly coincide with what can be sold; that resources get channeled out of sectors whose products are wanted in smaller quantities than before, and into sectors whose products are now in higher demand and indeed might not even have been imagined just a few years earlier; and that incomes are generated that enable the inhabitants of the system to purchase the goods that its productive activity has created. The system is, in other words, able to reproduce itself.[1] The mechanism that brings about this coordination is of course the intersectoral movement of capital in pursuit of its highest return, a process that, as described by Smith, manifests itself through the gravitation of market prices of goods toward long-period cost of production. None of this is meant to suggest that the mechanism unfolds seamlessly, or can be relied upon to generate optimal outcomes. The point is simply that this mechanism must play a part in any account of how a capitalist system provisions itself and how it evolves through history.

David Ricardo (1821) clarified and refined Smith's argument by demonstrating that real wages, the profit rate, and relative prices are connected to one another in a precise and systematic way. In particular, he showed that the wage rate and the profit rate vary inversely to one another, and that the specific effect of a change in distribution on the pattern of relative prices depends upon differences in the degree to which the production processes of the various sectors of the economy utilize produced means of production relative to labor. Ricardo's friend Thomas Robert Malthus (1820) raised prescient questions about the ability of a market economy to sustain aggregate demand at levels sufficient to prevent the system's stagnation or decline. Marx (1867, 1893, 1894) developed the surplus approach further, drawing directly upon the *Tableau Économique* to construct his Volume II reproduction schemes, which expose the roles that technical change, structural imbalances, and monetary phenomena may play in triggering crises.

The first few generations of neoclassical economists were no less concerned than the classicals and Marx with provisioning and economic structure. Alfred Marshall's famous definition of economics as "the study of mankind in the ordinary business of life" reflects his concern with the problem of material provisioning, and the attention he paid to the institutional framework is evidence of his recognition that the structural features of the economy are crucial to the provisioning process (Marshall 1920: 1). While Jevons (1879) and Walras (1926) directed their attention mainly to what we would call technical theoretical problems, they did so with a view to providing a tool to address real-world problems.[2] In his *Theory of Social Economy* (1932), Gustav Cassel presents a neoclassical general equilibrium model as part of an attempt to elucidate how markets coordinate production, which is conceived as a fundamentally collaborative activity aimed at provisioning the members of society. We find also in the Austrian School an acute awareness of the structural interconnections that underpin the provisioning process: Carl Menger's (1871) distinction between lower and higher order goods, Friedrich Hayek's (1931) production triangles, Eugene von Böhm-Bawerk's (1884) concept of the roundaboutness of production, and Ludwig Lachmann's (1956) emphasis on the complementarities among different capital goods as a factor in cyclical fluctuations—all these are indications that the Austrian tradition is duly mindful of the structural features of economic activity. Welfare economics and the socialist calculation debates are, if nothing else, a great hashing-out of the criteria by which to evaluate how effectively different institutional frameworks meet people's provisioning requirements.

Over the past three or four decades, though, the attention of mainstream economists has drifted away from problems of how the economy provisions itself, perhaps on the supposition that the main analytical issues have been mostly resolved. The shift is partly reflected in the current prominence of behavioral economics, which focuses on how economic actors make choices under various circumstances. The issue is of undeniable practical importance to policymakers, and is no doubt relevant to the provisioning process in so far as social outcomes are in an obvious sense the cumulative by-product of decisions taken by many individuals in a particular institutional context. But the focus has mainly been on choice behavior at the microeconomic level; less attention had been paid to how "individual behaviors and economic institutions interact to produce aggregate outcomes" (Bowles 2004: 8, an exception to the rule; for an overview of behavioral economics, see Altman 2004).

A Classical-Keynesian Model

From an economic standpoint the most fundamental problem is to identify the conditions required for the material continuation of society. If, in the long run, these conditions are not met, the social context that is today taken for granted will tomorrow be the subject of history. All economic activity takes place within a definite social setting comprised of institutions, laws, rights, social obligations, behavioral conventions, and so forth. The maintenance and reproduction of this social matrix requires that agents must somehow learn the rules imposed upon them by the existing mode of production; that is to say, they must learn what sorts of behavior will enable them to survive and flourish in a given social environment. Households, individuals, and firms are constrained not just by resource availability, but also by legal and moral rules and by the cognitive blinders that any social framework imposes upon the human mind (see Nell 1984; Lowe 1964).

Models of classical and Marxian provenance are particularly concerned with these structural features of economic activity. Such models focus upon the requirements for physical reproduction of the socioeconomic system rather than upon agents' behavioral responses to a particular set of conditions. Instead of treating the social context as a fait accompli, structural models attempt to discover what patterns of behavior are compatible with the existence and continuity of the institutions, class relations, and production processes that characterize the economic system. In the simplest constructions they determine the prices that reintegrate the economy's production processes and enable the system to reproduce itself. At higher levels of complexity, classical analysis attempts to show how capitalist institutions, class behavior, and production relations reinforce one another; it investigates the patterns of accumulation implicit in capitalist production; and it inquires into the relations connecting consumption, distribution, and accumulation. The objectives are, first, to explain the rules that preserve the system's viability, and then to determine the implications these rules have for the system's evolution over time. Marx's *Capital* (1867, 1893, 1894), which calls attention to the self-generated tensions, or contradictions, that accompany capitalist development, is perhaps the paradigmatic example of this approach. In this section we construct a simple structural model that incorporates classical and Keynesian elements.

The classical political economists and Marx sought to explain how a market economy generates and distributes a social surplus (see Garegnani 1984). Their interest in this question derived from the premise that the accumulation of capital is undertaken by the social class that receives the surplus in the form of profits, that is, the capitalist class. In classical surplus theories the process by which relative prices are determined does not simultaneously determine distribution and quantities; these are analyzed separately. The data of the classical theory are: (i) the size and composition of the social product; (ii) the technical conditions of production; and (iii) some distribution parameter—either the real wage or the profit rate. If we assume constant returns to scale, that all capital is circulating capital, that one method of production is available for the production of each commodity, that wages are paid *post factum*, that there is no joint production, and that all commodities are basic in the sense of Sraffa (1960),[3] then relative prices and the real wage are determined by the solution to the following system:

$$\begin{aligned} \mathbf{p} &= \mathbf{pA}(1+r) + w\boldsymbol{l} \\ p_1 &= 1 \\ r &= r^*, \end{aligned} \tag{1}$$

where $\mathbf{p}$ is a row vector of n prices; $\mathbf{A} = [a_{ij}]$ is an $n \times n$ matrix each element of which represents the amount of commodity i required to produce a unit of commodity j; $\boldsymbol{l}$ is a row vector of labor input requirements; w is the real wage, measured in terms of the *numeraire* (commodity 1); and $r = r^*$ is the profit rate, which we shall regard as parametric.[4] This system determines the $n-1$ relative prices and the real wage. Manipulation of Equation (1) yields the solution:

$$\mathbf{p} = w\boldsymbol{l}[\mathbf{I} - \mathbf{A}(1+r)]^{-1} \tag{2}$$

where $\mathbf{I}$ is the identity matrix. Implicit in this result is an inverse relationship between the wage rate and the profit rate. The trade-off has the form of a polynomial expression; its precise shape will depend upon the dimensions of **A**; on the technical conditions of production, that is, on the magnitudes of the elements of **A** and ***l***; and on the choice of *numeraire*. In general, the relationship will not be linear. The impact on relative prices of a change in distribution will likewise depend upon these same considerations (see Pasinetti 1977 for a more detailed discussion of the analytics).

In marginalist theory the function of the price mechanism is to clear markets by bringing quantities supplied into equality with quantities demanded. Prices perform a somewhat different task in the classical theory. The production of any commodity requires inputs from the various other sectors of the economy. During a round of production each industry, it is presumed, produces at least enough output to replace what is used up by itself and by other sectors. But at the end of each production period all of the output of any commodity is in the possession of the industry that produced it. Before another round of production can begin, the economy must somehow manage to transfer a portion of each output from the industry that produced it to the industries that use it as an input; this is accomplished through marketplace transactions. Competition causes the price vector to assume a configuration that permits the reproduction of the economy with a uniform profit rate. In both the classical and marginalist theories, prices play an indispensable coordinating role in the allocation of resources, but the nature of this role differs in the two cases. In the marginalist theory prices exist to enable the economy to accommodate the problem of scarcity, whereas classical prices of production make possible the swaps necessary for the economy to reproduce itself.

Implicit in the classical conception of a market economy is a set of quantity relations that must be satisfied in long-period equilibrium (see Walsh and Gram 1980; Kurz and Salvadori 1995). Let the elements of the column vector $\mathbf{q} = [q_1, \ldots, q_n]$ represent the gross outputs of commodities 1 through n. The elements of a second column vector $\mathbf{y} = [y_1, \ldots, y_n]$ are the net outputs or final demands for the various commodities. In any viable economy, **q** must be adequate to replace the commodities used up in production and to satisfy the final demand. In the long period, the economy will not produce more of any commodity than is demanded (demand for additions to inventories is included in **y**), so we have the equations:

$$\mathbf{q} = \mathbf{Aq} + \mathbf{y}, \text{ with solution} \tag{3}$$

$$\mathbf{q} = (\mathbf{I} - \mathbf{A})^{-1}\,\mathbf{y} \tag{4}$$

It can easily be shown that given **y** and *r*, the value of net output is equal to the sum of wages and profits distributed within the economy.[5] Unless the net output vector **y** (or some other *n*-component vector of gross and net outputs) is taken as parametric, the quantity system will be underdetermined (by *n* degrees of freedom) and no solution will be possible.

The quantity relations of Equation (3) simply reflect the condition that the quantity demanded of each commodity must match the amount of it produced. This equality of supply and demand refers only to produced goods and not to labor. The uniform profit rate condition and the implicit assumption that capitalists seek the highest possible rate of return imply that no entrepreneur will tend to produce more or less of a good than he can sell; but the same uniformity condition does not require that the supply and demand for labor be equalized. While the equality of supply and demand for commodities is a necessary feature of long-period equilibrium, neither long-period prices of production nor the outputs are here determined by the price-elastic supply and demand functions of marginalist theory.

The earliest attempt to disaggregate Keynes's model and express it in the form of a Leontief-type matrix was undertaken by Richard Goodwin (1949) in a paper that deserves more attention, especially from Post-Keynesians, than it has received. Several attempts have been made to construct formal models that integrate the classical and Keynesian theories (Pasinetti 1974; Kurz 1985). The model presented here (which I have utilized elsewhere; see Mongiovi 1991, 1992) draws upon these contributions and upon a less well-known paper by Miyazawa and Masegi (1963), who set up their model in terms of money-value transactions; we shall introduce some modifications to derive a model whose parameters and variables refer to physical quantities in order to derive a model of output determination that is compatible with the classical surplus approach.

As above, we consider an economy in which constant returns prevail, all goods are basics, only one technique is available for the production of any commodity, and all capital is circulating capital. We assume also that any final good can be used either to satisfy consumption demand or to expand the economy's stock of plant and equipment; this assumption can be taken into account if the vector of final demands is expressed as the sum of two sub-vectors:

$$\mathbf{y} = \mathbf{y}^c + \mathbf{y}^I \tag{5}$$

Each element y_i^c, $i = 1, \ldots, n$ of the column vector $\mathbf{y}^c$ represents the amount of commodity i demanded for consumption purposes; each element y_i^I of the vector $\mathbf{y}^I$ indicates how much of commodity i the economy wishes to channel into the expansion of productive capacity.[6]

Assume that there exist two social classes—workers, who receive wages, and capitalist-entrepreneurs, who receive profits. Each of these classes is presumed to allocate a certain proportion of its money income to the consumption of each of the commodities produced by the economy. Associating the subscripts w and π with the working class and capitalist class, respectively, we define the consumption coefficients c_{iw} and $c_{i\pi}$ as the number of additional units of commodity i demanded by the economy with each additional unit of wage or profit income, respectively; thus, $p_i c_{iw}$ (or $p_i c_{i\pi}$) is the marginal propensity of the wage-earning (or profit-receiving) class to spend its income on good i.

The consumption coefficients can be arranged into a matrix

$$\mathbf{C} = \begin{bmatrix} c_{1w} & c_{1\pi} \\ c_{2w} & c_{2\pi} \\ \vdots & \vdots \\ c_{nw} & c_{n\pi} \end{bmatrix}$$

which is subject to the following constraints: first, it must be true that $\mathbf{pC} \leq [1, 1]$; that is, the marginal propensity to consume of each class must be less than or equal to one, and the MPC of at least one class must be strictly less than one. We assume for simplicity that agents always spend the same proportion of their incomes on each good ($p_i c_{iw} = \gamma_{iw}$ and $p_i c_{i\pi} = \gamma_{i\pi}$ for $i = 1, \ldots, n$). These admittedly unrealistic assumptions are not essential, and little of substance would be changed by adopting more realistic hypotheses, although the analytics would become much more cumbersome.[7]

Let us now define a matrix **V** whose elements represent the values added by labor and by produced means of production to the price of each commodity:

$$\mathbf{V} = \begin{bmatrix} wl_1 & wl_2 & \ldots & wl_n \\ r\sum p_i a_{i1} & r\sum p_i a_{i2} & \ldots & r\sum p_i a_{in} \end{bmatrix}$$

where w, r, and p_i represent as before the real wage, the profit rate, and the prices of commodities. Each elements of **V** depends upon the prior solution of the economy's price equations. The profit rate is taken as a datum; and since production is, by assumption, characterized by constant returns, w and relative prices can also be considered given and fixed once a *numeraire* is chosen. The incomes of workers and capitalists are given by

$$\mathbf{Vq} = \begin{bmatrix} W \\ \Pi \end{bmatrix},$$

where W and Π are, respectively, the wage bill and aggregate profits in money terms. From this it follows that

$$\mathbf{y}^c = \mathbf{CVq} \tag{6}$$

We know that in equilibrium the gross output vector must satisfy the quantity relations of Equation (3) $\mathbf{q} = \mathbf{Aq} + \mathbf{y}$. Substituting Equations (5) and (6) into Equation (3) gives $\mathbf{q} = \mathbf{Aq} + \mathbf{CVq} + \mathbf{y}^I$. Manipulating this last expression, we obtain:

$$\mathbf{q} = [\mathbf{I} - \mathbf{A} - \mathbf{CV}]^{-1}\,\mathbf{y}^I \tag{7}$$

The inverse matrix in Equation (7) can be manipulated further, giving the result:[8]

$$\mathbf{q} = (\mathbf{I} - \mathbf{A})^{-1}\left[\mathbf{I} - \mathbf{CV}(\mathbf{I} - \mathbf{A})^{-1}\right]^{-1}\mathbf{y}^{I} \qquad (8)$$

Thus, given **A**, **C**, and the profit rate, a given vector of investment demand will determine a unique vector of gross outputs.

The first term—$(\mathbf{I} - \mathbf{A})^{-1}$—in the expression that multiplies $\mathbf{y}^{I}$ in System (8) is the familiar Leontief inverse. The interpretation of the expression $[\mathbf{I} - \mathbf{CV}(\mathbf{I} - \mathbf{A})^{-1}]^{-1}$ is less obvious, but it can be shown, with not too much effort, to be a perfect matrix analogue of the simple Kaleckian spending multiplier (see Miyazawa and Masegi 1963: 90–91).

By combining the Leontief and Keynes-Kalecki multipliers, System (8) captures the transmission mechanism by which autonomous changes in demand are translated into still larger changes in output. An autonomous increase in any of the elements of the investment vector will lead, via the operation of the Leontief inverse, to an increased demand for produced inputs. If the necessary labor is available, there will be an increase in the incomes of newly-hired workers and of the owners of newly-hired capital in those input sectors. Once this increase in incomes occurs, the spending multiplier becomes operative as the receivers of the new income begin to spend it on final goods. There follows an increase in the demand for inputs required to produce *those* final commodities. From this point on, the Leontief and Keynesian multipliers operate together until the initial increase in spending wears itself out in the usual way.

A few observations ought to be made here regarding the operation of the multiplier in this model. It is clear, first of all, that a change in investment need only occur in a single sector to set off a chain reaction throughout the economy. In the end we will find that the components of the consumption vector will not be what they were, and that the outputs of all basic commodities will have changed. If only one component of $\mathbf{y}^{I}$ changes, or if all changes in its components are in the same direction, then the outputs of basic commodities will all change in the same direction—increasing if the initial change was positive, decreasing if the initial change was negative. If, on the other hand, some elements of $\mathbf{y}^{I}$ increase while others decrease, the impacts on the outputs of basic commodities cannot be predicted *a priori.*

They may all move together, or some may rise while others fall, depending upon input requirements, the magnitudes of the initial changes in the investment demand vector, and the effects of the resulting changes in incomes on the pattern of consumption. One advantage of the matrix formulation is its ability to trace the complex consequences of an initial change, or set of changes, in parameters.

A second aspect of the model that is of interest is its explicit consideration of the influence exerted by the distribution of income (represented by the value-added matrix **V**) on the solution. Investment demand gives rise to a secondary consumption demand; since it is presumed that workers and capitalists have different consumption patterns, this secondary demand will vary according to how income is distributed between wages and profits. The secondary consumption demand will in turn determine what commodities will be required as inputs in the next round of production, and the input coefficients of these required means of production will determine, through **V**, how much the incomes of the working class and the capitalist class will change in that production period. Tertiary changes in the composition of consumer demand will naturally ensue, and so the process must continue until the multiplier runs its course. Moreover, owing to the layered nature of the production process, in which commodities are produced by commodities in a complicated circular network, a change—even a small one—in the profit rate or real wage can radically alter the composition of gross output. Any change in distribution will activate a complex sequence of adjustments the results of which cannot be known *a priori*. An increase, for example, in the profit rate may cause a particular q_i to either rise or fall; and the change in q_i can be large or small regardless of the size of the initial change in the profit rate. The result depends entirely upon the parameters **A**, ***l***, and **C**.

Associated with any gross output vector **q** is a level of employment $N = \boldsymbol{l}\mathbf{q}$. An implication of the matrix multiplier is that a change in the composition of demand can alter the level of employment, even if total expenditure remains constant; indeed, GDP and employment are as likely to move in opposite directions as in the same direction (Kurz 1985: 130–132 also makes this point). More importantly, there is no reason to suppose that the level of employment determined by the solution vector **q** will utilize all of the labor available at the going wage; no forces are at work to ensure that the economy will gravitate toward a position of full employment. One of the stylized facts of late capitalism is the weakening of the connection between employment growth and the growth of GDP: in the US, each of the last several economic recoveries have taken longer than the previous recovery to restore employment to its pre-recession level. The reasons for this phenomenon are in all likelihood connected to structural changes that have occurred in Western capitalism over the past three decades (see Basu and Foley 2011 for an analysis of the issue). Models like the one described here may cast some light on why GDP growth no longer readily generates sufficient employment growth to absorb new entrants to the labor market, or to reabsorb workers displaced by recession.

In the model described above, a reduction in the wage with no change in investment spending clearly will not provide a remedy to large-scale persistent unemployment. The decline in w will induce an increase in the profit rate, but since capitalists have a smaller propensity to consume than workers there will be a net decline in consumption demand, and consequently a net decline in gross output and employment. This result reinforces the traditional Keynesian skepticism about the efficacy of wage reductions as a remedy to unemployment. A solution might in fact require a *higher* wage rate, but even this would not guarantee full employment.

Some Dynamic Considerations

We turn briefly to the dynamic aspects of the matrix multiplier derived in the preceding section. The model deals with situations that are fully adjusted with respect to the price vector and therefore does not trace the sequential effects of a change in the exogenous distribution variable on outputs and employment. These sequential adjustments occur, by definition, outside of equilibrium, that is, in a sphere into which our analysis does not enter. It is supposed here that such adjustments do not exhibit the same regularity that can be attributed to the forces that determine the solution to System (8), and therefore are not susceptible, without the adoption of special assumptions, to an exact analysis. This does not imply that questions concerning the movements of the variables through time are of no interest; on the contrary, Goodwin (1949) has shown that these movements can have important consequences for the cyclical behavior of the economy.

More problematic, perhaps, is the question of the meaning of the notion of "long-period equilibrium" in a context in which investment represents changes in productive capacity, while long-period equilibrium has traditionally been regarded as a static position with productive capacity fully adjusted to aggregate demand. In *The General Theory* Keynes (1936: 47–48) describes the long-period level of employment as the level consistent with the existing state of long-term expectations. The model outlined here can be interpreted in an analogous way. The given vector $\mathbf{y}^I$ expresses the long-term expectations of entrepreneurs as well as the other factors, both objective and subjective, that influence investment at a particular historical moment. The solution of System (8) determines the gross outputs that will be generated by the demand for these investment goods. The analysis does not require that the investment vector be persistent or quasi-permanent. Given $\mathbf{y}^I$, we can identify the level of employment toward which the economy will gravitate. If it is legitimate to suppose (as we have implicitly done here) that the elements of $\mathbf{y}^I$ change slowly—that is, that the recursive effects of the gravitation process on investment are of negligible magnitude—then the static character of the model need not be problematic.[9]

Consumption Demand

We have noted the artificiality of our assumption that workers and capitalists devote a constant proportion of their income to expenditure on each good—a device adopted in order to make the model tractable. But a useful account of the social provisioning process requires a more realistic approach to the analysis of the composition of consumption demand. While such an analysis lies beyond the scope of this essay, a few tentative observations are relevant to the topic at hand.

There is a vast literature on the inadequacies of the conventional treatment of consumer demand, and on the need for an alternative framework. These critiques draw attention to the disparity between the structure of preferences on which the well-behaved price-elastic demand functions of orthodox theory are grounded, and what modern sociological and psychological research indicate about the actual structure of human preferences. The standard axioms of choice—completeness, transitivity, convexity, and so forth—are incompatible with empirical findings from behavioral economics. If human needs exhibit a hierarchical ordering such as that famously posited by A. H. Maslow (1943; see also Georgescu-Roegen 1966: 194–198), the marginalist theory of demand falls to pieces. Pierangelo Garegnani (1990: 131) has noted that consumption habits tend not to be reversible. It is usually the case, he argues, that when the normal quantity demanded of a good is affected by prices to any considerable degree, the impact of a price change will amount to "an *irreversible* . . . change in the habits of consumers, which even marginalist authors would have to treat as a change of 'tastes' and therefore by a stage of analysis *separate* from the 'general equilibrium' determination of prices [in terms of] demand functions, where tastes appear as given."[10] The example he cites is that of the expansion of the demand for automobiles in America in the 1920s when assembly-line technology brought the price of a car within the budget of the average household. In such a situation, consumers will not respond to a reversion of the price to its original level by resuming their earlier pattern of consumption. The argument echoes Georgescu-Roegen's observation (1966: 183) that the law of demand

> is not a quantitative law in the usual sense of the word, for it does not imply a reversible relationship between prices and quantities, but is simply a common feature of all demand laws, whether reversible or not. From this to the representation of the demand law by a curve relating prices and quantities is a very long way.

For as an individual moves from one position to another in commodity space, his preferences themselves undergo a transformation. Experience shapes an individual's tastes. The acquisition of information, through participation in markets, leaves a mark on the psyche that influences future behavior (Georgescu-Roegen 1966: 176–179).

Perhaps the most impressive attempt to incorporate this idea into a formal model of growth and structural change has been made by

Pasinetti (1981), who stresses that technical progress and the evolution of demand are intimately connected to one another:

> Consumers' preferences may . . . be widely manipulated, but they ultimately depend upon human nature, which represents, in the same way as the technical conditions of production do, a fundamental external datum for any meaningful economic investigation. . . . The relevance itself of technical progress depends on potential demand: an increase in productivity, however large it may be, loses much or even all of its meaning, if it takes place in the productive process of a commodity for which demand can only be small or negligible. This means that any investigation into technical progress must necessarily imply some hypotheses . . . on the evolution of consumers' preferences as income increases. (Pasinetti 1981: 68–69)

Pasinetti starts from the idea, compatible with the arguments of Garegnani and Georgescu-Roegen reported above, that real income has a greater bearing on consumption patterns than relative prices: one of the most solidly grounded stylized facts about consumption is that "the proportion of income spent on any type of good changes as per capita income changes" (Pasinetti 1981: 70). The composition of demand evolves in complex but partly systematic ways as an economy develops. For example, as per capita income rises—presuming that the benefits of productivity growth are spread broadly among members of the community—households tend to spend a smaller proportion of their incomes on basic necessities like food and clothing. This empirical regularity, known as Engel's Law—after Ernst Engel, the German statistician who first recorded it in the mid-19th century—provides one of the bases of Pasinetti's theoretical account of how the structure of demand evolves as an economy grows.

Early in the *Grundrisse*, Marx (1857–1858) calls attention, from a somewhat different perspective, to the fact that production and consumption are not strictly separable activities. Production entails the consumption of inputs—the means of production, including raw materials, fuel, and a portion of the constant capital; and workers' physical energy, which needs to be replenished. Consumption entails production, as when the consumption of raw materials results in the production of some commodity, or when the consumption of sustenance and shelter by a worker restores his depleted capacity to work: "consumption . . . in one way or another produces human beings in some particular aspect" (Marx 1857–1858: 91). Perhaps more pertinent to the topic at hand is Marx's observation that:

> Production not only supplies a material for the need, but it also supplies a need for the material. As soon as consumption emerges from its initial state of natural crudity and immediacy . . . it becomes itself mediated as a drive by the object [of consumption]. The need which consumption feels for the object is created by the perception of it. The object of art—like every other product—creates a public which is sensitive to art and enjoys beauty. Production thus not only creates an object for the subject [i.e., for the consumer], but also a subject for the object. Thus production produces consumption (1) by creating the material for it; (2) by determining the manner of consumption; and (3) by creating the products, initially posited by it as objects, in the form of a need felt by the consumer. It thus produces the object of consumption, the manner of consumption and the motive of consumption. Consumption likewise produces the producer's *inclination* by beckoning to him as an aim-determining need. . . . Without production no consumption; without consumption no production. [This identity] figures in economics in many different forms. (Marx 1857–1858: 92–93)

This passage warns us of the limits of formal analysis. The dialectical relationship between production and consumption that Marx describes cannot be fully captured by a system of equations. A deeply nuanced sociological and historical account is needed; for a perceptive example, see Pietrykowski (2009).

A Framework for Modeling Investment

If aggregate output is demand-constrained rather than supply-constrained, a useful investment theory will have to be compatible with the theory of effective demand. Here a difficulty arises. The classical writers and Marx saw the production of a physical surplus as a precondition for economic expansion. Growth takes place when part of an existing net product is ploughed back into the production process, so that output can be enlarged in the next period. But in order for the surplus to be ploughed back, a decision must be made to refrain from consuming it; the saving decision must be taken prior to any investment decision, which means that saving must be treated as *analytically* prior to investment.[11] This conflicts with the Keynesian understanding of how market economies operate. The classical view of accumulation appears to require causality to run from saving to investment. To ensure that this causal relation could be made consistent with the macroeconomic equilibrium condition that leakages from the expenditure flow must be matched by injections into it, the classicals, in the absence of a better alternative, had to fall back on a second un-Keynesian device, Say's Law (see Mongiovi 1990). In this section we shall outline a framework that reconciles the Keynesian and classical perspectives.

Marx assigned investment a crucial role in the competitive struggle for markets among different capitals. This aspect of the accumulation process suggests that there is a component to investment that is independent of the rate of return on capital. If a firm's survival depends upon its ability to innovate and expand, it will engage in a certain amount of investment regardless of what its rate of return happens to be. The degree to which any particular firm will be inclined (or compelled) to engage in such autonomous investment will depend upon its absolute size (measured, for example, by its productive capacity or by the average size of its labor force), its size relative to its competitors, and the degree of concentration of the industry in which it operates. It is probable that autonomous investment will be positively related to the degree of concentration, which is generally taken to reflect the degree of monopoly power. Where an industry is dominated by a small number of large firms, competition is apt to be far more intense and the penalties for laziness more severe (Clifton 1977; Schumpeter 1950).

If the broad competitive market structure of the economy is taken as given, we can conceive of a set of parameters α_{ij} $(i, j = 1, \ldots, n)$ that represent the amount of autonomous investment demand by sector j for commodity i. The magnitude of each such parameter will depend upon the competitive characteristics of sector j, with the α_{ij}s presumably increasing as the degree of market concentration increases,[12] and upon a variety of non-quantifiable considerations such as product characteristics and the "corporate culture" that characterizes the managements of the firms in that sector. This formulation is problematic in the sense that specification of the market structure presumes some notion of the scale of output in various sectors. We may get around the difficulty by supposing that agents take decisions against a background of particular historical circumstances, and that these circumstances establish broad levels of productive activity within and across sectors. This does not mean that we take productive capacity as fixed, but that managers take decisions in the context of an economy in which, for example, automobile production is on the order of 12 million units per year divided among three firms, rather than 300,000 units per year divided among 50 firms. We define $\alpha_i = \Sigma\alpha_{ij}$ and $\boldsymbol{\alpha} = [\alpha_i]$; this vector represents the autonomous component of $\mathbf{y}^I$, that is, the component of investment demand that is not dependent on the rate of return on capital.

The next issue that needs to be considered is whether the rate or the mass of profits should be used to explain investment. To use the mass of profits would be problematic for two reasons. First, given physical input requirements and the profit rate, the level of profits will vary with the level of productive activity. Taking the mass of profits as a datum pre-supposes that the output vector is known from the start, but since the purpose of the exercise is to explain the output vector, we cannot take it as known in order to model investment demand. Second, the demand for investment goods will depend not upon the total amount of profits present in the economy, but upon how these profits are apportioned among sectors. While aggregate investment spending appears to be highly correlated with aggregate profits (Eisner 1963), we are concerned with the determination of a vector of sectoral outputs; this means that the vector of induced investment demands cannot be treated as a simple function of Π, the sum of the economy's profits, but must depend upon the vector of sectoral profit levels ($\Pi_1, \Pi_2, \ldots \Pi_n$). This approach again runs into the difficulty that Π_i depends upon sectoral output q_i.

The profit rate is often presumed to provide a motivational rationale for investment; there is a tradition along this line within the Post-Keynesian literature, the most notable example being Joan Robinson's magnum opus, *The Accumulation of Capital* (1956). The rate of return on capital is an index of the benefits that can be expected to accrue from investment; thus the greater is the profit rate the greater will be the incentive for capitalists to take the trouble and run the risks associated with capacity expansion.

Let y_{ij} represent the amount of investment demand for commodity i induced by profitability in sector j; $y_{ij} = y_{ij}(r_j)$, where r_j is the rate of return on capital invested in sector *j*. We define $y_i = y_i(r_1, \ldots, r_n)$ as the total amount of induced investment demand for commodity *i*. Finally, we write $\mathbf{y}_r^I = \mathbf{y}(r_1, \ldots, r_n)$ for the vector of investment demand related to profitability. Under competitive conditions, the economy will gravitate toward a uniform profit rate; it is precisely through investment responses to differential profit rates, here modeled explicitly, that a uniform profit rate is established. We may therefore write $\mathbf{y}_r^I = \mathbf{y}(r)$, where r is the exogenously determined normal rate of profit. Thus we have $\mathbf{y}^I = \boldsymbol{\alpha} + \mathbf{y}(r)$. Combining this result with our matrix multiplier in System (8) gives:

$$\mathbf{q} = (\mathbf{I} - \mathbf{A})^{-1}\left[\mathbf{I} - \mathbf{CV}(\mathbf{I} - \mathbf{A})^{-1}\right]^{-1}[\boldsymbol{\alpha} + \mathbf{y}(r)] \tag{9}$$

When the profit rate and money wage are specified, the price Equation (1) and System (9) allow us to obtain a determinate solution for prices, the wage rate, investment, sectoral outputs, and employment.

The construction summarized in System (9) captures a number of key elements in the classical approach to investment, while avoiding the trap posed by Say's Law. The classical insight that a physical surplus must be present for accumulation to take place is retained, but in an obviously Keynesian fashion, *the surplus is itself called into existence by demand*, as represented by the vector $[\boldsymbol{\alpha} + \mathbf{y}(r)]$. Saving is determined by investment through the income generation process, rather than the other way round.

But the limitations of this formalization are also evident. For a start, the precise relationship between investment demand and the profit rate expressed by the equation $\mathbf{y}_r^I = \mathbf{y}(r)$ is a behavioral relation that is particularly likely to be contingent and inexact. There are no *a priori* reasons to expect the components of $\mathbf{y}_r^I$ to exhibit any substantial elasticity with respect to changes in the *general* rate of profit. The law of competition implies that intersectoral profit rate *differentials* will induce systematic adjustments in the investment vector, but this does not explain why there should be a significant correlation between investment demand and the general profit rate established by competitive market forces.[13] A positive correlation between investment and the profit rate, it will be recalled, has been supported on two grounds. First, all other things being equal, a higher profit rate entails a larger surplus available for expansion of the capital stock; second, the profit rate represents an incentive for capitalists to enlarge the stock of assets from which they derive their incomes. But since in our model it is demand (one component of which is investment) that calls forth the surplus, the latter cannot, *in the long run*, constitute a constraint upon accumulation; therefore, the profit rate cannot be regarded as an index of the economy's capacity to accumulate. And, while the profit rate clearly provides an incentive to investment when rates of return are not equalized, its ability to perform that function once competition has eliminated intersectoral differentials is by no means evident.

Furthermore, even if it were possible to defend the existence of a systematic positive relationship between the investment vector and the profit rate, the exact form of the relationship will depend upon expectations. Since we are mainly concerned with the long period, we need consider only long-term expectations; short-term expectations, which are particularly volatile, can be ignored. If the state of long-term expectations can be taken as fixed, it is possible at least to conceptualize a relationship of the form $\mathbf{y}_r^I = \mathbf{y}(r)$. But once that relationship is put to its intended use, in comparative static analysis, serious difficulties arise. It is inconceivable that long-term expectations will remain unchanged in the face of an autonomous change in the profit rate. Even a small change in expectations may radically alter the form of the relationship between $\mathbf{y}_r^I$ and r; at the same time, there is no way to know with any degree of certainty how changes in the profit rate will influence expectations. Thus we are deprived of the possibility of constructing a model of investment behavior that is both rigorous and simple.

Investment is a complex phenomenon that cannot be reduced to a set of neat mathematical formulae. This was recognized by the classicals, who, in their theoretical discussions, took care not to impose an artificial simplicity on economic behavior. How then is investment to be explained?

Investment depends upon a wide range of factors. Current profitability, particularly if it is high or low by historical standards, may exert some influence, as the classicals supposed. The availability and cost of financing (to which the level and structure of interest rates are relevant) will almost certainly also have a bearing on investment spending. But the connection between the conditions of financing and the level of desired investment is far more complex, and far less direct, than conventional theoretical and policy discussions suggest. The evidence on the relationship between investment spending and the interest rate is not encouraging for adherents to the neoclassical hypothesis. Tinbergen's results (1938–1939), and a host of studies since then, suggest that there is no clear and consistent inverse relationship between interest rates and investment. A well-known study by Meade and Andrews (1938), in which businessmen were questioned about the influence of interest rates on their decisions, found that interest rates were not a significant determinant of investment behavior.

There is, moreover, room for different views on the connection between investment and the financial environment in which firms operate. Marglin (1984: 88–93) argues, for example, that investment can crowd-out consumption, rather than the other way round, because the corporate sector—the capitalist class—has privileged access to finance; thus there is no real financial constraint on investment. Kalecki (1969: 91–95), on the other hand, has pointed out that the current value of a firm's assets sets a practical limit on the amount that it may borrow: "The most important prerequisite for becoming an entrepreneur is the *ownership* of capital." Similar constraints, he continues, limit the firm's ability to expand by issuing additional shares of common stock.

Other considerations are likely to exert a comparable influence on investment. The competitive conditions within which firms operate impose certain broad requirements upon firms regarding research and development expenditures and investment—requirements that can be ignored only at the risk of a loss of market share. In the mathematical formulation of Equation (9) these influences are captured in the parameters $\boldsymbol{\alpha}$, which, since they carry equal weight with the induced components of investment, can no longer be left unexplained. Treating them as givens, in a sense, amounts to kicking the can a little bit further down the road: since the elements of $\boldsymbol{\alpha}$ are crucial to how the system performs, we cannot fully understand the working of the system without understanding what determines these parameters. The corporate cultures and the managerial philosophies of different industries or firms will also have a substantial impact on investment decisions. Expectations, of course, cannot be ignored. But if they are to form part of any real explanation they need to be grounded in observable phenomena, such as the age composition of the population, the pattern of income distribution, the geographical distribution of the population, or the ability of sellers to manipulate preferences through advertising.

A useful explanation of investment, therefore, entails much more than the econometric evaluation of the significance of the usual independent variables. A more flexible interdisciplinary approach, which can take account of historical evidence and can exploit the vast literature on the sociology of organizations, is required. Any explanation of investment along these lines must be specific to particular historical and institutional circumstances. But what might at first appear to be a lamentable loss of generality is in fact no loss at all; for the preceding discussion suggests that the generality of orthodox investment theory is spurious. The investigation of historical and social processes in all their complexity and richness is bound to produce conclusions that are less clear-cut and more difficult to interpret than the results derived from orthodox theory.

Notes

1. "Reproduction" does not preclude structural evolution. Social systems never exactly reproduce themselves: the process of structural reintegration always involves some modification of the material and institutional features of the community. Simple models that abstract from structural change can expose significant aspects of how economic systems function, which need to be understood before more complex transformative processes can be analyzed. Luigi Pasinetti's ambitious project, begun half a century ago, to model the structural dynamics of a modern economy pushes the tools of formal analysis about as far as they can go in this direction (see Pasinetti 1981, 1993).

2. Curiously, in his *Éléments d'Économie Pure*, Walras makes only passing reference to the *Tableau Économique*, and he acknowledges no influence of the *Tableau* on the formulation of his own intersectoral model, though he does remark that Quesnay's tabular description of an economic system "is . . . analogous to our own" (Walras 1926: 393). The precursors Walras esteemed most highly were Antoine Cournot, Jules Dupuit, and Hermann Heinrich Gossen—all partial equilibrium theorists! Marx, in contrast, explicitly

identified the *Tableau* as "the first systematic conception of capitalist production," and drew upon it directly in constructing the reproduction schemes of *Capital*, Vol. II (see Marx 1893: 364).

3. A basic commodity is one that enters directly or indirectly into the production of every commodity in the system.

4. In treating the profit rate as the given distribution variable we follow Sraffa (1960: 33). The classical economists and Marx took the real wage as given in order to explain the profit rate. The logic of classical surplus models is compatible with either approach. What distinguishes this theoretical outlook from the alternative neoclassical framework is the idea that distribution is regulated not by the interaction of price-elastic factor demand and supply functions, but by the opposition of class interests in a particular historical and institutional setting (see Garegnani 1984).

5. From the price equations, $\mathbf{pA} + r\mathbf{pA} + w\boldsymbol{l} = \mathbf{p}$, or $\mathbf{p}(\mathbf{I} - \mathbf{A}) = w\boldsymbol{l} + r\mathbf{pA}$. Post-multiplication of the latter by $\mathbf{q}$ gives $\mathbf{p}(\mathbf{I} - \mathbf{A})\mathbf{q} = w\boldsymbol{l}\mathbf{q} + r\mathbf{pAq}$. Thus, we have $\mathbf{py} = w\boldsymbol{l}\mathbf{q} + r\mathbf{pAq}$, or $\mathbf{py} = W + \Pi$, where W is the economy's wage bill and Π the amount of profits paid to the owners of capital.

6. The elements of $\mathbf{y}^c$ and $\mathbf{y}^I$ must be non-negative. In many instances, though, we can expect that various elements of the two vectors will be zero. For example, the demand for machine tools for consumption purposes is bound to be zero. All goods are basics, but they may not enter *directly* into the investment demand vector. Corn may be a basic commodity because it enters into the production of ethanol; yet there may be no direct investment demand for it. Thus the entry for corn in the consumption demand vector will be positive, but the corresponding entry in the investment demand vector will be zero.

7. A change in incomes or prices will almost always entail complicated changes in $\mathbf{C}$ that are apt to be unpredictable in magnitude and perhaps direction. The second set of conditions on $\mathbf{C}$ is simply a convenient way of managing the complexity of consumption behavior; if we are prepared to make detailed assumptions, based, for example, on Engel curve data, about how the elements of $\mathbf{C}$ respond to income and price changes, we can substitute another set of conditions for the simple ones given here.

8. The derivation is obtained as follows:

$$\begin{aligned}[\mathbf{I}-\mathbf{A}-\mathbf{CV}]^{-1} &= \left[(\mathbf{I}-\mathbf{A}-\mathbf{CV})(\mathbf{I}-\mathbf{A})^{-1}(\mathbf{I}-\mathbf{A})\right]^{-1}\\ &= \left[(\mathbf{I}-\mathbf{A})(\mathbf{I}-\mathbf{A})^{-1}-\mathbf{CV}(\mathbf{I}-\mathbf{A})^{-1}(\mathbf{I}-\mathbf{A})\right]^{-1}\\ &= \left\{\left[\mathbf{I}-\mathbf{CV}(\mathbf{I}-\mathbf{A})^{-1}\right](\mathbf{I}-\mathbf{A})\right\}^{-1} = (\mathbf{I}-\mathbf{A})^{-1}\left[\mathbf{I}-\mathbf{CV}(\mathbf{I}-\mathbf{A})^{-1}\right]^{-1}.\end{aligned}$$

This last step follows from a rule of linear algebra stating that $(\mathbf{AB})^{-1} = \mathbf{B}^{-1}\mathbf{A}^{-1}$.

9. The solution to System (8) can be conceived as stationary state. But without an explicit theory of investment there is no reason to suppose that the elements of $\mathbf{y}^I$ would remain constant outside of particular historical

circumstances—that is, outside of a situation of extremely limited duration. Naturally if the elements of $\mathbf{y}^I$ change rapidly with the passing of time, the static formulation would be useful mainly as a heuristic device to illustrate the effects on production and employment of a change in investment. But it would be possible to modify the model to take account of dynamic considerations along lines laid out by Goodwin (1949) and Pasinetti (1981).

10. The ramifications of this idea for the cyclical behavior of the economy are developed in Garegnani and Trezzini (2010).

11. The origins of this idea can be traced at least as far back as the physiocratic literature. That economic growth requires both the production of a surplus and the application of part of that surplus to accumulation is not in question. We shall argue, however, that it is demand that calls the surplus into existence in the first place and that therefore provides the ultimate impetus to growth.

12. The supposition here, in line with the Schumpeterian understanding of competition as a rivalrous process, is that the higher the degree of market concentration in an industry, the greater will be the pressure on firms in that sector to expand market share.

13. The same point holds when long-period equilibrium is characterized by intersectoral profit rate differentials due to institutional impediments to the mobility of capital, such as monopolistic forces, barriers to entry, and government regulations. Once the long-period position is established, the rationale for a systematic behavioral relationship leading from the vector of sectoral profit rates to the vector of investment demands lose much of its force.

References

Altman, M. (2004). "The Nobel Prize in Behavioral and Experimental Economics: A Contextual and Critical Appraisal of the Contributions of Daniel Kahneman and Vernon Smith." *Review of Political Economy* 16(1): 3–41.

Basu, D., and D. K. Foley (2011). "Dynamics of Output and Employment in the US Labor Market." PERI Working Paper 248 [*http://www.peri.umass.edu/fileadmin/pdf/working_papers/working_papers_201-250/wp248.pdf*].

Böhm-Bawerk, E. von (1884). *Capital and Interest* (W. Smart, tr.). London: Macmillan [1890].

Bowles, S. (2004). *Microeconomics: Behavior, Institutions, and Evolution.* Princeton: Princeton University Press.

Cassel, G. (1932). *The Theory of Social Economy.* London: Ernest Benn.

Clifton, J. (1977). "Competition and the Evolution of the Capitalist Mode of Production." *Cambridge Journal of Economics* 1(2): 137–151.

Eisner, R. (1963). "Investment: Fact and Fancy." *American Economic Review* 52(2): 237–246.

Garegnani, P. (1984). "Value and Distribution in the Classical Economists and Marx." *Oxford Economic Papers* 36(2): 291–325.

——. (1990). "Sraffa: Classical Versus Marginalist Analysis." In *Essays on Piero Sraffa: Critical Perspectives on the Revival of Classical Economics*. Eds. K. Bharadwaj and B. Schefold, pp. 112–158. London: Unwin-Hyman.

Garegnani, P., and A. Trezzini (2010). "Cycles and Growth: A Source of Demand-Driven Endogenous Growth." *Review of Political Economy* 22(1): 119–125.

Georgescu-Roegen, N. (1966). *Analytical Economics*. Cambridge, MA: Harvard University Press.

Goodwin, R. (1949). "The Multiplier as Matrix." *Economic Journal* 59(4): 537–555.

Hayek, F. A. (1931). *Prices and Production*. London: Routledge and Keegan Paul.

Jevons, W. S. (1879). *The Theory of Political Economy*. 2nd edition. London: Macmillan.

Kalecki, M. (1969). *Theory of Economic Dynamics*. 2nd edition. New York: A. M. Kelley.

Keynes, J. M. (1936). *The General Theory of Employment, Interest and Money*. London: Macmillan.

Kurz, H. D. (1985). "Effective Demand in a 'Classical' Model of Value and Distribution: The Multiplier in a Sraffian Framework." *Manchester School* 54(2): 121–137.

Kurz, H. D., and N. Salvadori (1995). *Theory of Production: A Long-Period Analysis*. Cambridge: Cambridge University Press.

Lachmann, L. M. (1956). *Capital and Its Structure*. London: G. Bell and Sons.

Lowe, A. (1964). *On Economic Knowledge*. New York: Harper and Rowe.

Malthus, T. R. (1820). *Principles of Political Economy*. London: John Murray.

Mandeville, B. (1724). *The Fable of the Bees*. Ed. F. B. Kaye. Oxford: Clarendon Press [1924].

Marglin, S. (1984). *Growth, Distribution and Prices*. Cambridge, MA: Harvard University Press.

Marshall, A. (1920). *Principles of Economics*. 8th edition. London: Macmillan.

Marx, K. (1857–1858). *Grundrisse: Foundations of the Critique of Political Economy* (M. Nicolaus, tr.). New York: Vintage Books [1973].

——. (1867). *Capital*. Vol. I. New York: International Publishers [1967]

——. (1893). *Capital*. Vol. II. New York: International Publishers [1967].

——. (1894). *Capital*. Vol. III. New York: International Publishers [1967].

Maslow, A. (1943). "A Theory of Human Motivation." *Psychological Review* 50(4): 370–396.

Meade, J., and P. S. Andrews. (1938). "Summary of Replies to Questions on the Effects of Interest Rates." *Oxford Economic Papers* (Old Series) 1: 14–31.

Menger, C. (1871). *Grundsätze der Volkswirtschaftslehre.* Wien: Wilhelm Braumüller.

Miyazawa, K., and S. Masegi. (1963). "Inter-Industry Analysis and the Structure of Income Distribution." *Metroeconomica* 15(2–3): 89–103.

Mongiovi, G. (1990). "Notes on Say's Law, Classical Economics and the Theory of Effective Demand." *Contributions to Political Economy* 9: 69–82.

——. (1991). "Keynes, Sraffa and the Labour Market." *Review of Political Economy* 3(1): 25–42.

——. (1992). "Domanda Effettiva, Occupazione ed il Modello Classico Ricostruito." *Note Economiche* 22(3): 396–413.

Mun, T. (1664). *England's Treasure by Forraign Trade.* Oxford: Blackwell [1928].

Nell, E. J. (1984). "Structure and Behavior in Classical and Neo-Classical Theory." *Eastern Economic Journal* 11(2): 139–155.

Pasinetti, L. L. (1974). *Growth and Income Distribution.* Cambridge: Cambridge University Press.

——. (1977). *Lectures on the Theory of Production.* New York: Columbia University Press.

——. (1981). *Structural Change and Economic Growth: A Theoretical Essay on the Dynamics of the Wealth of Nations.* Cambridge: Cambridge University Press.

——. (1993). *Structural Economic Dynamics: A Theory of the Economic Consequences of Human Learning.* Cambridge: Cambridge University Press.

Petty, W. (1662). *A Treatise of Taxes and Contributions.* In: *The Economic Writings of Sir William Petty.* Ed. C. H. Hull. New York: A. M. Kelley [1986].

Pietrykowski, B. (2009). *The Political Economy of Consumer Behavior: Contesting Consumption.* London: Routledge.

Quesnay, F. (1759). *Tableau Économique.* Eds. M. S. Kuczynski and R. L. Meek. London: Macmillan [1972].

Ricardo, D. (1821). *On the Principles of Political Economy and Taxation.* 3rd edition. Ed. P. Sraffa. Cambridge: Cambridge University Press [1951].

Robinson, J. (1956). *The Accumulation of Capital.* London: Macmillan.

Schumpeter, J. (1950). *Capitalism, Socialism and Democracy.* 3rd edition. New York: Harper.

Smith, A. (1776). *An Inquiry into the Nature and Causes of the Wealth of Nations.* Ed. E. Cannan. Chicago: University of Chicago Press [1976].

Sraffa, P. (1960). *Production of Commodities by Means of Commodities.* Cambridge: Cambridge University Press.

Walras, L. (1926). *Elements of Pure Economics* (W. Jaffe, trans.). London: George Allen & Unwin.

Walsh, V., and H. Gram. (1980). *Classical and Neoclassical Theories of General Equilibrium.* New York: Oxford University Press.

Modeling the Economic Surplus in a SAM Framework

By ERIK K. OLSEN*

ABSTRACT. This paper derives the Marxian social accounting aggregates, including surplus value, using a social accounting matrix. The derivation assumes a three sector economy and consists of a set of discrete operations applied to conventional national aggregates. It demonstrates that the Marxian aggregates are fully consistent at the economy-wide level, and that the mapping from conventional to Marxian aggregates is well-defined. This mapping relies on Marxian class theory, and it is this class theory that distinguishes the Marxian aggregates from the conventional and Sraffian alternatives. It is shown that the Marxian surplus has no necessary relation to the conventional measures of either net operating surplus or net product, and hence that neither of these serve as useful proxies for the Marxian aggregates.

Introduction

The concept of an economic surplus is something that Marxian and Sraffian economics share in common. Both theories recognize the existence of a surplus that is produced and subsequently utilized for various purposes, but each defines this surplus in very different ways. The surplus of Sraffian theory is the net product of the economy as defined in conventional national accounts. The surplus in Marxian theory is defined through its class theory.

From the Marxist perspective the surplus created in production provides the resources that support the array of nonproduction activities associated with capitalist enterprises as well as many activities and individuals that might otherwise seem quite distant from these enterprises. Shareholders of a corporation, for example, receive an income

*Department of Economics, University of Missouri Kansas City, 5100 Rockhill Rd., Kansas City, MO 64110; olsenek@umkc.edu

American Journal of Economics and Sociology, Vol. 70, No. 5 (November, 2011).

derived from the surplus created in production, but this is simply one of many potential uses. Identifying the connection between the surplus created in production and the subsequent recipients is the task of Marxian class theory. Class theory provides a means to understand how the surplus created in production circulates and thus plays a role in the reproduction of the economic system itself. This emphasis on a complex class structure that is part of the fabric of the economy is what distinguishes Marxian class theory from the Sraffian one, and it is also what distinguishes their two different theories of surplus.

These two theories of surplus are different, but they are not inherently incomparable with one another. This paper focuses on defining the Marxian surplus as it is produced and circulates in the economy as a whole. It will also be shown how this differs from the conventional net product, and thus the Sraffian surplus. The primary technique for doing this is a social accounting matrix (SAM). The SAM makes it possible to first define the conventional national accounting aggregates and then systematically derive the Marxian aggregates through a class analysis of these conventional accounts. A SAM is simply a way of organizing the transactions in an economy into a set of accounting aggregates, and it has the advantage of connecting these aggregates together in a way that maintains mutual consistency among them. It can be cast at any level of detail, from highly disaggregated to complete aggregation, according to the task for which it is intended. This flexibility is especially useful for deriving the Marxian income and product aggregates from the conventional ones because neither complete aggregation nor fine-grained disaggregation are necessary or useful in this process.

The derivation of the Marxian accounting aggregates presented here draws from two very different literatures. The first is Resnick and Wolff's theory of class and their Marxian analysis of the capitalist enterprise (1987). Their work provides a sophisticated microeconomic analysis of the flows of value within an enterprise, and a basic understanding of the flow of value between enterprises. They do some rudimentary national accounting (1987: 180–183), but focus primarily on the microeconomics of the production, appropriation, and distribution of surplus. The second important influence on this work is the literature on Marxian interpretations of conventional national accounts and, in particular, the work of Shaikh and Tonak

(1994). Some readers may find the juxtaposition of Resnick and Wolff's work with Shaikh and Tonak's curious. But despite important differences on many points, with regard to many of the basic issues involved in this paper they have much in common.

This paper contains two primary sections. The next section presents a very simple SAM and uses it to show how it defines the conventional national accounting aggregates. The following section then systematically derives the Marxian aggregates from the conventional ones and analyzes some of the important similarities and differences. The final section summarizes the basic findings of the paper.

Social Accounting Matrix

A SAM is simply an accounting device that registers the flows of value between different economic units. This does not, however, imply that the construction of a SAM is theoretically neutral. There is no taxonomy, classification, or observation without theory, and one of the objectives of this section is to show that the construction of a SAM, and the accounting aggregates that this generates, is always an expression of an underlying theory.

A SAM is like an input-output (IO) transactions table in that it uses single-entry accounting. The rows and columns of the matrix represent accounts for a specific sector in the economy, and every element in the SAM is a revenue when read in the row context and an expenditure in the column context. Each element in the matrix depicts a flow from one accounting unit (establishment, industry, sector, etc.) to another. But a standard IO transactions table is limited to inter-industry transactions, while a SAM includes a more comprehensive set of transactions in order to encompass the entire circular flow of income and product. In fact, a SAM need not include inter-industry transactions at all and can instead be used to describe only transactions between different sectors rather than within a sector.

A Very Basic SAM

Table 1 is the first SAM published by Stone and Brown (1962),[1] and depicts the national accounts for the U.K. in 1960. All of the

Table 1

Stone and Brown's Proto SAM for U.K. 1960 (Millions of Pounds Sterling)

	(1) Domestic Product	(2) Income/Outlay	(3) Capital Transactions	(4) Balance of Payments	Totals
(1) Domestic Product	0	20,797	4,694	5,102	30,593
(2) Income/Outlay	23,038	0	0	179	23,217
(3) Capital Transactions	2,015	2,334	0	1	4,350
(4) Balance of Payments	5,540	86	−344	0	5,282
Totals	30,593	23,217	4,350	5,282	

entries in the matrix are flows per unit time (year) reckoned in money units.

Each of the four rows/columns in the Stone and Brown SAM are designed to account for four different types of economic activity:

1. Production
2. Current income/expenditure
3. Capital accumulation and depreciation
4. Transactions with the rest of the world (ROW)

Each of the cells in Table 1 presents a national accounting aggregate. Reading along the first row shows that the total revenues from the sale of domestically-produced final goods and services consists of household and government consumption ($CON_h + GOV = 20{,}797$) in cell (1,2), gross domestic fixed investment and net change in business inventory ($I^+ = 4{,}694$) (1,3), and sales to ROW ($EX = 5{,}102$) (1,4). Column one lists the total outlays by business in producing this output: domestic factor payments and indirect taxes net of subsidies ($F_d + T = 23{,}038$) (2,1), depreciation of fixed assets ($D = 2{,}015$) (3,1), and imports ($IM = 5{,}540$) (4,1). Gross domestic product (GDP) is easily found in the SAM as $CON_h + I^+ + GOV + (EX - IM) = GDP$, and net domestic product (NDP) is $GDP - D = NDP$. Similarly, using the income measures, gross domestic (GDI) income is $F_d + T + D = GDI$ and net domestic income (NDI) is $GDI - D = NDI$. The two fundamental national accounting identities $GDP \equiv GDI$ and $NDP \equiv NDI$ are definitionally true, and hence either the product or income aggregates provide equivalent measures of domestic production.

The second row and column of Table 1 describe the current income and expenditures by the two domestic final users, households and government. Current income includes both domestic factor payments and net indirect taxes ($F_d + T = 23{,}038$) (2,1) plus net factor payments from abroad ($F_{row} = 179$) (2,4). The uses of current income are described by column two: household and government consumption ($CON_h + G = 20{,}797$) (1,2), saving ($SAV = 2{,}334$) (3,2), and net current gifts (foreign aid, remittances, etc.) to the rest of the world ($GIF_{row} = 86$) (4,2). One of the unique features of the SAM is that it imposes the same source-use consistency that is familiar from the $GDP \equiv GDI$ or $NDP \equiv NDI$ identities on each of the four activities considered in the SAM. In this case consistency requires that the total current income must be consumed, saved, or gifted abroad. This says simply that the current income in the economy can be described either as income or expenditures.

The third row and column of Table 1 describe capital transactions in the economy. The inflow (sources) of revenues into the capital account consists of depreciation ($D = 2{,}015$) (3,1), saving ($SAV = 2{,}334$) (3,2), and net capital gifts from abroad ($CGA = 1$) (3,4); the outflows (uses) are gross domestic fixed investment and net change in business inventory ($I^+ = 4{,}694$) (1,3), and net foreign lending ($LEN_{row} = -344$) (4,3). Once again, the SAM requires that the income into the account equal the expenditures.

The fourth row and column describe domestic balance of payments.[2] The inflows (sources) of revenue for this account consist of imported goods ($IM = 5{,}540$) (4,1), net current gifts to the rest of the world ($GIF_{row} = 86$) (4,2), and net foreign lending ($LEN_{row} = -344$) (4,3). Outflows consist of exports ($EX = 5{,}102$) (1,4), net factor payments from abroad ($F_a = 179$) (2,4), and net capital gifts from abroad ($CGA = 1$) (3,4).

In the Stone and Brown SAM all of the transactions within a particular account are suppressed (so the principal diagonal of the matrix contains all zeros). This assumption means that inter-industry transactions, transfers of current income among households and government, and flow-of-funds transactions are all omitted.

Disaggregation and Intrasectoral Flows

The SAM in Table 1 provides a useful way of integrating and ensuring consistency in economic data, but it gives just the basic outline of a SAM. To develop certain analytic properties of interest to this paper the assumptions of complete aggregation and omission of all intra-account transactions need to be dropped.

Table 2 presents another simple SAM that distinguishes between businesses and households and includes inter-industry transactions. Government and the ROW are omitted here, and throughout the remainder of the paper, to simplify exposition. Excluding the ROW from the SAM reduces the types of economic activities from the four

Table 2

A Basic IO-NIPA SAM

		Production	**Current**		**Accumulation**	
		Business	Business	Household	Business	Σ
Production	Business	Inter-industry Transactions (M)	0	Household Consumption (CON_h)	Gross Investment (I^+)	Total Product (TP)
Current	Business	Net operating surplus (NOS)	—	0	0	NOS
	Household	Wages and salaries (W)	Interest, dividends, rent (IDR)	—	0	W + IDR
Accumulation	Business	Depreciation (D)	Undistributed profit (SAV_b)	Household saving (SAV_h)	—	$D + SAV_b + SAV_h$
Σ		Total Outlay (TO)	$IDR + SAV_b$	$CON_h + SAV_h$	I^+	

in the Stone and Brown SAM to three: production, receipt/expenditure of current income, and capital accumulation/depreciation. Table 2 is therefore not a comprehensive depiction of flows in the economy, but it is perhaps the simplest possible one that still has enough detail to be useful for the purposes of this paper.

Table 2 defines the standard national accounting aggregates for this simplified economy using the conventions common to both the US National Income and Product Accounts (NIPA) (Bureau of Economic Analysis 2009) and the US Input-Output (IO) Accounts (Horowitz and Planting 2006). Since these different accounts are designed to be mutually consistent, these are referred to in this paper as the "IO-NIPA" conventions.

Including inter-industry transactions (*M*) makes it possible to define the familiar IO aggregates total product (*TP*) as $GDP + M \equiv TP$, and total outlay (*TO*) as $GDI + M \equiv TO$. These represent the sum of the first row and column of the matrix, respectively, and are equal by definition:

$$\underbrace{M + CON_h + I^+}_{TP} \equiv \underbrace{M + NOS + W + D}_{TO} \tag{1}$$

In Equation (1) the domestic factor payments have been disaggregated into wage income (*W*) and net operating surplus (*NOS*), which is the IO-NIPA measure of "profit-like income" before it is either distributed to households as interest, dividends, and rent payments (*IDR*) or retained as undistributed profits (Bureau of Economic Analysis 2009: 2–9, 2–25, 2–26, 2–28).

Row and column two show the total profit income in the economy *NOS* as either distributed to households as *IDR* payments or retained by the enterprises to fund capital accumulation:

$$NOS \equiv IDR + SAV_b$$

Row and column three describe the revenues and expenditures of the households. Household income consists of *W* and *IDR* payments from business, and households use this to fund either consumption or saving:

$$W + IDR \equiv CON_h + SAV_h$$

Finally, row and column four show an identity between savings (gross of depreciation) and gross investment:

$$D + SAV_b + SAV_b \equiv I^+$$

At this level of abstraction, where all business establishments are assumed to be engaged in production, the mapping between the IO-NIPA aggregates and the Marxian aggregates for constant capital (C^*), variable capital (V^*), and surplus value (S^*) is one-to-one (Shaikh and Tonak 1994: 44–45).[3] The IO-NIPA aggregate TO is equal to its Marxian analog total value (TV^*), as are the individual components of these aggregates:

$$TO = TV^* = \underbrace{M + D}_{C^*} + \underbrace{W}_{V^*} + \underbrace{NOS}_{S^*} \qquad (2)$$

TP consists of production inputs ($M + D$) plus net final product (FP). Again, when all establishments are understood to be engaged in production, the Marxian total product aggregate (TP^*) is identical to the IO-NIPA TP, and all of the individual components are also. But an additional distinction can be made in the Marxian aggregates, which is that FP can be divided into its *necessary* and *surplus* portions. This requires that investment be treated on a net rather than a gross basis ($I^+ - D = I$), and that total consumption CON_b be disaggregated into consumption out of wage income (CON_b^w) and consumption out of profit-type income (CON_b^p):

$$TP = TP^* = \underbrace{M + D}_{\text{inputs}} + \underbrace{CON_b^w}_{\text{necessary}} + \underbrace{CON_b^p + I}_{\text{surplus}} \qquad (3)$$

Since $TO = TV^*$ and $TP = TP^*$, then the fundamental accounting identity of Equation (1) also holds for the Marxian aggregates,

$$\underbrace{M + D}_{C^*} + \underbrace{W}_{V^*} + \underbrace{NOS}_{S^*} \equiv \underbrace{M + D}_{\text{inputs}} + \underbrace{CON_b^w}_{\text{necessary}} + \underbrace{CON_b^p + I}_{\text{surplus}} \qquad (4)$$

It is worth noting that in the IO-NIPA conventions assumed in Table 2 businesses are categorically excluded from consuming any portion of the final income/product. By assumption all expenditures on goods and services by enterprises, including interest and dividend payments between enterprises but exclusive of labor services from households, are treated as intermediate inputs and counted among *M*. Furthermore, all of the payments to employees of the enterprise are excluded from *NOS*. These two assumptions express a more basic premise that underlies the IO-NIPA national accounting conventions: *all* activities of business are assumed to be production. This perspective excludes a possibility, which was commonly accepted in classical political economy and by Marx, that some of the activities of business, and hence the establishments and employees that carry them out, are final uses that consume resources without creating new goods or services. These are the nonproduction activities of business.

Marx, like Ricardo, Smith, and others in the classical tradition, used the term "unproductive" to refer to economic activities like this, and they considered them forms of social consumption rather than production. This difference is what distinguishes the Marxian aggregates from their conventional counterparts, and once one introduces this distinction the symmetry between the Marxian and the IO-NIPA aggregates disappears. In his economic writings Marx analyzed some unproductive activities in detail and concluded that these nonproduction activities consume portions of the economic surplus. These nonproduction activities are connected to production by virtue of their reliance on the surplus produced there, and making this connection visible is a central concern of Marxian class theory. Marxian social accounting is one way of identifying these connections.

A Marxian SAM

This section presents a SAM that embodies the Marxist conception of the economy and its class structure. In a market economy the surplus exists both as a physical quantity of output and as a quantity of value. Marx, writing to Engels in 1867, concluded that one of the "best points" of *Capital* is ". . . the treatment of *surplus-value regardless of its particular* forms as profit, interest, ground rent, etc." (Marx 1987). His advance over classical political economy, he argues, is that the classical writers failed to consistently identify these various forms of income as parts of the surplus, and hence lacked a clear understanding of what the surplus is and its role in the economy. The SAM provides a useful way to both identify surplus value in the economy and make clear its connections to the other commodity and value flows that make up the process of economic reproduction.

Previous Literature on Marxian Interpretation of National Accounts

There is a long tradition of using conventional national accounts to derive estimates of the Marxian accounting aggregates. Shaikh and Tonak (1994: ch. 6) provide a comprehensive survey of this literature, and here I simply discuss several works that are especially germane to this paper.

The connection between Marxian value categories and conventional accounting is first developed by Marx in *Capital.* Marx demonstrates a sensitivity to the issues that arise when interpreting conventional accounting statements reckoned in price terms from the perspective of a labor theory of value (1967a: 220), but he routinely develops his value quantities in units of money, and frequently interprets conventional business accounting statements in terms of his value categories. Likewise, Engels referred to the economic data then published by the US census as a source for estimating Marxian value categories empirically (Marx 1967c: 76).

Data about manufactures in the US have been collected in some form since at least 1810, and Varga (1928, 1935) used this data to produce some of the earliest estimates of Marxian value aggregates in the US economy. His methodology has been influential. It provides a basis for number of subsequent studies and is still used today. Gillman (1958) used a variant of it to produce estimates of the Marxian aggregates for the US for the period 1849–1952. He worked directly from the price data reported by federal agencies, but also introduced a distinction between productive and unproductive activities not found in Varga's work.

A significant development in the evolution of the use of US national accounts to estimate Marxian value aggregates was Wolff's (1975) use of disaggregated IO data, which allows for a much more detailed analysis than is possible when working from economy-wide aggregates. Wolff uses a methodology developed by Okishio (1959), which estimates the Marxian aggregates using labor values rather than prices, and this requires industry-level rather than aggregate data. In later work Wolff (1987: ch. 3) also introduces a relatively complete taxonomy of productive and unproductive activities in the economy, and the focus of his worked changed from estimating labor values to analyzing the impact of unproductive activity on economic performance.

Wolff's decision to use labor values rather than prices was not adopted by later writers. Weisskopf (1979: 343), for example, develops estimates of the Marxian aggregates directly from price data without reference to labor values.

By the mid 1980s several people were producing estimates of the Marxian aggregates for the US economy from conventional accounts. Moseley (1986) identified two important theoretical issues that define the different perspectives of people working in this field: (i) whether the Marxian aggregates should be estimated in money or in labor units, and (ii) whether or not the distinction between productive and unproductive labor should be recognized.

Like Weisskopf, Moseley (1991: section 2.1) takes the position that the Marxian aggregates should be estimated in price terms rather than labor values, but he does not accept that these are simply proxies for labor values. Instead, taking inspiration from Foley (1982), he argues that Marx defines his value categories in terms of abstract labor time rather then concrete labor times, and that money is the measure of abstract labor time. Hence Marx's value categories refer directly to quantities of money rather than direct labor times, and these money measures are the entries in the income statements and balance sheets of capitalist firms and national accounts.[4] Moseley, like Gillman and Wolff's later work, also argues that the concepts of productive and unproductive activities are integral to Marx's value categories, and hence that these must be integrated in any estimate of the Marxian aggregates.

The methodology for estimating the Marxian aggregates from conventional accounts reaches its highest level of sophistication in the work of Shaikh and Tonak (1994). Like Wolff and Weisskopf they take the position that Marx's value categories refer to quantities of embodied labor, but they also find that empirically prices serve as reasonable proxies for labor values, so it is not necessary to transform the price data reported in conventional accounts into embodied labor times. They recognize the deviation of prices from labor values as a theoretical problem, but since empirically these deviations are found to be small (1994: 84, 141–144) it is not necessary to transform the price data to labor values in order to estimate the Marxian aggregates. Also, like Gillman, Moseley, and Wolff's later work, they distinguish between productive and unproductive labor. In fact, they argue that since the price-value deviations are small, it is precisely this distinction that sets the Marxian aggregates apart from their conventional analogs.

Production and Nonproduction Activities

The most basic distinction in national income accounting is to establish whether a type of economic activity is an act of production, consumption, accumulation, or a transaction with the ROW (Stone and Stone 1962: ch. 2). As shown in Tables 1 and 2, these four activities serve to define all of the primary conventional national accounting aggregates as well as several secondary flows.

Marxian social accounting shares with conventional social accounting the idea that value is created only in production (US BEA 2009: 2-1–2-2), but it draws the production boundary more narrowly than do the conventional accounts. In conventional national accounting almost any activity that receives remuneration is considered production.[5] So, for example, the retail and financial sectors, whose primary activities are trading claims to existing commodities or financial intermediation, are treated symmetrically with manufacturing and service enterprises, which produce goods and services. All of these things are characterized as different forms of production in the conventional accounts, and hence establishments in any of these sectors would enter into the SAM in Table 2 as simply different parts of national business activity.

The Marxian approach is different, and understanding how it is different is perhaps the most fundamental aspect of defining the economic surplus in the Marxian accounts. The basic point is that, unlike the conventional accounts, not all types business activity that receive remuneration are considered production in the Marxian approach, and not all employees who are remunerated add value. Instead, some payments to businesses and employees are shares of the value created in production, which is subsequently distributed to them.

Marx divides the value added in production into two parts, variable capital and surplus value. Variable capital is relatively straightforward: it is the compensation of production workers. But surplus value plays a much more complicated role in the economy. In Marxian economic theory the surplus accrues initially to the industrial capitalist (or board of directors in a modern corporation), and it is subsequently distributed in various forms to others who do not produce, but rather perform nonproduction activities that support the production activities, or, more broadly, provide the conditions of existence for the capitalist.

Marx is reasonably clear in the presentation of this class theory, but he develops it progressively across all three volumes of *Capital*, and hence this class-analytic vision of the economy is often overlooked by readers who focus instead on one or another of the many individual topics in these books—the forest is often overlooked because of the trees. He notes in volume one, for example,

> The capitalist who produces surplus-value—i.e., who extracts unpaid labour directly from the labourers, and fixes it in commodities, is, indeed, the first appropriator, but by no means the ultimate owner, of this surplus-value. He has to share it with capitalists, with landowners, &c., who fulfil other functions in the complex of social production. Surplus-value, therefore, splits up into various parts. Its fragments fall to various categories of persons, and take various forms, independent the one of the other, such as profit, interest, merchants' profit, rent, &c. It is only in Book III. that we can take in hand these modified forms of surplus-value. (Marx 1967a: 564)

This production-appropriation-distribution process is the first stage that surplus value passes through as it circulates from its initial creation in production to its final disposition in consumption or accumulation. The task of Marxian social accounting is to clearly distinguish the various forms the surplus takes as it passes through the entire process from creation to final disposition. In so doing Marxian social accounting identifies the various forms that surplus value takes, and is a tool for analyzing the roles that the surplus plays in a class structure and in the process of social reproduction.

The distinction between "productive" and "unproductive" labor in Marxian economics distinguishes the source of value from the subsequent distributions. Marx's definition of productive labor involves two criteria. The first is whether the concrete tasks that a laborer performs is production, and the second is whether production is carried out in the service of capital:

> That labourer alone is productive, who produces surplus-value for the capitalist, and thus works for the self-expansion of capital. . . . Hence the notion of a productive labourer implies not merely a relation between work and useful effect, between labourer and product of labour, but also a specific, social relation of production, a relation that has sprung up historically and stamps the labourer as the direct means of creating surplus-value. (1967a: 509)

Similarly, Shaikh and Tonak (1994: 30) adopt a two-fold definition and give these two criteria for defining productive labor: (a) it is labor that is first exchanged against capital (and thus capitalistically employed); (b) it is labor that creates or transforms use values (it is production labor). Resnick and Wolff also define productive labor as "when the direct laborer produces surplus value for a capitalist employer" (1987: 133). According to these definitions unproductive labor can be either nonproduction labor or production not undertaken under capitalist social relations (for example, production for use rather than sale, etc.).

In order to simplify the analysis in this paper I assume a purely capitalist economy. Therefore, the question of distinguishing productive from unproductive labor reduces to simply whether or not it is labor engaged in production or nonproduction activity.

There are many things that are classified in conventional accounts as forms of production that are nonproduction from the Marxist perspective. Very broadly, nonproduction labor in a capitalist economy can be categorized as either the labor of circulation or management and supervisory labor. Circulation labor is associated with trading and financial activities, while management and supervisory labor is required for the management of capitalist enterprises, as well as the supervision and disciplining of workers.[6] Nonproduction activity may occur alongside production processes within an enterprise, or, as with trading and financial firms, it may be the enterprise's sole activity. Marx recognized this possibility, and indeed goes to some lengths to explain that if an industrial capitalist chooses to contract for a nonproduction activity rather than performing it himself, this does not change it into production activity (1967b: 131). In other words, nonproduction activity does not become production simply because it becomes the exclusive occupation of, say, a merchant enterprise rather than an incidental occupation of an industrial (productive) capitalist enterprise. This is what makes it possible for there to be capitalist enterprises that do not engage in production at all. These firms employ workers, earn profits, and behave in ways that are entirely similar to productive capitalists, enterprises, but they do not engage in production. Understanding how this can occur is best done by looking at specific industries in the context of deriving the Marxian aggregates from the IO-NIPA accounts.

Nonproduction Activities and the Marxian Aggregates

Distinguishing production from nonproduction activities within the SAM makes it possible to derive the Marxian aggregates as distinct from the conventional aggregates discussed earlier. In the following sections three different types of nonproduction activity are introduced: trading activities (wholesale and retail trade), finance, and management and supervision. This requires that the single aggregate national business accounts shown in Table 2 be further disaggregated.

This disaggregation generally follows the conventions of the US IO accounts with two notable exceptions. First, the disaggregation assumed here is simply into three sectors: production, trade, and finance. While not comprehensive it is sufficient to illustrate the basic similarities and differences between the Marxian and conventional aggregates. Second, since the late 1960s the US BEA publishes rectangular Make and Use tables rather than the more analytically useful symmetric inter-industry tables. But these Make and Use tables can readily be converted into an inter-industry table, and the following discussion assumes that the primary IO table is an inter-industry table.

Trading Activities

Trading activities, the buying and selling of commodities or merchanting, are considered circulation activity in Marxian theory, not production. They consume labor and nonlabor inputs, but produce neither new commodities or value. Marx refers to these activities as among of the "*faux frais*" (false costs) of capitalist production (1967b: 131).

This cost is paid by the distribution of surplus value either within an enterprise, if the enterprise handles the merchanting of its output itself, or a distribution from one capitalist enterprise to another if merchanting becomes the primary occupation of a separate enterprise (Marx 1967b: 126–135, 1967c: chs. 16–17; Resnick and Wolff 1987: 125–127). Since merchanting may be the primary occupation of a particular type of capitalist enterprise, Marx introduces two different terms to distinguish different types of capitalist enterprises. He refers to "industrial capitalists," who use their capital for production, and "merchant capitalists," who use their capital simply to buy and sell produced commodities. Both of these types of firms are capitalist in that they seek to expand their capital through their activities, but they are distinguished by whether their predominant activity is production or trading.

Since merchants do not produce, the value they realize in trade must originate in production and be distributed to them by an industrial capitalist. This typically occurs through an unequal exchange between producing and trading establishments. The industrial capitalist sells the commodity to the merchant capitalist below its value, and in so doing allows the merchant to realize a portion of the surplus value created in the production process (Shaikh and Tonak 1994: 45–51; Resnick and Wolff 1987: 127; Marx 1967b: ch. 6, 1967c: chs. 16–17). This is the familiar difference between the "wholesale" and "retail" price of a commodity, though it should be noted that there may be several sales and purchases between the producer and the final consumer. For example, a producer may sell to a wholesale trader at one price (the producer's price), which realizes a portion of the value of the commodity for the producer; the wholesale trader sells to a retail trader at an even higher price and thereby realizes another portion of the total value of the commodity; and finally the retailer sells the commodity to a consumer for still another higher price, and thus realizes another portion of the value of the commodity. In this series of transactions the value of the produced commodity is shared-out among both the producing and the trading sectors. This series of transactions between the producing and the trading sector, and between the wholesale and retail trade industries, is the method through which this distribution of surplus value occurs. This distribution of surplus value from the production sector to the trading sector is what makes it possible for *merchant capital* to exist as something distinct from *industrial capital.*

In IO-NIPA conventions the price paid by the final consumer of a commodity sold in the market (the purchaser's price) is decomposed into four parts, the producer's price, the transportation costs, and the trade margins (wholesale and retail). The IO-NIPA accounts then show these components of the value of a commodity as four separate purchases by the user of the commodity: one from the industry that produced the commodity, one from the transport industry, and one each from the wholesale and retail trade industries (Streitwieser 2009: 42). This is known as "unbundling" and "forward shifting" the various components of market value of the commodity as it is realized by the different industries (Horowitz and Planting 2006: 5–4). Since the trading industries are treated just like any other industry in IO-NIPA conventions, the producer's price, the transport cost, and the trade margins are all treated symmetrically and hence all register as measures of production. The producer's price measures the contribution of the producing industry; the transport costs measures the contribution of the transport industry; and the trade margins represents the contribution of the wholesale and retail trade industries.

From the Marxist perspective counting the trade margin as a measure of production is inappropriate and should be corrected. To do this the wholesale and retail trade industries can be grouped together into one combined Trade sector and all production industries into one Production sector. In the IO-NIPA conventions this Trade sector produces a product that it sells to the Production sector as an intermediate input M_{tp}, to the Trade sector itself as an intermediate input M_{tt}, to households as a final consumption good CON_{th}, and to businesses as a final investment good I_t^+. The sum of these sales is the total product of the Trade sector TP_t.

$$TP_t \equiv M_{tp} + M_{tt} + CON_{tb} + I_t^+$$

To produce this product the Trade sector is understood to purchase intermediate inputs from the Production sector M_{pt} and from itself M_{tt} (the trade mark-up on M_{pt}), labor power from households W_t, and incur depreciation of fixed capital D_t. The profit-type income of this sector is its net operating surplus NOS_t. The sum of these outlays is the income measure of the total product of this sector, the total output of the Trade sector TO_t:

$$TO_t \equiv M_{pt} + M_{tt} + D_t + W_t + NOS_t$$

The Marxian accounting for this set of transactions is significantly different. The producer's price and transport cost do measure the value of production activity (transport being counted among the production industries). The trade margins, on the other hand, represent the distribution of surplus value from the Production sector to the Trade sector as described above.

Since trading activities involve no production the Trade sector produces no output,[7] so TO_t and TP_t simply record the portion of the income and product created in the Production sector that passes to the Trade sector through unequal exchange and is realized by that sector. The "unbundling" done in the IO-NIPA accounts, which splits the purchaser's price of a commodity into the various components falling to the different sectors, makes it possible to identify the portion of surplus value that passes from Production to Trade sectors.

Therefore, in an economy with only Production and Trade sectors the IO-NIPA product measure TP and the Marxian analog TP^* are equal, but TP^* is understood to be entirely output of the Production sector, even if some portion of it is realized by the Trade sector. For this reason Shaikh and Tonak (1994: 39) refer to Production and Trade as the "primary" sectors because it is through their combined operation that the product of the economy is produced and realized.

Since trading activities are not production they have no production inputs; instead, the Trade sector's commodity purchases, M_{pt} and M_{tt}, represent the consumption of final goods and services by the trading activities. This creates a new category of final consumption in the

Marxian aggregates that does not exist in the IO-NIPA aggregates: consumption by business (CON_b^*).

Shifting M_{pt} and M_{tt} from M to CON_b^* is the first discrete operation performed on the IO-NIPA aggregates in order to derive the Marxian aggregates. In order to clearly identify this and subsequent operations used to derive the Marxian aggregates they are listed individually. Together these operations represent the algorithm for deriving the Marxian aggregates from the IO-NIPA accounts in this simplified three-sector economy.

T.1 Trade sector purchases from the Production sector M_{pt}, and the trade mark-up on these purchases M_{tt}, are classified as current consumption of business CON_b^*.

Distinguishing trading activities from production activities requires a similar change to the outlay (value) side of the accounts. In the IO-NIPA conventions the Trade sector purchases labor and nonlabor inputs W_t, and $M_{pt} + M_{tt}$, incurs depreciation of fixed capital D_t, and has a net operating surplus NOS_t. The sum of these items constitutes the total output of the trade sector TO_t. Since in the Marxian accounts the revenues of the Trade sector simply realize the portion of the surplus value distributed to them from the Production sector through unequal exchange, TO_t is classified as part of aggregates surplus value.

T.2 All of the components of the total output of the trading sector ($TO_t = M_{pt} + M_{tt} + NOS_t + W_t + D_t$) are classified as parts of aggregate surplus value.

Remark 1 *Operations T.1 and T.2 leave the equalities $TO = TV^*$ and $TP = TP^*$ intact, but increase the Marxian measures of gross value added (GVA*) and gross final product (GFP*) relative to the IO-NIPA analogs ($GVA^* > GVA$ and $GFP^* > GFP$).*

Proof. Remark 1 follows immediately from the descriptions of T.1 and T.2. T.1 annexes Trade sector purchases $M_{pt} + M_{tt}$ from M to CON_b^*, which is a type of final consumption. Marxian gross final product is therefore $GFP^* = CON_b^* + CON_b + I^+$, which is strictly greater than the IO-NIPA $GFP = CON_b + I^+$. T.2 shifts $M_{pt} + M_{tt}$ from intermediate use M to the S^* portion of value added and makes it strictly greater than NOS. The Marxian measure of gross value added $GVA^* = S^* + V^* + D$ is thus strictly greater than the IO-NIPA $GVA = NOS + W + D$. Therefore, operations T.1 and T.2 increase GFP^* and GVA^* relative to GFP and GVA, and reduce M by an equivalent amount, but leave the equalities $TV^* = TV$ and $TP^* = TP$ from Equations (2) and (3) unchanged. ■

Finance

The Finance sector consists of financial establishments that receive deposits and make loans.[8] Their primary source of income is the interest rate spread between deposits and loans.

As with the Trade sector, the Finance sector is treated just like any other in the IO-NIPA accounts. It is understood to produce a product (financial intermediation) that it sells to other sectors and to households. Interest payments from the Production and Trade sectors to the Finance sector are treated as purchases of intermediate inputs by these sectors (M_{fp} and M_{ft}, respectively), and interest payments from households to the Finance sector CON_{hf} are treated as the purchase of a final commodity. Finance sector purchases from the Production sector M_{pt}, and the Trade mark-up on these purchases M_{tf}, are treated as the intermediate inputs of the Financial sector. The gross "value added" of this sector (GVA_f) consists of compensation paid to employees (W_f), net operating surplus (NOS_f), and depreciation (D_f).

Again, from the Marxian perspective this sector and its place in the aggregates is quite different. Financial enterprises do not engage in production, and they produce neither value nor product. Shaikh and Tonak refer the Finance sector as a "secondary" sector along with real estate, government agencies, and several others, and characterize them as

> . . . defined by the fact that they derive their revenues from the recirculation of the money flows generated by the primary sectors (Production and Trade), or from the circulation of socially validated claims upon portions of these primary flows, or both. (Shaikh and Tonak 1994: 52)

Shaikh and Tonak refer to the interest paid by the Production and Trade sectors to Finance as a "business royalty payment." Royalty payments are typically understood to be paid out of value added, and adopting this nomenclature in the Marxian accounts signals that this is a distribution of the surplus realized by the primary sectors. Similarly, Resnick and Wolff (1987: 219–226) characterize interest payments from productive capitalist enterprises to financiers as a distribution of the surplus value created in production and subsequently distributed to this sector in order to gain access to capital. Interest payments and fees from households, on the other hand, are interpreted as expenditures of household current income. These exchanges between Finance and the nonfinancial sectors, or between Finance and households take place outside of the production sphere of the economy, and hence outside of the Production account in the SAM. These transactions are simply the circulation of current income, and register entirely in the Current account of the SAM.

The key point of this analysis for the Marxian aggregates is that the Finance sector produces no product and adds no value. Instead, the interest payments M_{fp} and M_{ft} are portions of the surplus realized by the Production or Trade sectors, and distributed as business royalty payments to the Finance sector. To derive the Marxian aggregates these payments must be reclassified both as an outlay of the primary sectors and as an income of the Finance sector. M_{ff}, interest payments that circulate revenue within the Finance sector, must likewise be shifted out of M.

F.1 Intermediate inputs are reduced by M_{fp}, M_{ft}, and M_{ff}. These transactions are reclassified in the Marxian aggregates as business royalty payments RY_b^* and surplus value S is increased by $M_{fp} + M_{ft}$.

Also, since the Finance sector does not engage in production, its purchases of goods and services from the primary sectors (M_{pf} and M_{tf}) are a part of final demand in the Marxian aggregates rather than an intermediate input. These purchases are a part of CON_b^* rather than intermediate transactions, and this reduces intermediate output and increases final output by an equivalent amount.

F.2 Purchases by the Finance sector from Production and Trade M_{pf} and M_{tf} are shifted from M to CON_b^*.

The transactions between the Finance sector and households must similarly be modified in the Marxian aggregates. Interest payments from households to the Finance sector CON_{fh} are classified as royalty payments from the household RY_h^* to the Finance sector in the Marxian accounts. This reduces final consumption but increases the current income of business by an equivalent amount.

F.3 Household consumption is reduced by the amount CON_{fh} and household royalty payments $RY_h^* = CON_{fh}$ are added at the intersection of the Current row of Business and the Current column of the Household division.

Finally, the IO-NIPA gross value added for the Finance sector ($W_f + NOS_f + D_f = GVA_f$) must be deducted from the Marxian measure of gross value added. This is because the Finance sector does not engage in production and hence it adds no value. These outgoings from the Finance sector do not disappear from the aggregates entirely, but rather are treated only when they are paid-out as Current expenditures by this sector. In the Marxian accounts the Finance sector has revenues $RY_h^* + RY_b^* \equiv M_{fp} + M_{ft} + CON_{fh}$ and expenditures $W_f + IDR_f + SAV_f + D_f \equiv W_f + NOS_f + D_f$. But what is treated as production revenues and outlays in the IO-NIPA accounts are simply secondary circulations of value in the Marxian accounts and must be treated accordingly.

F.4 Gross value added is reduced by the amount $GVA_f \equiv D_f + NOS_f + W_f$.

Remark 2 *Operations F.3 and F.4 eliminate the equality between TV^* and TO and the equality between TP^* and TP.*

These conclusions follow immediately from the description of the operations, which provide adequate proof of Remark 2. F.3 reduces the size of the Marxian product measure TP^* relative to TP by the amount $CON_{fh} \equiv RY_h$, and F.4 and reduces the Marxian income measure TV^* relative to TO by the amount GVA_f. Since none of the other operations offset these changes, then $TP^* \neq TP$ and $TV^* \neq TO$ when secondary sectors, and their associated secondary flows, are included in the economy.

Remark 3 *The net effect of operations F.1–F.4 on GVA and GFP may be greater than, less than, or equal to zero, but the size of these effects will be the same on both, and therefore these operations maintain the identity $GVA^* \equiv GFP^*$ in the Marxian aggregates.*

Proof. The following outlay/income identity must hold for the Finance sector:

$$M_{pf} + M_{tf} + M_{ff} + GVA_f \equiv M_{fp} + M_{ft} + M_{ff} + CON_{fb} \tag{5}$$

The right-hand side of Equation (5) is the IO-NIPA definition of the total product of Finance sector TP_f, the left-hand side is the IO-NIPA definition of total outlays of the Finance sector TO_f. Simple manipulation of Equation (5) yields

$$M_{fp} + M_{ft} - GVA_f = M_{pf} + M_{tf} - CON_{bf} \tag{6}$$

Operation F.1 increases GVA^* relative to GVA by $M_{fp} + M_{ft}$ and F.4 reduces it by GVA_f. F.2 increases GFP^* relative to GFP by $M_{pf} + M_{tf}$ and F.3 reduces it by CON_{bf}. According to Equation (6) these net changes will always be equal to one another, and therefore operations F.1–F.4 maintain the identity $GVA^* \equiv GFP^*$ in the Marxian aggregates. ■

Remark 4 *Operations F.1–F.4 do not affect the total income or outlay from the Finance sector, they simply re-classify these transactions.*

Proof. According to F.1–F.3 the revenues of the Finance sector, M_{fp}, M_{ft}, M_{ff}, and CON_{bf}, are classified as RY_b^* and RY_b^*, and the outlays M_{pf}, M_{tf}, M_{ff} register as portions of CON_b^* and RY_b^*. According to F.4 (and the associated discussion) all of the outlays associated with GVA_f continue to appear in SAM, though only as parts of the current expenditure of business rather than flows associated with production. ■

The effect of the operations on the Finance sector is to show its revenues and outlays as secondary circulations of current income entirely within the Current account of the SAM. This sector receives business royalty payments from businesses and households, and uses this revenue to consume final commodities, compensate employees, make interest, dividend, and rent payments, etc. It does all of this without engaging in production. This illustrates the case of a nonproduction capitalist business sector.

Management and Supervision

The third type of nonproduction activity considered here is the management of enterprises, including the supervision of labor, within the Production establishments. No such production/nonproduction distinction was necessary or possible within the Trade or Finance sectors because, as nonproduction sectors, *all* of the labor performed there is nonproduction labor. But the Production sector is different. Only some of the employees in this sector engage in production, while others engage in associated nonproduction activities such as corporate management and the supervision and disciplining of production workers.

Resnick and Wolff (1987: 174–176) present a concise Marxian analysis of the class position of managers and supervisors within the firm. They note that since they engage in nonproduction activities rather than production their compensation consists of shares of the surplus value produced by the productive laborers in that enterprise. Similarly, Shaikh and Tonak (1994: appendix F) classify nonproduction workers as unproductive laborers whose compensation is paid out of the surplus value of the firm.

There are quite a few theoretical issues that arise when trying to estimate the size of managerial and supervisory labor from published accounts. Wolff (1987), Moseley (1991), and Shaikh and Tonak (1994) take slightly different approaches to this, but all ultimately rely on the occupational distinctions made in the Bureau of Labor Statistics Standard Occupational Classification (SOC) system. Since the SOC distinguishes management and supervisory occupations from production occupations ("persons engaged in production") it is possible to use them to estimate the Marxian equivalent of production and nonproduction employees, as well as to estimate the compensation of these employees.[9]

Using this approach the total wage and salary income in the SAM can be divided into the portion paid to production workers in the

Production sector ($(W_p)^p$) and the portion paid to nonproduction workers in that sector ($(W_p)^u$). They key idea here for the purposes of the Marxian aggregates is that $(W_p)^p$ is constant capital, while $(W_p)^u$ is paid out of surplus value. In order to identify the surplus in the Marxian aggregates $(W_p)^u$ must be deducted from the labor cost portion of production inputs W_p and added to the surplus.

M.1 W_p is split into $(W_p)^p$ and $(W_p)^u$, and $(W_p)^u$ is annexed to S^*.

Remark 5 *M.1 shifts a portion of GVA* from V* to S*. This does not change TV* or TP*, affect the relation between TV* and TV, TP* and TP, GVA* and GVA, or GFP* and GFP.*

Remark 6 *Total household income remains unchanged, but* $(W_p)^u$ *now registers in the aggregates as a distribution of surplus from the Production sector rather than as cost of production.*

Summary Accounting

The SAM in Table 3 shows a Marxian SAM for this three-sector economy. It is derived by applying the discrete operations specified above to the basic IO-NIPA SAM in Table 2. Several important conclusions about the Marxian aggregates and their relation to the conventional equivalents can be deduced from this.

Remark 7 *The Marxian aggregates maintain the necessary identity* $TP^* \equiv TV^*$.

Proof. Remark 1 establishes that T.1 and T.2 preserve the identity $TP^* \equiv TV^*$, and Remark 5 notes that M.1 has no effect on either TP^* and TV^*. Therefore, it only remains to be proven that F.1–F.4 preserve the identity $TP^* \equiv TV^*$. To prove this observe that $TV^* \equiv GVA^* + M^*$ and $TP^* \equiv GFP^* + M^*$. Since Remark 3 proves that F.1–F.4 maintain the identity between $GVA^* \equiv GFP^*$, then the identity $TP^* \equiv TV^*$ is also maintained in the Marxian aggregates. ■

Remark 8 *The Marxian measures TP* and TV* are strictly less than their IO-NIPA analogs TP and TO.*

Table 3

A Marxian SAM

		PRODUCTION	CURRENT		ACCUMULATION	
		Business	Business	Household	Business	Σ
PRODUCTION	Business	$C^*_m = M_{pp} + M_{tp}$	$CON^*_b = M_{pt} + M_{tt} + M_{pf} + M_{tf}$	$CON^*_h = CON_{hp} + CON_{ht}$	$I^+ = I^+_p + I^+_t$	TP^*
CURRENT	Business	$S^* = NOS_p + TO_t + M_{fp} + (W_p)^u$	$RY^*_b = M_{fp} + M_{ft} + M_{ff}$	$RY^*_h = CON_{hf}$	0	$S^* + RY^*_b + RY^*_h$
	Household	$V^* = (W_p)^p$	$IDR + WU^* = IDR + (W_p)^u + W_t + W_f$	—	0	$V^* + IDR + WU^*$
ACCUMULATION	Business	$C^*_d = D_p$	$SAV_b + D_t + D_t$	SAV_h	—	$C^*_d + SAV_b + D_t + D_f + SAV_h$
Σ		TV^*	$CON^*_b + RY^*_b + IDR + WU^* + SAV_b + D_t + D_f$	$CON^*_h + RY^*_h + SAV_h$	I^+	

Proof. This property of the Marxian aggregates can easily be shown from Table 3. TP^* is defined in the first row of Table 3:

$$TP^* \equiv M_{pp} + M_{tp} + M_{pt} + M_{tt} + M_{pf} + M_{tf} + CON_{bp} + CON_{bt} + I_p^+ + I_t^+$$

This defines TP^* as the sum of the IO-NIPA measures of the gross product of Production sector TP_p and the trade mark-up on that product TP_t. This is strictly less than the economy-wide TP for this model economy, which has Production, Trade and Finance sectors:

$$TP^* \equiv TP_p + TP_t < TP_p + TP_t + TP_f \equiv TP \tag{7}$$

TV^*, which is also decomposable into the Marxian value categories for constant capital C^*, variable capital V^*, and surplus value S^*, is defined by the production column of Table 3:

$$TV^* \equiv \underbrace{M_{pp} + M_{tp} + D_p}_{C^*=C_m^*+C_d^*} + \underbrace{(W_p)^p}_{V^*} + \underbrace{NOS_p + TO_t + M_{fp} + (W_p)^u}_{S^*}$$

This defines TV^* as the sum of the IO-NIPA measures TO_p and TO_t. This is strictly less than the economy-wide TO for this model economy, which has Production, Trade and Finance sectors:

$$TV^* \equiv TO_p + TO_t < TO_p + TO_t + TO_f \equiv TO \tag{8}$$

Therefore, according to Equation (7) $TP^* < TP$ and Equation (8) $TV^* < TO$. ■

Remark 9 *The Marxian economy-wide measures GVA^* and GFP^* may be greater than, less than, or equal to the IO-NIPA measures GVA and GFP.*

Remark 9 is a corollary of Remarks 1, 3, and 5. Each of these deals with the effect that the operations used to derive the Marxian aggregates from the IO-NIPA ones has on gross value added and gross final product. Remark 1 proves that T.1 and T.2 result in $GVA^* > GVA$ and $GFP^* > GFP$, and Remark 5 notes that M.1 has no effect on the size of GVA^* or GFP^* relative to GVA and GFP. But Remark 3 proves that the effect of F.1–F.4 on the size of GVA^* and GFP^* relative to GVA and GFP

is ambiguous. Since the effect of F.1–F.4 may reinforce or counteract that associated with T.1 and T.2, the cumulative effect of these operations on GVA^* and GFP^* relative to GVA and GFP is likewise ambiguous.

Remark 10 *The Marxian measure of surplus value S^* may be greater than, less than or equal to the IO-NIPA measure NOS.*

Proof. According to the IO-NIPA conventions *NOS*, the conventional measure of profit-type income, is the sole current income of business. This income is exhausted by the current expenditures of this sector:

$$NOS \equiv IDR + SAV_b \tag{9}$$

In contrast, the current income of business in the Marxian accounts is $S^* + RY_b^* + RY_b^*$, and this is used to satisfy several different end uses:

$$S^* + RY_b^* + RY_b^* \equiv CON_b^* + RY_b^* + IDR + WU^* + SAV_b \tag{10}$$

where WU^* is the wages of unproductive labor. Solving Equation (10) for S^* and then equating this with the IO-NIPA definition of current expenditures (the right-hand side of Equation (9)) gives:

$$CON_b^* + IDR + WU^* + SAV_b - RY_b^* = IDR + SAV_b$$

This implies that the following condition must be met for the equality $S^* = NOS^*$ to hold:

$$RY_b^* = CON_b^* + WU^* \tag{11}$$

But RY_b^* and $CON_b^* + WU^*$ have no necessary relation to one another. CON_b^* and WU^* are competing demands for surplus value, and hence may be expected to be inversely related, but RY_b^* is a type of expenditure of household revenue and will vary independently of CON_b^* and WU^*. Condition (11) will be satisfied only by coincidence, and therefore, S^* may be greater than, less than, or equal to *NOS*. ■

Remark 11 *The ratio* $\frac{NOS}{W}$ *may be greater than, less than, or equal to the Marxian rate of surplus value* $\frac{S^*}{V^*}$.

Proof. $V^* = (W_p)^p$ is strictly less than $W = (W_p)^p + (W_p)^u + W_t + W_f$, but Remark 10 proves that $S^* \gtreqless NOS$. Therefore, $\frac{S^*}{V^*} \gtreqless \frac{NOS}{W}$. ■

Remark 12 *The Marxian measure of surplus value S^* may be greater than, less than, or equal to the IO-NIPA measure of net final product NDP.*

Proof. The IO-NIPA definition of *NDP* for this three-sector economy is:

$$NDP \equiv CON_{bp} + CON_{bt} + CON_{bf} + I \tag{12}$$

Here I is net rather than gross investment. To relate *NDP* to S^* note that S^* can be defined in terms of the equality between Marxian net value added and Marxian net final product:

$$S^* + V^* \equiv CON_b^* + CON_{bp} + CON_{bt} + I \tag{13}$$

Definition (13) shows S^* as the Marxian net final product minus V^*. Equating this with the IO-NIPA definition of *NDP* from Definition (12) and simplifying gives the following condition for equality between S^* and *NDP*:

$$CON_b^* - V^* = CON_{bf} \tag{14}$$

Since CON_b, V^*, and CON_{bf} $(= RY_b^*)$ are all free to vary independently of one another, then this condition will be satisfied only by coincidence and $S^* \gtreqless NDP$. ■

Conclusion

The Marxian surplus S^* has no necessary relation to either the IO-NIPA *NOS* or *NDP*. Neither of these conventional aggregates serve as useful proxies for the Marxian one, and it is an empirical question which will be larger. But even though they are analytically distinct, the mapping between these quantities is well-defined.

The Marxian aggregates are based on a theory that is different in important ways from the one that underlies the IO-NIPA accounts and the Sraffian concept of surplus. The primary difference between them is Marxian class theory. The distinction between production and nonproduction activity makes it possible to distinguish the producers from the subsequent receivers of surplus, and thus to classify positions in the economic system according to their relation to the surplus created by workers engaged in production activities. In a capitalist economy the surplus is appropriated by employers who then use it to maintain and develop the enterprise. This gives rise to a class structure established by this network of relations involved with the production, appropriation, and distribution of surplus. It is through this that Marxian theory demonstrates how the exploitation of workers in production provides the means for the system of class relations to be reproduced. Rather than a question of simply maintaining an enterprise as a going concern, the Marxian theory of surplus enables us to understand how a capitalist class structure is maintained.

These relations can be observed in the transactions that participants engage in and these transactions form the basis for both the IO-NIPA aggregates illustrated in Tables 1 and 2, and also the Marxian aggregates illustrated in Table 3. Each of these aggregates groups these transactions according to an underlying theory of the social and economic relations involved. They are not pre-theoretic or theoretically neutral. But since the basis for both accounts is the same universe of transactions, there should be a consistent mapping from one to the other. This is done here by the set of discrete operations outlined in the paper. This class analysis of the national accounts provides the method to derive one set of aggregates from the other, and shows that the Marxian aggregates are both comprehensive and consistent. The method presented here is limited to an economy with only three sectors (Production, Trade, Finance), but it can be extended to include the full array of sectors and activities in a modern capitalist economy and published national accounts.

Notes

1. Phillips's (1955) interpretation of Quesnay's *tableau economique* using a transactions table might also be called the first SAM.

2. Stone and Brown show the balance of payments from the perspective of the rest of the world.

3. Variables in the Marxian accounting system are distinguished with an asterisk. Variables that exist only in the IO-NIPA accounts, or are common to both sets of accounts, have no asterisk.

4. Mohun (2004) provides a highly useful analysis of the issues involved with this point.

5. The exception to this rule is a transfer payment, which is defined as a payment that receives nothing in exchange, *no quid pro quo*. Both businesses and households can receive transfer payments, but not as compensation for a good or service. Examples include social welfare payments and insurance claims. These are excluded from production in the national accounts.

6. This is by no means an extensive description of these categories, which would require a book-length treatment. Indeed, a large part of the literature on estimating the Marxian aggregates from published accounts is taken up with just this issue.

7. Even in the IO-NIPA conventions the trade sectors are defined as simply buying and reselling merchandise without providing any additional fabrication (Horowitz and Planting 2006: 5–4). Despite this the trade margin is interpreted as a measure of "production."

8. The benchmark US IO accounts group Finance, Insurance, Real Estate, Rental, and Leasing together into one sector. This paper considers only financial establishments, specifically bank or bank-like institutions that take deposits and lend money at interest. This corresponds with industry 52A0 Monetary Authorities, Credit Intermediation, and Related Activities in the summary IO tables. The analysis here can, however, be generalized for other similar industries.

9. Mohun (2005) provides a detailed discussion of this methodology.

References

Foley, D. (1982). "The Value of Money the Value of Labor Power and the Marxian Transformation Problem." *Review of Radical Political Economics* 14(2): 37–47

Gillman, J. M. (1958). *The Falling Rate of Profit*. New York: Cameron Associates.

Horowitz, K. J., and M. A. Planting. (2006). *Concepts and Methods of the Input-Output Accounts*. Washington, DC: US Department of Commerce, Bureau of Economic Analysis. Available at: <http://www.bea.gov/papers/pdf/IOmanual_092906.pdf> (accessed January 10, 2007).

Marx, K. (1967a). *Capital* vol. 1. New York: International Publishers.

——. (1967b). *Capital* vol. 2. New York: International Publishers.

——. (1967c). *Capital* vol. 3. New York: International Publishers.

——. (1987). "Letter to Engels dated August 24, 1867." In *Marx and Engels Collected Works* vol. 42: 407. New York: International Publishers.

Mohun, S. (2004). "The Labour Theory of Value as Foundation for Empirical Investigations." *Metroeconomica* 55(1): 65–95.

——. (2005). "On Measuring the Wealth of Nations: The US Economy, 1964–2001." *Cambridge Journal of Economics* 29(5): 799–815.

Moseley, F. (1986). "Estimates of the Rate of Surplus-Value in the Postwar United States Economy." *Review of Radical Political Economics* 18 (1&2): 168–189.

——. (1991). *The Falling Rate of Profit in the Postwar United States Economy.* New York: St. Martin's Press.

Okishio, N. (1959). "Measurement of the Rate of Surplus Value." *Economic Review*, Hitotsubashi University Institute of Economic Research 10: 1–9.

Phillips, A. (1955). "The Tableau Economique as a Simple Leontief Model." *Quarterly Journal of Economics* 69(1): 137–144.

Resnick, S. A., and R. D. Wolff. (1987). *Knowledge and Class.* Chicago and London: University of Chicago Press.

Shaikh, A. M., and E. A. Tonak. (1994). *Measuring the Wealth of Nations.* Cambridge U.K. and New York: Cambridge University Press.

Stone, R., and A. Brown. (1962). *A Programme for Growth: vol. 1 A Computable Model of Economic Growth.* Cambridge, MA: MIT Press.

Stone, R., and G. Stone. (1962). *National Income and Expenditure.* Chicago: Quadrangle Books.

Streitwieser, M. L. 2009. "A Primer on BEA's Industry Accounts." *Survey of Current Business* 89(6): 40–52.

US Department of Commerce, Bureau of Economic Analysis. (2009). "Concepts and Methods of the U.S. National Income and Product Accounts" chapters 1–5. Available at: <http://www.bea.gov/national/pdf/NIPAhandbookch1-4.pdf> (accessed January 15, 2010).

Varga, E. (1928). *The Decline of Capitalism: The Economics of the Decline of Capitalism After Stabilization.* London: Communist Party of Great Britain.

——. (1935). *The Great Crisis and Its Political Consequences 1928–1934.* London: Modern Books Limited.

Weisskopf, T. E. (1979). "Marxian Crisis Theory and the Rate of Profit in the Postwar U.S." *Cambridge Journal of Economics* 3 (4): 341–378.

Wolff, E. N. (1975). "The Rate of Surplus Value in Puerto Rico." *Journal of Political Economy* 83 (5): 935–950.

——. (1987). *Growth, Accumulation and Unproductive Activity.* Cambridge U.K. and New York: Cambridge University Press.

Integrating the Social Structure of Accumulation and Social Accounting Matrix with the Social Fabric Matrix

By F. GREGORY HAYDEN*

ABSTRACT. The purpose here is to elaborate on the social fabric matrix approach (SFM-A), and to assess the possibility of integrating it with the social structure of accumulation and the social accounting matrix.The SFM-A to analysis and policy evaluation allows for cultural values, social beliefs, institutions, attitudes, technology, and the ecological system to be modeled into a system. The guiding goal is to work toward a more complete model of the provisioning process.

There is a society[1] and there is an ecological system. And they are united, in a manner by which they benefit and damage each other. And both are unified in all provisioning processes. Neither the current society nor ecological entities can exist without the other. They are embedded in each other, processing together. The set of societal relationships and transactions provides for goods and services, and, therefore, bads and disservices (because all provisioning produces bads and disservices). The components relevant to societal activities are cultural values, social beliefs, institutions, attitudes, technology, and ecological systems. All institutions include the influence of all of those components, so all provisioning of goods, services, bads, and disservices includes the processing of all those components. Production is the result of all those components processing together; therefore, nothing has ever been produced without the use and/or abuse of the ecological system. Provisioning takes place as those six components and their elements are coordinated, although not necessarily in a manner consistent with the improve-

*Department of Economics, University of Nebraska–Lincoln, Lincoln, NE 68588-0489, ghayden1@unl.edu

American Journal of Economics and Sociology, Vol. 70, No. 5 (November, 2011).

ment of the general welfare. The social fabric matrix approach (SFM-A) to analysis provides a way to model, describe, explain, and analyze coordination through deliveries among those six component sets (see Hayden 2006; Natarajan, Elsner, and Fullwiler 2009).

Social scientists regularly state that the economy is embedded in societal systems. That description is sometimes made as if the economy is an entity separate from society that is then embedded as a separate set of institutions in society.[2] In such descriptions, the idea of "embedded" has been used as it was with the embedded media reporters who were added to military units when the United States invaded Iraq in 2003. Reporters were there and drew provisions from the units, but were not directly involved as a unified part of the units' combat mission. Since the idea of the economy as a separate entity is found in literature dealing with the embedded economy, there is sometimes discussion of the economy becoming disembedded or unembedded because, logically, as a separate entity, it can function separately from society, just as reporters can function separately from soldiers. More correctly, economic processes are the parts of society that are united with other parts and identified by analysts as the economy. There is not an economy that exists as a separate functioning entity. Economic processes are the result of the unification of the components and elements of societal systems.[3] The concept of embeddedness is now recognized even in the popular media as is clear in John Kay's recent statement in the *Financial Times*: "We need to put out of our minds this widely held notion that there is such a thing as 'the economy', a monster outside the door that needs to be fed and propitiated and whose values conflict with things . . . that make our lives agreeable and worthwhile" (August 11, 2010: 7).

Furthermore, ecological problems exist as a result of the social system being embedded in and united with the ecological system. In early human history, societal activities barely impacted on the ecological system, but, as society changed technology and accumulated a larger and more powerful technological base, ecological systems—upon which provisioning is dependent—become more impacted, sometimes to the point of complete destruction of some of the systems.

Elaboration of the Digraph of the Social Fabric Matrix Approach

The purpose of this article is to elaborate on the SFM-A, and to assess the possibility of integrating that approach with the knowledge bases of the social structure of accumulation and the social accounting matrix, given other contextual concerns. The elaboration of the SFM-A is adumbrated with the digraph in Figure 1.

Social beliefs, attitudes, technology, and the ecological system function together within social institutions in a society. They, along with cultural values, are expressed as separate parts in Figure 1 because of

Figure 1

The Social Fabric Matrix Approach: Relationships Among Values, Beliefs, Attitudes, Institutions, Technology, and the Ecological System

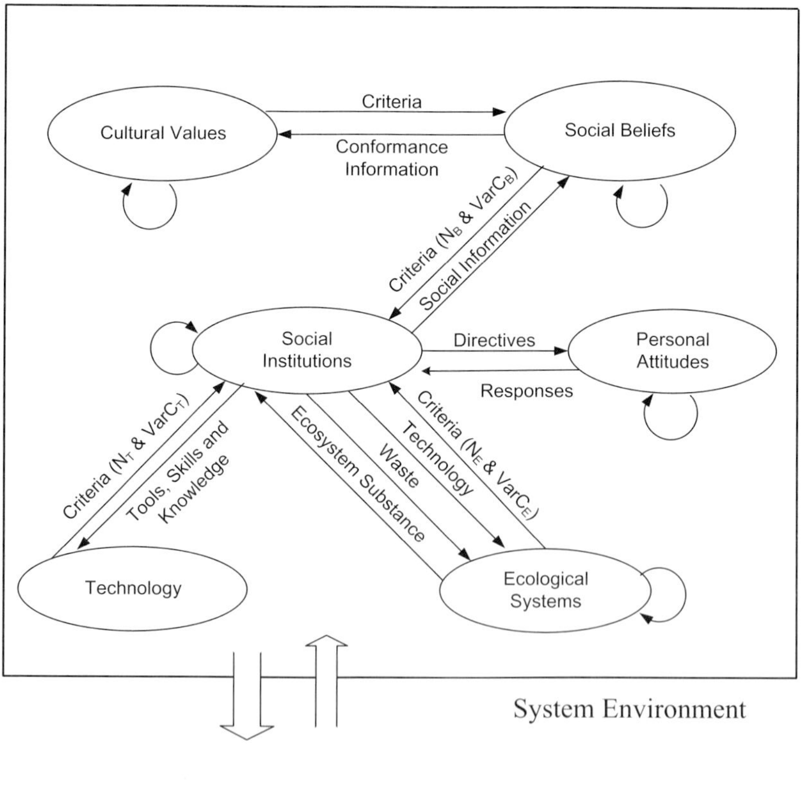

the extensive study that has been completed on each, not because they are separate from institutions in reality.[4] Delivery loops in Figure 1 that return to their own component are the first item for discussion. Those loops indicate delivery among the parts within each of the components.

The delivery loop among cultural values is included in Figure 1 with a note of caution. This author feels insecure about that loop because, in the literature reviewed about cultural values, nothing specific was found about whether and how different values might be related to other values. Delivery loops among component parts are indicated for social beliefs, attitudes, institutions, and ecological systems. However, with regard to social beliefs, it should be noted that when normative criteria (N_B) from social beliefs are adopted by institutions for a particular case, deliveries of social criteria and their elements (rules, regulations, requirements) are made by social institutions.

Ecological criteria (N_E) should not be interpreted to mean criteria designed so that judgments are made to protect the natural environment. Ecological criteria can be the opposite—they usually are. In modeling a system, the ecological criteria are criteria that exist in reality. For example, judgments are regularly made to dispose of toxic waste in a river, based on criteria to reduce monetary cost and increase profit.

There is no loop that indicates direct deliveries among technologies in Figure 1 because technologies do not make direct deliveries to each other. Technology is innovated, implemented, and operated by institutions. The only delivery from technology is the delivery of normative criteria (N_T) to institutions; criteria that become enforced due to the implementation of the technology by the institutions. Technology, in turn, as indicated in both figures, is applied as a direct delivery by institutions to biological and physical ecological systems for extraction, destruction, and disposal. Implicit in Figure 1 is the regular delivery of technology among institutions; for example, through sales, foreign aid, and systems of negative reciprocity. (Variant criteria $VarC_B$, $VarC_E$, and $VarC_T$ in Figure 1 are explained below.)

Finally, the system digraph of the SFM-A is enclosed in Figure 1 to indicate that the SFM-A system, like all systems, is open to its environment with inputs from and outputs to the environment as indicated at the bottom of Figure 1 (Adkisson 2009). This means that at least one row and column, or rows and columns, representing the system's environment should be included in the social fabric matrix (SFM) used to articulate the SFM-A.

Criteria, Rules, Regulations, and Requirements

Given the dominant importance of normative criteria and the rules, regulations, requirements, and attitudes activated by criteria, a brief review follows about those entities and the SFM. A general demonstration of the relationships among these entities is found in the SFM in Figure 2 and its digraph in Figure 3.

Figure 2

Social Fabric Matrix of Normative Criteria and Institutions

Delivering Components \ Receiving Components		Social Belief Norms (N_B)	Technological Norms (N_T)	Ecological Norms (N_E)	Authority Institutions (I_{A1})	Authority Institutions (I_{A2})	Processing Institutions (I_p)	Attitudes for I_p
		1	2	3	4	5	6	7
Social Belief Norms (N_B)	1				1			
Technological Norms (N_T)	2				1			
Ecological Norms (N_E)	3				1			
Authority Institutions (I_{A1})	4					1		
Authority Institutions (I_{A2})	5						1	
Processing Institutions (I_p)	6							1
Attitudes for I_p	7						1	

Figure 3

Social Fabric Matrix Digraph of Figure 2 with Deliveries Specified

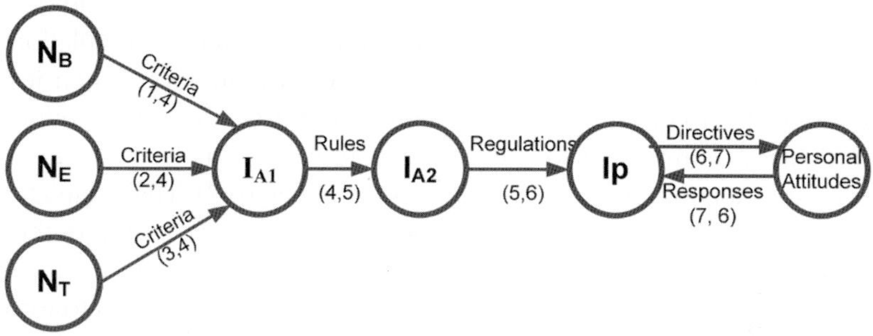

Relationships Among Normative Criteria, Rules, Regulations, and Required Attitudes

Figure 2 demonstrates that the normative criteria of social belief norms (N_B), technological norms (N_T), and ecological norms (N_E) are considered together by authority institutions (I_{A1}) in order to provide criteria elements, such as rules, laws, and court decisions, to other authority institutions (I_{A2}). The other authority institutions, in turn, formulate regulations for various institutions consistent with the rules, and deliver those regulations to processing institutions, for example, production institutions (I_P). The production institutions formulate requirements consistent with the regulations for persons working on production teams. In Figure 2, the requirements are expressed as directives to persons about how they are to respond to different signs and symbols. These directives become personal attitudes and are expressed as responses to the signs and symbols by persons functioning in institutions, to include production institutions.

As stated above, the digraph for Figure 2 is found in Figure 3, with cell numbers and deliveries designated on the edges. Reading each row from left to right, the cell deliveries are expressed as directed edges between the components' rows and columns. Cell (1,4) is the delivery of social belief criteria from social beliefs to authority institutions I_{A1}, cell (2,4) is the delivery of technological criteria from technology to authority institutions I_{A1}, and cell (3,4) is the delivery of ecological system criteria to authority institutions I_{A1}. I_{A1} uses those criteria to make judgments about the kind of rules to create. Cell (4,5) is the delivery of rules from authority institution I_{A1} to authority institutions I_{A2}. In turn, authority institutions I_{A2} formulate regulations that are delivered in cell (5,6) to processing institutions I_p. Then it is the task of I_p to design operating routines and procedures that require particular actions by persons in response to various signs and symbols in the production process. This delivery is in cell (6,7). These directed requirements form personal attitudes (see Figure 2) that are then expressed as attitudinal responses in the processing institutions in cell (7,6). Requirement descriptions are broader than the directives to form personal attitudes, but requirements always include directives to persons if the work is to get done. Figure 3 is presented as a one-directional sequence here. There will, of course, be feedback deliveries as well. (For a more complete explanation of Figures 2 and 3, see Hayden ([1998] 2009a). This explanation, although simple, demonstrates that social provisioning cannot be understood without recognizing and accounting for normative criteria, rules, regulations, and attitude requirements. The failure of this recognition is one of the main reasons for the failure of economic models.

Ongoing Conflict

Three conflicts exist because of the structure and processes of normative criteria and their elements. First, there is conflict in a pluralistic society because different groups have different normative criteria. In the United States, for example, the Amish wheat farmers of Pennsylvania have different technological norms than other wheat farmers. Such differences can usually be accommodated in a society that respects pluralism, but it makes for conflict situations nonetheless. The conflicts are more intense in societies where pluralism is not respected. Second, conflict is inherent among the normative criteria because of regular change, especially because of changes in technology. Technological change leads to a conflict between the old and new technological criteria, and between the new technological criteria and the established belief and ecological criteria. In a modern technological society, technological change is a regular occurrence; thus, constant conflict and adjustment are inherent. In a similar manner, new ideas can lead to new normative belief criteria, which can lead to conflict with existing belief, technological, and ecological criteria. The same is the case when there is a change in ecological criteria. Third, conflict happens when society is forced to live by criteria other than what is conceived to be normative criteria, as is the case with variant criteria.

Variant Criteria

Given the importance of normative criteria, one should not conclude that institutions are guided only by legitimate normative criteria that are consistent with what society believes to be appropriate—the community standards, so to speak. That is not the real-world case. Many criteria, rules, regulations, requirements, and attitudes that guide institutional and organizational operations are variant criteria, rules, regulations, and requirements. Although variations from normative ones, they are enforced to guide the working of institutional processes. They deviate from legitimate community standards, but are enforced in relevant societal settings. Some are not considered moral, but are legal. Some may be common practice without being stated in legal codes or court orders. Examples are practices of corporations when corporate campaign funds and lobbyists are used to establish variant laws and court decisions through legislative actions and court cases. Or they may be cases in which variant criteria are not legal, for example, the illegal abuse of workers in a factory setting. Variant criteria and rules with long-term application can be observed in an array of very different settings and spatial extension. One is when a farmer uses illegal pesticides. Another is when illegal aliens are hired by corporations. Still another is the imposition of neoliberal Western criteria and laws onto second- and third-world economies. Variant criteria are represented as $VarC_B$, $VarC_T$, and $VarC_E$ in Figure 1. They can be added to Figures 2 and 3 both as variant criteria and the concomitant variant rules, regulations, requirements, and attitudes. Variant criteria need to be included in economic and policy analysis in order to know their effect on social, economic, and technological flows.

Variant criteria usually depend on power to override laws and community standards. Conflict is established in institutions between normative criteria and variant criteria—the greater the variance of variant criteria from societal norms, the greater the level of resources that must be expended to maintain them through propaganda, security personnel, workforce turnover, lobbying expenses, instruments of violence, and so forth. All modern societal institutions, whether market, Islamic, socialist, or other orientation, have conflicts between normative criteria and variant criteria. This is the case with belief, ecological, and technological criteria. Since rapidly advancing technology leads societies to become more complex, hierarchical, and in a constant state of flux, there are more opportunities for various special interests to establish niches for variant criteria sets.[5]

Contracts Establish Criteria

Much of rule-making, regulation, and requirement articulation to establish criteria is completed through contracts among different parties. Thus, contracts become very important in the fulfillment of policies and plans. Therefore, contracts, including those between so-called private parties, need to be evaluated with the assistance of the SFM.[6] A principle to remember for societal systems in general and for the articulation of a societal concern in a SFM is that rules, regulations, and requirements do not deliver themselves to institutional entities. Institutional organizations deliver rules, regulations, and requirements to other institutional organizations. When a contract is established, it means that normative and variant criteria rows in a SFM make deliveries to the SFM column cells of the parties of the contracts. Then the rows of the parties of the contract make deliveries of the terms of the contract to cells of the columns of the same parties. The contract specifies which parties have responsibilities for different parts of the contract. In turn, the SFM rows of those parties make deliveries to the cells in the columns of other institutional organizations that are to carry out the responsibilities. (See Figures 2 and 3 for the sequence of different kinds of institutions involved in carrying out the rules, regulations, and requirements delivery in the SFM because of the negotiation of a contract.)

Consistent with the SFM-A, directives are delivered by institutions to form different attitudes and knowledge in order to call forth responses and knowing activities. If groups have the wrong attitudes and knowledge, the response will be wrong, thereby engendering institutional failure. An example is presented in the SFM study of the Nebraska school aid distribution formula completed by this author. In Figure 4, the authority institution Nebraska Department of Education (in row 12) delivers directives to processing institutions (in columns 9 and 14 through 40) about the data to collect or use, the formula calculations to make with the data, and instructions about where to deliver the calculations after completion. Particular knowledge and knowing are necessary to complete these tasks. Upon receipt of the directives and the application of knowledge by the institutional groups, those groups, in turn, become row entries to deliver their findings to other appropriate institutions (Hayden 2009b: 212–213).

Whenever rules, regulations, and requirements are delivered to the columnar cell of an institution, that institution must then become a row entry in the study or the process ends with that cell. For example,

Figure 4

Digraph of Overlapping Processes

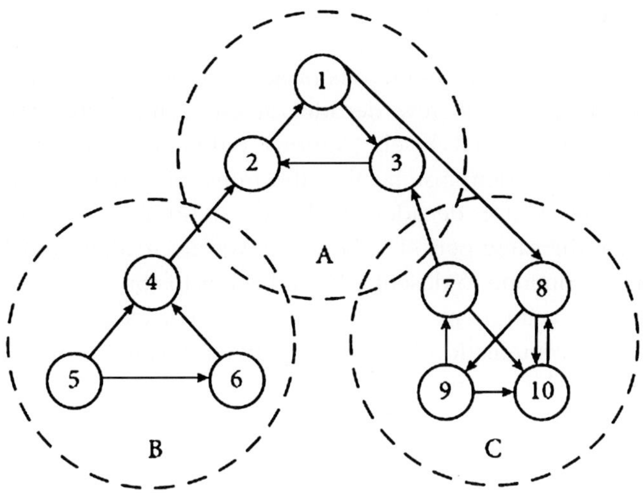

if a corporate headquarters sends a corporate regulation to a production subsidiary that obligates the subsidiary to dump toxic waste into a nearby river, the study cannot demonstrate the dumping into the river in a SFM unless the subsidiary is made a row entry with the waste delivered to the cell of the column representing the river. Most economic studies leave out the latter step because of the narrow interest in the production of goods and services, without concern for criteria antecedents and consequences.

Context is the Enemy of a Basic Ideological Component of Macroeconomics

Real-world context and the many measures of that context have led to an obvious growing credibility chasm between reality and economic models, to include macroeconomic models. We have been, and continue to be, in an intense period of degradation, depletion, depreciation, deterioration, decompression, destruction, deindustrialization, and deaccumulation.[7] Those deleterious processes are a unified part of production that are generally neither discussed nor measured in macroeconomics because the analysis of macroeconomics has been organized so that the economy is defined as an entity that is disembedded from its social and ecological context.[8]

"Context is the enemy of gullibility" (Byrd 2008: 126). The more knowledgeable policymakers are about real-world contexts, the less likely they are to be misled by ideology. The reality of the current context is clarified with numerous progress indicators that have been constructed in the last few decades at the community, city, state, regional, and national levels. Various different kinds of genuine progress indexes demonstrate that the trend of general welfare has been downward for decades while the trend for GDP has been upward for the same period.[9] These indexes are readily available, yet economists continue to describe United States history with terms such as growth, development, and accumulation. For example, the social structure of accumulation literature has been devoted to the relationship between the structure of institutions and economic accumulation, mainly for a period that has been a time of deaccumulation.

The reason economists continue to act as if economic welfare is growing in the face of the overwhelming evidence to the contrary[10] appears to be because of a concept that is held by both conservative and liberal economists. N. Gregory Mankiw, in his *Macroeconomics*, succinctly states the concept, as follows: "Of all the measures of economic performance the one that best measures economic wellbeing is GDP. Real GDP measures the economy's total output of goods and services and, therefore, a country's ability to satisfy the needs and desires of its citizens" (2010: 568). The ecology is not even mentioned in Mankiw's book, and there is no mention of the positive relationship between GDP and disease, resource waste, and ecological destruction. This case is made by both liberal and conservative economists. Although these economists hold different ideological positions, they both hold to the idea that the narrow measure of GDP indicates—ignoring evidence to the contrary—an increase in economic wellbeing. Generally, both support policies and activities to increase employment and production.

In that simple yet powerful concept, there is no recognition of the importance to consult belief criteria to determine if the production and employment are socially legitimate or to recognize ecological system destruction that accompanies employment and production.[11] "'In order to ascertain the meaning of an intellectual conception,' writes Peirce (1931–1958: Vol. 5, para. 9) 'one should consider what practical consequences might conceivably result from the truth of that conception; and the sum of these consequences will constitute the entire meaning of the conception.' The point is that the pragmatists believed that the 'truth' of a statement can be tested adequately only by the consequences of adopting the assertion" (Verma and Churchman 1997: 671). Most macroeconomists adopt the intellectual conception of macroeconomics and its production and employment policies without respect to many of its consequences.

Relating the Social Fabric Matrix to Social Structure of Accumulation and Social Accounting Matrix

To move beyond the narrow approach, such as has been mentioned with regard to macroeconomics, we know it is necessary to turn to the analysis of whole systems. This has led to various different models and tools for policy analysis. They include the Action Impact Matrix,

Sustainable Development Assessment, System Dynamics, Social Fabric Matrix, Social Structure of Accumulation, and the Social Accounting Matrix. This article discusses the latter two in conjunction with the SFM.

Relating the Social Fabric Matrix to the Social Structure of Accumulation

The social structure of accumulation (SSA), as an approach to analysis, is most concerned with the explanation of the relationships between institutions and historical periods rather than with designing plans or policies. However, its concern for the long period is consistent with the concerns of planning and policymaking. SSA is consistent with the SFM-A, as both are concerned with institutions broadly to include economic, political, financial, government, religious, and educational institutions, and with the integration of institutions (see McDonough, Reich, and Kotz 2010). The SFM-A would serve SSA well for those concerns. SSA has also been concerned with normative criteria, especially social beliefs as expressed through ideological analysis. The SFM-A would serve SSA well to further refine the definition of social belief criteria in particular cases and to refine the relationship between belief criteria and institutions. In addition, the SFM-A would allow for normative technological and ecological criteria to be added to the explanation of the social structure. Additionally, the integration of institutions in the SFM would help solve the problem of the "lack of specificity about the exact character of SSAs themselves" (McDonough 1994: 74). Furthermore, the use of the SFM-A for the analysis of institutions and normative criteria would provide a framework for social indicators in general and for genuine progress indicators in particular in order to measure accumulation and stagnation.

To this author's knowledge, the SFM-A has not been utilized to model change for long-term periods but it has been for shorter periods to describe and analyze change within a process (Hayden and Bolduc 2000; Hayden 2009b), and there is an explanation of how to model longer periods of successional time and evolutionary time in Hayden (2006: 178–181). Such use of the SFM would allow for the construction of the SSA in a way to mark points and dates of expansion and stagnation.

The SFM can be used to model change and evolution by monitoring deliveries among the components and elements of the matrix. Through such monitoring, it is possible to observe changes in levels of deliveries that lead to cumulative changes in the components. The delivery changes can be from the components in the SFM system, from the system's environment, and/or from new components that have developed. Illustrations are found in Figures 5 and 6. Figure 5 represents a SFM digraph of components 1 through 10 from a SFM. They are organized in three overlapping processes, the overlaps being the result of deliveries between components. System changes can be observed in Figure 6. Figure 6 illustrates a system that has become more complex, has developed new components and deliveries, and has lost particular components and deliveries. The birth and death of SFM components and cells is an expression of evolutionary changes. A well-monitored SFM allows for the observation of such changes. Victor Lippit explains such changes from the work of Martin Wolfson. Lippit explains that Wolfson argues "that 'the financial component of the postwar social structure of accumulation contributed to strong economic growth in the United States. . . .' Wolfson places special emphasis on the financial reforms of the 1930s" (2010: 51). Changes came about as "many of these reforms were reversed in the 1980s and 1990s" (2010: 51). The details of such changes in financial institutions and the normative criteria expressed through rule changes can be modeled and monitored with the SFM (as Scott Fullwiler has done, 2009). Such information would be very useful to planners, as they could observe the buildup or decrease of deliveries among components that can forecast system changes.

Relating the Social Fabric Matrix to the Social Accounting Matrix

The social accounting matrix (SAM) is the most technically refined of the approaches being considered here, has been applied more extensively, and is generally consistent with the SFM-A in that a basic concern of both is with regard to deliveries among the various sectors included in their respective matrices. To integrate SAM into the SFM-A will make for the kind of planning, policymaking, and monitoring paradigm now needed. Such integration will lead to the inclusion of

Figure 5

Social Fabric Matrix of Nebraska State Aid for a Local K–12 Public School System, 2006–2007

Delivering Components ↓		Receiving Components →	Social Beliefs: Equity 1	Adequacy/Sufficiency 2	Cost/Efficiency 3	Comprehensive Size 4	Consolidation 5	Local Control 6	Authority Institutions: Courts/Legal System 7	Neb. Legislature/Govenor 8	Local K-12 Public Sch System 9	Property Tax Program 10	Property Wealth 11	Neb. Dept. of Education 12	Neb. Dept. of Revenue 13
Social Beliefs	Equity	1							1	1					
	Adequacy/Sufficiency	2							1	1					
	Cost/Efficiency	3							1	1					
	Comprehensive Size	4							1	1					
	Consolidation	5							1	1					
	Local Control	6							1	1					
Authority Institutions	Courts/Legal System	7								1	1	1	1	1	1
	Neb. Legislature/Govenor	8									1	1	1	1	1
	Local K-12 Public Sch System	9							1					1	
	Property Tax Program	10									1		1		
	Property Wealth	11													
	Neb. Dept. of Education	12									1				
	Neb. Dept. of Revenue	13										1		1	
Processing Institutions for Regulations and Requirements	Fall Membership	14													
	Formula Students	15													
	Weighted Formula Students	16													
	Limited English Proficiency	17													
	Indian Land Factor	18													
	Remoteness Factor	19													
	Proverty Factor	20													
	Adj Weighted Formula Stu	21													
	Excluded TGFOE Accts	22													
	Transportation Allowance	23									1				
	Special Receipts	24									1				
	Adjusted GFOE	25													
	Cost Factor Growth	26													
	Aggregate Stu w/o Remoteness	27													
	Cost Group Cost/Student	28													
	Cost/Stu X Local Students	29									1				
	Temporary Aid Adj	30									1				
	Yield from Local Tax	31									1				
	Net Option Students	32													
	Net Option Funding	33									1				
	Allocated Income Tax Fund	34									1				
	Processing Actual Receipts	35									1				
	Minimum Levy Adj	36									1				
	Lop Off	37									1				
	Small Sch Stabilization Adj	38									1				
	Stabilization Factor	39									1				
	Prior Year Deficiency & Correction	40									1				

Figure 5 *Continued*

Processing Institutions for Regulations and Requirements																										
Fall Membership	Formula Students	Weighted Formula Students	Limited English Proficiency	Indian Land Factor	Remoteness Factor	Poverty Factor	Adj Weighted Formula Stu	Excluded TGFOE Accts	Transportantion Allowance	Special Receipts	Adjusted GFOE	Cost Factor Growth	Aggregate Stu w/o Remoteness	Cost Group Cost/Student	Cost/Stu X Local Students	Temporary Aid Adj	Yield from Local Tax	Net Option Students	Net Option Funding	Allocated Income Tax Fund	Other Actual Receipts	Minimum Levy Adj	Lop Off	Small Sch Stabilization Adj	Stabilization Factor	Prior Year Deficiency & Correction
14	15	16	17	18	19	20	21	22	23	24	25	26	27	28	29	30	31	32	33	34	35	36	37	38	39	40
																	1									
1	1	1	1	1	1	1	1	1	1	1	1	1	1	1	1	1	1	1	1	1	1	1	1	1	1	1
	1																									
		1			1	1						1														
							1						1					1								
							1						1													
							1						1													
							1																			
							1						1													
															1											
											1															
											1					1							1	1	1	
											1					1					1		1	1	1	
														1												
														1												
														1												
															1				1							
																1							1	1	1	
																			1	1			1	1	1	
																							1	1	1	
																			1							
																				1			1	1	1	
																							1	1	1	
																							1	1	1	
																				1			1	1	1	
																								1	1	
																									1	
																							1			

Figure 6

Evolution of Figure 5 with Acquisition and Loss of Nodes and Deliveries. Loss of Nodes Indicated by Shaded Circles. New Deliveries Indicated by Dotted Lines. Nodes Lost are 3, 9, and 10. Nodes Gained are 11, 12, 13, 14, and 15

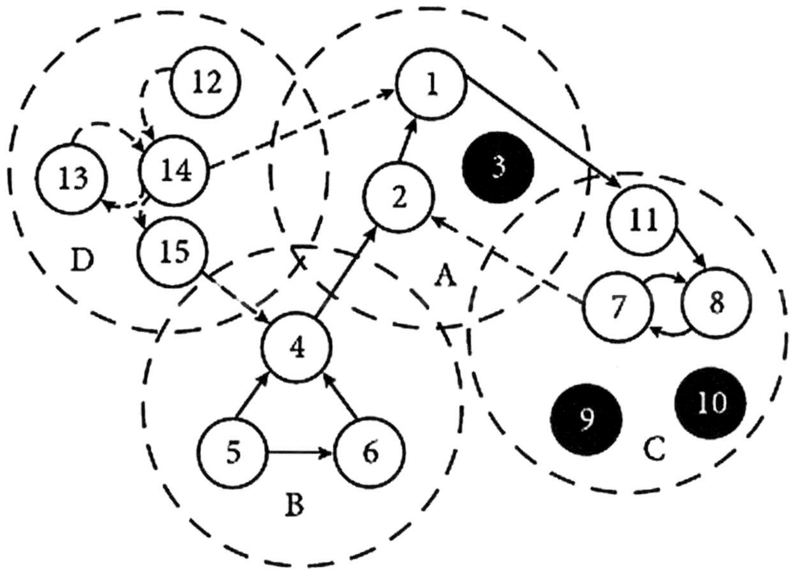

normative criteria, rules, attitudes, social institutions, ecological entities, and progress indicators not included in SAM today.

The SFM was developed "to allow the convergence and integration of conceptual works in instrumental philosophy, general systems analysis, Boolean algebra, social system analysis, ecology, policy analysis, and geobased data systems (Hayden 2006). It allows multiple forms of data to be incorporated into one analytical tool. While not comprehensive, it identifies and incorporates six main components in examining a problem and in attempting to develop a policy to solve the problem" (Sturgeon 2009: 42). The six components were outlined above. Each component is analyzed with an eye toward determining the flow and delivery of one component to another. By conducting the analysis in this manner, the SFM can "express the attributes of the parts as well as the integrated process of the whole" (Hayden 2006). There are seven major characteristics of the SFM itself: (1) it is based on the concept of delivery, (2) rows deliver to the columns, (3) it is a noncommon-denominator matrix (meaning that all kinds of data can be incorporated), (4) cell observations are the flows of the system (that is, a 1 in a cell represents a direct delivery; therefore, indirect deliveries are not counted (in a cell), (5) the number of cells is dependent on the study at hand, (6) the matrix defines the system as it exists, and (7) the matrix allows for model building and data collecting consistent with theory (Sturgeon 2009: 42).

SAM, as currently constructed, is consistent with some SFM characteristics and inconsistent with others. Generally, when inconsistent, as now constructed, SAM can be made consistent by being integrated into the SFM. First, SAM and SFM share the basic input/output matrix. Second, although SAM is narrowly defined to be based only on monetary expenditures, a SAM can be incorporated into a SFM to take advantage of the latter's multiple forms of data resulting from the components that are included. Third, the problems of interest to SAM users can be extended to fit normal policy concerns if SAM is fitted into a SFM. Fourth, both SAM and SFM are based on the concept of delivery. Fifth, SAM is a common-denominator matrix; thus, it needs to be integrated into a SFM to determine the relationships between expenditures and deliveries of other important components of the system for which there is not a common denominator. Sixth, SAM does not attempt to define and explain the system that is creating the problem of interest. Seventh, the integration of SAM and SFM will allow for model building and data collection consistent with transdisciplinary systems theory and socioecological systems.

What is included in a SAM varies with different conceptual presentations and applications so all discussion that follows does not apply to all SAM studies, but is generally relevant. One difference among different SAMs is what is included in the rows and columns of the matrix. Although very different kinds of entries are made in the rows and columns, they are treated as if they have the same character of deliveries. An example is when business institutions, investment, and wages are each entered in a SAM as different rows and columns, and are all treated as institutions making monetary expenditure deliveries. Investment is not an institution and it does not make direct monetary deliveries. Investment is plant and equipment, and it is usually delivered by institutions such as corporations and government agencies to other corporations and government agencies. Wages are a delivery from corporations, government agencies, nonprofits, religious organizations, universities, and so forth made to households and families.

The basic information in a SAM is usually presented as (1) having rows and columns always directly exchanging deliveries with each other so that if row A delivers to column B then row B will also make a delivery to column A, and (2) having each cell containing only one kind of delivery. These assumptions do not hold in real-world processes so a SAM, as it is traditionally constructed, is insufficient for planning. This set of methodological assumptions and characteristics of a SAM is consistent with the assumption that the economy in general, and markets in particular, are disembedded, and therefore ignores the complex web of social and ecological relations that can be included if a SAM is embedded in a SFM.

A real-world SAM in a SFM will not necessarily have institutions making direct exchange of deliveries with each other. For example, social beliefs deliver criteria directly to corporations without receiving a return delivery. The same is the case for other normative criteria. In a similar manner, a corporation may deliver unwanted pollution to another corporation without a return delivery. The same is the case when a corporation delivers cancer to households or toxic waste to a river. There usually is no return delivery in the opposite direction, from households or river to the corporation.

A problem in much of economics that has already received serious attention in numerous publications is the assumption that it is possible to have a common denominator in complex systems. Beyond that general assumption, a more serious mistake is that commercial prices could possibly serve as a common denominator. The SFM-A explicitly rejects any endorsement of a common denominator (and SAM can be expanded to do the same). It is not possible to aggregate all the entries in a row or column—pollution, cancer, and monetary payments may all be in the same row or column. When undertaking macro or system planning, it is unlikely that many of the cells used to define real-world deliveries would all be the same kind. The same corporation, for example, may deliver investment goods, consulting services, consumer goods, government rules, and pollution in the same cell to another corporation. A different corporation will, during the same period, make a different set of deliveries to the same receiving corporation. Relevant research needs to take account of all these different deliveries in order to calculate relationships among them. This is important, for example, in determining what industries macroeconomic stimulus funds should be diverted from in order to protect the environment or prevent cancer. This became a real issue between some state governors and the Obama Administration in the United States in 2009. Governors were demanding that stimulus funds be released without respect to the environmental damage that would be caused by particular projects in their respective states. The Obama Administration appropriately emphasized that funds should be withheld until being assured that production operations and technologies were changed in order to protect the environment.

SAM has been constructed in some cases so that monetary expenditures are divided according to the amount of money received by different industries (see Pyatt and Round 1985). Pollution studies have also documented the amount of pollution from different industries. These two kinds of studies provide two sets of deliveries that can be related in a SFM, along with policies to adjust production to low-pollution industries. Thus, needed changes in laws (often to change variant criteria and laws) for particular industries can be identified.

In a like manner, SAM has been constructed to measure the distribution of income by looking at the amount of wage expenditures going to different kinds of households from different industries (see Pyatt and Round 1985). With the benefit of that information, a SFM can identify what kinds of wage rules or regulations need to be changed to impact on the wages paid by low-income industries.

Any real-world problem of interest is embedded in an array of different institutions along with concomitant criteria, rules, technologies, and ecological entities of those institutions. For economic planning to be relevant, these entities should all be included in the matrix. For example, if the concern of interest is hospital care, institutional roles may be played by environmental protection advocates and agencies, orders of nuns, corporations, government agencies, research universities, labor unions, banks, insurance corporations, nurses' training organizations, and so forth. All those institutions are involved in the production and delivery of the goods, bads, services, and disservices associated with hospital care. Without a means to understand their relationships and determine which deliveries make a positive contribution and which deliveries make a negative one, it is unlikely that we can be successful in providing an efficient system of hospital care. Deliveries of bads need to be included in the matrix along with the criteria, rules, and regulations that allow for and obligate the production and distribution of bads.

Macroeconomists are rightly concerned about multipliers, as monetary expenditures are multiplied through different societal institutions in response to expenditure changes. For planning purposes, it is also necessary to define the relationships between expenditure multipliers and other multipliers. As production, employment, and inflation levels change, the impact of those changes filter through society and change institutions. The physical infrastructure will change as homes and buildings are destroyed through "urban renewal" in cities and home abandonment in rural areas and small towns. Additionally, impacts will be multiplied through the ecological system. Production generates (1) direct ecological damage on the resource input side through habitat degradation and loss of species, (2) direct ecological damage from the output side through pollution, and (3) indirect ecological damage as the consequences of habitat degradation and pollution impact on each other. Mohan Muniasingh and Wilfrido Cruz outline some of these impacts in an action impact matrix (AIM) (Muniasingh and Cruz 1994; Munasingh 2010: 155–158). However, an AIM is not an interactive matrix but a table that summarizes impacts. It does not assist in discovering relationships and calculating impacts. The purpose of the SFM and SAM is to discover relationships among components and calculate impacts that are the consequence of changes in deliveries. A SAM integrated into a SFM would be able to define the relationships between changes in monetary expenditures and changes in social and ecological components and their deliveries.

A technical difference between the multiplier effects of expenditure streams in macroeconomics and multiple ecological effects in ecological systems is that ecologists do not suggest that we collapse ecological deliveries into a common denominator. Ecological effects are different in origin, kind, level of delivery, and long-term impact. The same differences exist for monetary expenditures, but they are hidden with the assumed common denominator of money. A common denominator can be assumed if the only interest is how fast dollars turn over through the system. We know, however, the meaning and consequences of the dollar expenditures are not the same when spent on crop production cultivation that protects the soil as when spent on crop production cultivation that destroys the soil. Such differences can be researched and recognized in a SAM/SFM approach that will make it possible for economic planning to be successful.

Conclusion

The conclusion reached in the discussion about the possibility of integrating the concepts from the SFM, SSA, and SAM is that such integration is not only possible but necessary in order to provide for the kind of analysis needed for understanding, planning, and policymaking. It is necessary in the context of what this paper outlines as important for such an endeavor to be successful. The context includes a recognition that (1) holistic theory of socioecological systems, similar to that displayed in Figure 1, is necessary; (2) the six components of cultural values, social beliefs, institutions, personal attitudes, technology, and ecological systems need to be integrated because they are embedded together to provide for the provisioning process; (3) the six components are guided and held together by both normative and illegitimate variant criteria, thus, both need to be included in modeling and analysis; (4) criteria in conjunction with advancing technology and new ideas establish a constant stream of new societal conflicts that need to be monitored and addressed in policymaking; and (5) we need to move beyond the idea that fate will bring progress and enhance welfare if we just undertake production.

Notes

1. The sociologist Nicole Biggart, during a Karl Polanyi symposium about embeddedness, stated that economists often begin talks with the remark,

"assume a market." They do not mean a real market, but, rather, a fictional construct that includes additional assumptions like perfect information, independent firms and actors, homogenous products, rational actors with complete information, the existence of utility and its maximization by actors, and equilibrium. Biggart wondered what it would be like if, in response, sociologists opened with "assume a society" (Krippner et al. 2004: 119).

2. See discussion in Krippner et al. (2004).

3. Thus, as John Dewey emphasized, analysts need to identify the problem of interest before they can know what to study. That study can be called economic if it is understood that what is considered economic will change with the identification of each different problem. This means that to assume that any particular problem is to be solved with either microeconomics or macroeconomics does not follow because real-world problems include both detailed activities within institutions and transactional aspects across various system components.

4. For a more complete description of the six components, see Hayden (2006: 75–85).

5. It may be the case that the more important variant criteria become in a system, the more protean the variant guidelines because of the constant pressure and conflict within the institutions and constant battles in legislative bodies and courts to change the variant criteria that are seen as being illegitimate.

6. For an example, see Hayden and Bolduc (2000).

7. Some specific examples of those processes in the United States are as follows: mountains destroyed to get coal; coal burned that creates climate change; water systems disrupted; water resources destroyed; water quality diminished; soil denuded, eroded, and its nutrients depleted; use of pesticides that cause extinction of species and industries; huge rural regions and urban neighborhoods depopulated; disintegration of families; urban sprawl; buildings depreciated by air pollution; wages, incomes, and wealth decompressed; pension funds underfunded and raided; deterioration of the physical infrastructure of bridges, dams, streets, highways, railroad service, and pipelines; ethanol produced for fuel; donut production; arms production for export; website universities; disappearance of knowledge bases and skills; manufacturing industries downsized; energy resources depleted, depreciated, and wasted; leaking toxic waste disposal sites; the Katrina flood; antibiotic overuse; and so forth. This list could be continued to book length.

8. Our goal should be to follow the precautionary principle, which means to avoid approving production activity until it is possible to document its safety through system modeling and studies of the relevant socioecological context.

9. *The Index of Social Health of the United States* is based on 16 indicators. They are infant mortality, child poverty, child abuse, teenage suicide, teenage

drug abuse, high school dropouts, unemployment, weekly wages, health insurance coverage, poverty among the elderly, out-of-pocket health costs among the elderly, homicides, alcohol-related traffic fatalities, food stamp coverage, access to affordable housing, and income inequality. In 2008, the Index was 55.5 out of a possible 100. "Overall, between 1970 and 2008, the Index declined from 66.2 to 55.5, a drop of 16 percent" (Institute for Innovations in Social Policy 2010: 1–2).

10. The idea that it is best to take action without respect to consequences seems to be a traditional trait of Western society. More than once, corporate executives have appeared before a public commission or committee on which this author was a member and testified, in response to questions about some ill-conceived action, to the effect that, "I would rather do something wrong than do nothing at all." George Bernard Shaw is reported to have advised: "A life spent making mistakes is not only more honorable but more useful than a life spent doing nothing." Worse advice is rarely stated. It makes the life of former Vice-President Dick Cheney appear very honorable. The illusion that taking action, without respect to whether it is a mistake, will lead to progress appears to be consistent with the Western "Idea of Progress," which Robert W. Merry explains as the belief that progress is inevitable and inexorable (2005: 39–44). It is "a fundamental reality of current Western thinking—namely that the Idea of Progress remains for many the central underlying philosophical precept and the wellspring for much of what we see today in the way of perceptions, outlooks, predictions, and convictions" (Merry 2005: 41). Consistent with the idea that progress is fated, macroeconomists adopted GDP as an indicator for progress that they knew was inevitable. The long-term rise of GDP need not be questioned because it is consistent with the idea of the inevitability of progress.

11. There are examples to the contrary. A source of contrary literature that is also a good source for references is *Twenty-First Century Macroeconomics: Responding to Climate Change*, edited by Jonathan M. Harris and Neva R. Goodwin (2009).

References

Adkisson, R. V. (2009). "The Economy as an Open System: An Institutionalist Framework for Economic Development." In *Institutional Analysis and Praxis: The Social FabricMatrix Approach*. Eds. T. Natarajan, W. Elsner, and S. T. Fullwiler, pp. 25–38. New York: Springer.

Byrd, R. C. (2008). *Letter to a New President: Commonsense Lessons for Our Next Leader*. New York: Thomas Dunne Books.

Fullwiler, S. T. (2009). "The Social Fabric Matrix Approach to Central Bank Operations: An Application to the Federal Reserve and the Recent Financial Crisis." In *Institutional Analysis and Praxis: The Social Fabric Matrix Approach*. Eds. T. Natarajan, W. Elsner, and S. T. Fullwiler, pp. 123–170. New York: Springer.

Harris, J. M., and N. R. Goodwin, eds. (2009). *Twenty-First Century Macroeconomics: Responding to the Climate Challenge*. Cheltenham, UK: Edward Elgar Publishing Ltd.

Hayden, F. G. (2006). *Policymaking for a Good Society: The Social Fabric Matrix Approach to Policy Analysis and Program Evaluation*. New York: Springer.

——. ([1998] 2009a). "Normative Analysis of Instituted Processes." In *Institutional Analysis and Praxis: The Social Fabric Matrix Approach*. Eds. T. Natarajan, W. Elsner, and S. Fullwiler, pp. 103–120. New York: Springer.

——. (2009b). "Utilization of the Social Fabric Matrix to Articulate a State System of Financial Aid for Public Schools and to Derive Conceptual Conclusions." In *Institutional Analysis and Praxis: The Social Fabric Matrix Approach*. Eds. T. Natarajan, W. Elsner, and S. T. Fulwiller, pp. 209–235. New York: Springer.

Hayden, F. G., and S. R. Bolduc. (2000). "Contracts and Costs in a Corporate/Government System Dynamics Network: A United States Case." In *Industrial Policies After 2000*. Eds. W. Elsner and J. Groenewegen, pp. 235–284. Boston: Kluwer Academic.

Institute for Innovation in Social Policy. (2010). *The Index for Social Health, 2008*. Poughkeepsie, NY: Vassar College. Online. Available at: http://iisp.vassar.edu/index.html (accessed August 12, 2010).

Kay, J. (2010). "A Good Economist Knows the True Value of the Arts." *Financial Times* August 11: 7.

Krippner, G., M. Granovetter, F. Block, N. Biggart, T. Beanish, Y. Hsing, G. Hart, G. Arrighi, M. Mendell, J. Hall, M. Burawoy, S. Vogel, S. O'Riain. (2004). "Polanyi Symposium: A Conversation on Embeddedness." *Socio-economic Review* 2: 109–135.

Lippit, V. D. (2010). "Social Structure of Accumulation Theory." In *Contemporary Capitalism and Its Crises*. Eds. T. McDonough, M. Reich, and M. Kotz, pp. 45–71. Cambridge: Cambridge University Press.

Mankiw, G. (2010). *Macroeconomics*. New York: Worth Publishers.

McDonough, T. (1994). "Social Structures of Accumulation, Contingent History, and Stages of Capitalism." In *Social Structures of Accumulation: The Political Economy of Growth and Crisis*. Eds. D. M. Kotz, T. McDonough, and M. Reich, pp. 72–84. Cambridge: Cambridge University Press.

McDonough, T., M. Reich, and D. Kotz. (2010). *Contemporary Capitalism and Its Crises: Social Structure of Accumulation Theory for the 21st Century*. Cambridge: Cambridge University Press.

Merry, R. W. (2005). *Sands of Empire: Missionary Zeal, American Foreign Policy, and the Hazards of Global Ambition*. New York: Simon & Schuster.

Munasinghe, M. (2009). "Macroeconomics and Sustainable Development: Applying the Sustainomics Framework." In *Twenty-First Century Macroeconomics: Responding to the Climate Challenge.* Eds. J. M. Harris and N. R. Goodwin, pp. 138–168. Northhampton, MA: Edward Elgar Publishing, Inc.

Munasinghe, M., and W. Cruze. 1994. *Economywide Policies and the Environment: Lessons from Experience.* Washington, DC: World Bank.

Natarajan, T., W. Elsner, and S. Fullwiler. (2009). *Institutional Analysis and Praxis: The Social Fabric Matrix Approach.* New York: Springer.

Pyatt, G., and J. I. Round. (1985). "Accounting and Fixed-Price Multipliers in a Social Accounting Matrix Framework." In *Social Accounting Matrices: A Basis for Planning.* Eds. G. Pyatt and J. I. Round, pp. 186–206. Washington, DC: World Bank.

Sturgeon, J. I. (2009). "The Social Fabric Matrix, the Principles of Institutional Adjustment, and Individual Action." In *Institutional Analysis and Praxis: The Social Fabric Matrix Approach.* Eds. T. Natarajan, N. Elsner, and S. T. Fullwiler, pp. 39–54. New York: Springer.

Verma, N., and W. Churchman. (1997). "The Theory of the Firm: An Epistemological Analysis." *Systems Practice* 10(6): 657–675.

Social Structures of Accumulation: A "Punctuated" View of Embeddedness

By TERRENCE MCDONOUGH*

ABSTRACT. This article starts from the institutional/evolutionary insight that economic processes are necessarily embedded in broader sets of social institutions and that these institutions change over time. It uses a Marxian framework, the Social Structure of Accumulation school, to argue that this change is not gradual or continuous. Rather, wide-ranging institutional transformations follow periods of capitalist crisis, setting the stage for renewed accumulation and, eventually, new crises. This leads to a punctuated pattern of successive stages of capitalism.

By now it is almost uncontroversial that the capitalist economy is embedded in a range of institutions. Further, it is recognized that the market economy cannot function without the effective functioning of its embedding institutions. This insight is, of course, one of the founding principles of the Institutional school of economics. Marxian economics has always seen capitalism as an historical mode of production in a complex dynamic relationship with various institutional conditions of existence at the economic, political, and ideological levels. Post Keynesian economics is rooted in the recognition of the essential importance of money and accompanying financial institutions, demand and consumption, and the institutional responses to the inevitable uncertainty of economic decision-making. Even the neoclassical mainstream has interpreted the failure of "shock therapy" in Eastern Europe as due to insufficient attention to the institutional context of markets.

Thus it is widely accepted within economics that capitalism exists in relationship to a number of conditioning institutions.[1] It would be possible to adopt a strictly static approach to this relationship. Indeed,

*terrence.mcdonough@nuigalway.ie

American Journal of Economics and Sociology, Vol. 70, No. 5 (November, 2011).

there is a strong temptation within some wings of the neoclassical, Post Keynesian and Marxian tradition to conceptualize capitalism in a "pure form" and then conceptualize the somewhat invariant institutional preconditions that must accompany this pure form. This facilitates both mathematical modelling and the hypothesizing of teleological trajectories to optimal equilibrium in the case of the neoclassicals, to socialist transition in the case of some Marxists. Nevertheless, much of the theorizing about embeddedness in economics assumes that institutions change over time and that this change contributes to the creation of a more concrete history of capitalist development than more abstract theoretical models allow. Thus both the embeddedness of capitalism in social institutions and a development of this relationship over time are widely accepted.[2] The question I wish to address is whether or not it is possible to say something more specific than this about the relationship between capitalism and its institutional environment.

I will situate the proposed answers within the Marxian tradition and more specifically within the Marxian tradition of stage theory. Marxism was never proposed primarily as a theory of what we characterize today as "economics." Rather, it was a theory of history in general with a "political economic" aspect of that history, the class struggle, as its principal dynamic force.[3] Thus Marxism is a significant current in historiography and Marx is widely regarded as one of the founders of both modern sociology and political science. A comprehensive presentation of cultural studies cannot afford to ignore the Marxian tradition. Arguably, the bulk of the work in the Marxian tradition exists outside of efforts to further Marx's treatment of the economy strictly speaking.[4]

Thus a concrete consideration of the capitalist mode of production quickly becomes a consideration of the broader "social formation," including its political, ideological, and cultural aspects. Marx himself had at one time included a volume on the state as one of the six-book plan for what later became the series on *Capital.* Wolff and Resnick (1987) have elaborated a conception of subsumed classes, groups characterized by the supply of one of the conditions of the capitalist class process. This includes political and ideological conditions, thus bringing the institutional embedding of capitalism into class analysis itself. The Marxian tradition of capitalist stage theory brings these factors into the heart of the Marxian analysis of the capital accumulation process.

There is a fundamentally continuous tradition of Marxian stage theory from the beginning of the 20th century until the present day. The Marxian stage theory tradition is intimately linked to turning points in the historical process of capital accumulation. These turning points mark the inauguration of a period of relatively unproblematic reproduction of capitalist social relations or, symmetrically, the beginning of a period of stagnation and crisis. Simply put, the alternating periods of growth and crisis that describe the transition from one capitalist stage to another have left a strong imprint on the history of the Marxian theory of capitalist stages.

This history begins with the first crisis of Marxism. This crisis was precipitated by the recovery of the capitalist economy from the first Great Depression at the end of the 19th century. Seeing capitalism recover from what was thought to be its final crisis, Marxist activists searched for a way of explaining this recovery without abandoning the revolutionary implications of Marx's analysis of the contradictory character of capitalist social relations. This explanation was to be found in the pioneering work of Rudolf Hilferding (1980) on finance capital, Nicolai Bukharin (1973) on the world economy, and V. I. Lenin (1968) on imperialism. All three argued that the capitalist economy had, with the advent of monopoly capitalism, entered into a new and higher stage of capitalism. This new stage underlay the recovery but it had not transcended the basic Marxian dynamics of capital accumulation.

Hilferding's, Bukarin's, and Lenin's (HBL) analysis would be carried into the post World War II era through the work of Paul Sweezy (1968) and Ernest Mandel (1970). In their influential expositions of Marxian economics, the HBL analysis of monopoly capitalism was treated by each as essentially a fourth volume of capital. Their descriptions of the transition to monopoly capital consolidated stage theory as an accepted component of Marxian theoretical practice. Both would be influential in forming the basis for the second wave of Marxian stage theory.

The second wave of Marxian stage theorizing emerged with the end of the post World War II expansion. Ernest Mandel's Long Wave

Theory (LWT) (1975, 1980), the Social Structure of Accumulation Framework (SSAF) (Gordon, Edwards, and Reich 1983), and the Regulation Approach (RA) (Aglietta 1979) analyzed the stagflationary crises of most of the advanced capitalist countries as the end of a long wave of growth following the end of the war. This long wave of accumulation was underpinned by the emergence of a new stage of capitalism that was analogous to the reorganization brought about by monopoly capital at the turn of the century. Since this new stage was the resolution of the crisis of the monopoly stage, these new schools were reluctant to predict the non-resolution of the then current crisis, thus opening up the possibility of further stages of capitalism in the future. This identification of a new stage following on from HBL's monopoly stage and the possibility of subsequent stages in the future elevated Lenin's theory of the highest stage to a general theory of stages of capitalism. The SSAF built on Sweezy's contribution and that of the American Monopoly Capital school. Mandel's LWT, not surprisingly, was founded on his earlier analysis of monopoly capital. The RA claimed no precursors apart from Althusser, though Althusser's admiration for Lenin and specifically his *Imperialism* is well known.

This tradition has contended that a full analysis of capitalism cannot be satisfied with an understanding of the general transhistorical dynamics of capitalism as a mode of production nor with the analysis of particular historical conjunctures. Stage theory undertakes an intermediate level of analysis in the sense that it identifies periods intermediate in length between the conjuncture and overall capitalist history. This intermediate period of analysis is founded on the observation that while all economies are embedded in the broader array of social institutions, this is especially important in the capitalist era because of the conflictual foundations of capitalism in class division and capitalist competition. For accumulation to proceed relatively smoothly these sources of instability must be countered through the construction of a set of stable institutions at not only the economic but also the political and ideological levels.

The construction of such a social structure underpins the profit rate and creates the secure expectations that make long term investment possible. Nevertheless, as accumulation proceeds the institutions are undermined by class conflict, capitalist competition, and accumulation itself. These forces and the interdependence of the institutions lead to a breakdown of the institutions, a fall in the profit rate, and the collapse of accumulation, initiating a period of crisis and stagnation that is only overcome with the construction of a new set of institutions. Thus capitalist stages are constituted by the sets of interdependent economic, political, and ideological institutions that underpin relatively successful accumulation separated by intervening periods of crisis. The following section considers the SSAF wing of the second wave of theorizing in more detail.

The Social Structure of Accumulation Framework[5]

At the end of the 1970s, David Gordon (1978, 1980) published two articles linking long cycle theory with the concept of stages of capitalism. In this context, the advent of monopoly capital at the turn of the century coincides with the completion of the long wave trough at the end of the 19th century and the inauguration of the long wave expansion that ended with the Great Depression of the 1930s. The new question that the adoption of a long wave perspective posed to the monopoly stage of capitalism tradition was whether the postwar expansion was associated with a similar set of multidimensional institutional changes. Gordon (1978) answers this question by proposing a set of postwar institutions whose establishment accounted for the long period of postwar prosperity. These institutions included among others multinational corporate structures, dual labor markets associated with a bread-and-butter industrial unionism, American international economic and military hegemony, easy credit, conservative Keynesian state policy, and bureaucratic control of workers.

In this way, Gordon established the possibility of articulating a postwar set of institutions that conditioned the subsequent expansion of the economy in a way similar to the manner in which the set of institutions analyzed by Hilferding, Bukharin, and Lenin accounted for the turn of the century expansion. Thus the multi-institutional analysis of monopoly capital is implicitly used by Gordon as a model for explaining the postwar expansion.

The repetitive use of this kind of explanation raised the question of whether the assembling of such sets of institutions could be generalized as the basis of a comprehensive theory of stages of capitalism. Gordon (1978, 1980) answers this question by proposing that both the institutions comprising monopoly capital and those making up the postwar social order constituted examples of social structures of accumulation (SSAs). The construction of a new SSA provided the basis for a new stage of capitalism. The disintegration of this set of institutions marks the end of each stage.

The SSA approach achieved its definitive form shortly thereafter with the publication of Gordon, Edwards, and Reich's *Segmented Work, Divided Workers* (1982). This volume used Gordon's SSA approach to capitalist stages to reformulate these authors' earlier analysis of the history of capital-labor relations in the U.S (Reich, Gordon, and Edwards 1973). The authors' exposition of the SSA, which dominated the capitalist world at the beginning of the 20th century, clearly owes a great deal to HBL's original description of the era of imperialism.

Developments within the SSA school have brought the SSA framework closer to the HBL position. The notion of long cycles or long waves has been deemphasized in favor of a conception of periods of alternating growth and stagnation in capitalist history. The length of these periods is not determined in advance. They do not follow on from one another with the strict logic that a cycle theory would demand. The eclipse of the long cycle argument refocuses attention on Lenin's concept of stages of capitalism (see McDonough 1994a, 1994b).

SSA theory is rooted in both Marxian and Keynesian macroeconomic insights. Marxian economics sees capitalism as an inherently conflictual system, characterized by crisis tendencies brought about by such factors as the conflict between classes, most prominently between workers and capitalists, and competition among capitalists. These crisis tendencies can appear in a number of concrete blockages to the accumulation process. Keynesian economics sees the investment decision as inherently unstable, subject to large fluctuations due to changing expectations and periodic imbalances between the financial and real economies, as well as being prone to self-reinforcing periods of stagnation and depression.

SSA theory argues that these inherent problems can be attenuated through the construction of sets of institutions that mitigate and channel class conflict and stabilize capitalists' long-run expectations. Institutions in this sense are conceived of broadly and can be economic, political, ideological, or cultural in character. [6] The particular organization of markets and the structure of competition are examples of economic institutions. The state, including its various organs and associated policies, is the most prominent example of a political institution. Ideological and cultural institutions include political ideologies, the higher education system, and systems of religious belief. The economic, political, ideological, and cultural institutions of any social structure of accumulation are mutually compatible and generally supportive of each other as well as supportive of the accumulation process. Thus each SSA constitutes a relatively unified structure.

When a social structure of accumulation is in place, many of the determinants of the profit rate are secured and long-run expectations of profitability are stabilized. Higher levels of investment lead to expansion and growth. Initially, this expansionary dynamic reinforces the SSA and provides resources that can be devoted to its consolidation. However, over time the process of expansion eventually undermines the accumulation process. This undermining can result from intensifying class conflict, increasing competition in product and resource markets, the saturation of markets, or any of a number of other causes, some of which are general tendencies of capitalism, while others are specific to individual SSAs. As institutions are destabilized, profits and profit expectations fall, leading to declines in investment rates. The decline in resources then further undermines the institutions of the SSA. The integrated character of the SSA accelerates the decline as failing institutions destabilize each other. The SSA ceases to underpin accumulation and the economy enters into a long period of stagnation.

Under conditions of stagnation, conflict increasingly focuses on restoring the conditions for renewed profitability and accumulation. Since different classes and social forces favor different programs, new initiatives are often tentative and may be blocked. A successful set of institutions must include political and ideological innovations as well as economic ones. The construction of the new SSA therefore requires a long period of time and as a result the period of stagnation is usually lengthy. Eventually, however, one political-economic program is able to defeat its rivals or an historic compromise might be reached. A new SSA is constructed and more rapid accumulation begins again.[7]

U.S. history illustrates this dynamic process. In the mid to late 19th century, a competitive SSA was dominated by a market structure of small and medium size firms. Labor control strategies were simple and direct, resisted eventually through craft union organization. The state provided infrastructure but overall maintained a laissez faire position. Trade constituted the dominant form of international economic relations, and the dominant ideology consisted of classical liberalism. While there are some differences in the SSA school over which factors were most important in undermining this SSA, analysts have pointed to falling prices due to unrestrained competition, rising real wages, excess capacity created in the competitive struggle, and conflicts over the role of gold and the structure of finance, which led to a profit squeeze. This crisis was resolved through the creation of a new monopoly SSA, characterized by an oligopolistic market structure, weak unions, U.S. expansionism in Latin America and Asia, and the creation of the Federal Reserve System. This SSA then ended in the Great Depression, with the SSA literature citing such causes as inadequate demand due to wages rising more slowly than profits, the collapse of a speculative bubble in the stock market, and the exclusion of the U.S. from areas of further overseas expansion.

The Great Depression then led to a long period of institutional reform, including new regulations in finance and a heightened role of the state in the economy. The economy did not revive fully until the economic stimulus of war production in the 1940s. The new SSA was consolidated at the end of World War II, with the institution of the Keynesian welfare/warfare state, industrial unions strong enough to impose a limited "capital-labor accord," U.S. international dominance, and a new Cold War ideology. The boom period lasted until the Great Stagflation. The decline and disintegration of the postwar SSA was visible in the 1970s, with an end to the capital-labor accord, a price/wage spiral, and rising international disorder due to increasing European and Japanese competition, the end of the Bretton Woods system of fixed exchange rates, and two episodes of very rapid increases in oil prices. In the 1980s and 1990s a new SSA, global neoliberalism, was established.

Global neoliberalism is characterized by the creation of a transnational capitalist class that faced nationally divided working classes, decisively weakened by capital's ability to cross borders. Capital acquired the ability to site each portion of the accumulation process in the location most conducive to profitability. Domestic policy moved from the Keynesian welfare state to what Bob Jessop characterizes as the Schumpeterian workfare state (Jessop 2002). At the transnational level, tentative moves have been made in constructing a transnational state apparatus (Nardone and McDonough 2010). The pursuit of competitiveness has become the touchstone of more and more areas of policy. Capitalist class and market relationships have spread worldwide with the imposition of structural adjustment programs on less developed countries and the capitalist transitions in Eastern Europe and China. All of these developments are legitimated and partially driven by neoliberal ideology. Overproduction due to the aggressive merging of markets and deficient consumption as a result of stagnating wages set the stage for economic collapse. In 2008 the collapse of a property bubble driven by neoliberal finance may well have initiated the crisis of the global neoliberal stage of capitalism.

Table 1 summarizes these historical developments.

What are the implications of the Marxian stage theoretic approach to capitalist history? At a general theoretical level, Marxian stage theory integrates the institutionalist conception of the embedding of capitalist markets with the Marxian analysis of the contradictions and crisis tendencies of capitalism. This integration succeeds in explaining alternating periods of capitalist stability and crises. It explains how it is possible for capitalism to generate crises that are deeper than business cycle declines but short of the final crisis of capitalism. It brings the analysis of politics and ideology into the heart of the Marxian analysis of capital accumulation.

At the level of current conjunctural analysis, its understanding of the nature of capitalist crisis is crucial in coming to an understanding of the current situation. Is the current crisis *the* crisis of capitalism in

Table 1

SSAs in American History

	Competitive [1865–1898]	Crisis	Monopoly [1898–1945]	Crisis	Postwar [1945–1982]	Crisis	Global Neoliberalism [1982–2008]
Capital Capital	Competition		Oligopoly		Oligopoly		Transnational Capitalist Class
Capital Labor	Craft Unions	Prices Decrease	Weak Unions	Demand Decrease	Strong Unions	Popular Unrest Rises	Nationally Divided, Weakened Working Class
State	Laissez Faire Infrastructure	Wages Increase	Mildly Regulatory	Financial Fragility	Keynesian Welfare State	Stagflation	Schumpeterian Workfare State Transnational State Apparatus
Ideology	Classical Liberalism	Excess Capacity Increases	Corporatism		Cold War Liberalism	International Competition Increases	Neoliberalism Competitiveness
International	Trade Investment	Profits Decline	Imperialism		US International Dominance		Russia, China Structural Adjustment Programs

that it precedes and conditions the transition to a new mode of production? It is too early to tell. While the crisis may not be the crisis of capitalism, it is increasingly safe to say it is the crisis of the current stage of capitalism. That is, it is the crisis of global neoliberalism. It is not simply or even primarily a crisis of finance. It is a crisis of the total set of institutions that have conditioned capital accumulation over the last 25 to 30 years and must be analyzed as such.

Finally, what can the SSAF specifically contribute to the creation of a heterodox model of the economy? Certainly, any such model must incorporate the institutional conditions of economic activity. This is to some extent the purpose of the employment of the social fabric matrix (Hayden 2011). The central insights of stage theory are that, on the one hand, the institutional framework within which the capitalist economy is embedded is not constant and, on the other hand, that change is not continuous. The succession of one capitalist stage by another is marked by the installation of a new and different institutional structure whose changes ramify across the economic, political, and ideological levels of society. Institutional change is characterized by periods of relative stability punctuated with episodes of comprehensive change. Within this overall pattern each stage has a period of relatively healthy conditioning of the accumulation process and a period of breakdown and crisis.

The evolutionary biologist and historian of science Stephen Jay Gould has written extensively about the debate between gradualism and catastrophism within historical sciences like geology and evolutionary biology. This debate bears directly on one of his major contributions to evolutionary biology, the theory of punctuated equilibrium (Gould 2007). Evolutionary conceptions of the origin of species had replaced a conviction of momentary creation with a conception of gradual change and adaptation. Gould and his co-authors realized that the fossil record does not seem to support this gradual conception. Instead, species seem to be stable in form for long periods of time and then undergo a shorter period of rapid change leading to a renewed period of stability. Gradual incremental change is not absent and to some extent characterizes the stable periods. Nevertheless, major changes, including speciation, do not seem to be the cumulative result of gradual changes.

Gould's notion of punctuated equilibrium in evolution has been greeted with considerably controversy due to the appeal of the progressive conception of gradual, adaptive, and cumulative change. Versions of gradualism still have considerable appeal within the social realm. Marxian stage theory breaks with gradualist conceptions of change not only at the traditional boundaries between modes of production, but also within capitalist development.[8] This is good news for the heterodox modeling project. Periods of stability mean the embedded character of capitalist economies can be described (and modeled) beyond the particular conjuncture. Stadial theory insists, nevertheless, that close attention be paid to the temporally bounded nature of such models.

Notes

1. It is perhaps appropriate to observe at this point that most social sciences would hardly regard this as an insight and generally treat the existence and importance of institutions as a "common sense" background.
2. In the case of the neoclassical mainstream, it is another question whether these insights have had more than marginal significance in modifying its fundamental world view.
3. This is only one reading of "historical materialism" and other interpretations can find specific textual support in Marx's work and have been subsequently developed within the Marxian tradition.
4. I have argued elsewhere that admission to the canon of the history of economic thought is organized around attempts to found economics as a science separate from the broader social sciences (McDonough 2000). Thus within the history of economic thought only a truncated version of Marxist "economics" has been admitted.
5. For a useful collection of articles explaining, reviewing, and applying the SSA approach see McDonough, Reich, and Kotz (2010).
6. Lippit (2005: 27–28) discusses the concept of institutions:

> We can think of an institution in two principal ways. The first is essentially as an organization, like the World Bank or a university. The broader sense of an institution refers to the habits, customs and expectations that prevail in a particular society. While both senses of the term are used in SSA analysis, it is this second usage that is emphasized. The second usage, moreover, can be employed narrowly or broadly, and it is the broader form that is usually more helpful. A union for example, is an institution in the first sense. Collective bargaining would be an example of an institution in the second sense, employed narrowly. A national system of labor relations

would also be an example of an institution in the second sense, but one employed broadly.

This is more or less consistent with the American Institutionalist tradition in economics.

7. Another way of characterizing this movement is to divide SSAs into three phases, first, exploration, second, consolidation, third, decay. See Carlson, Gillespie, and Michalowski (2010).

8. The connection between punctuated equilibrium and Marxian conceptions of history is perhaps not accidental. Gould avowed Marxist politics for much of his life.

References

Aglietta, M. (1979). *A Theory of Capitalist Regulation.* London: NLB.

Bukharin, N. [1915] (1973). *Imperialism and World Economy.* New York: Monthly Review Press.

Carlson, S. M., M. D. Gillespie, and R. J. Michalowski. (2010). "Social Structures of Accumulation and the Criminal Justice System." In *Contemporary Capitalism and Its Crises.* Eds. Terrence McDonough, Michael Reich, and David M. Kotz, 239–266. Cambridge: Cambridge University Press.

Gordon, D. M. (1978). "Up and Down the Long Roller Coaster." In *Capitalism in Crisis.* Ed. Union for Radical Political Economics, pp. 212–235. New York: Union for Radical Political Economics.

——. (1980). "Stages of Accumulation and Long Economic Cycles." In *Processes of the World System.* Eds. Terence Hopkins and Immanuel Wallerstein, pp. 9–45. Beverly Hills, CA: Sage Publications.

Gordon, D. M., R. C. Edwards, and M. Reich. (1982). *Segmented Work, Divided Workers.* Cambridge: Cambridge University Press.

Gould, S. J. (2007). *Punctuated Equilibrium.* Boston: Belknap Press.

Hayden, G. (2011) "Assessment of the Possibility of Integrating the Social Structure of Accumulation and Social Accounting Matrix with the Social Fabric Matrix Approach." *American Journal of Economics and Sociology* 70(5): 1208–1233.

Hilferding, R. [1910] (1980). *Finance Capital.* London: Routledge and Kegan Paul.

Jessop, B. (2002). *The Future of the Capitalist State.* Cambridge: Polity Press.

Kotz, D. M., T. McDonough, and M. Reich, Eds. (1994). *Social Structures of Accumulation: The Political Economy of Growth and Crisis.* Cambridge: Cambridge University Press.

Lenin, V. I. [1917] (1968). *Imperialism, The Highest Stage of Capitalism.* In *Selected Works,* pp. 169–262. Moscow: Progress Publishers.

Lippit, V. (2005). *Capitalism.* Oxon: Routledge.

Mandel, E. (1970). *Marxist Economic Theory.* New York: Monthly Review Press.

——. (1978) [1975]. *Late Capitalism.* London: Verso.

——. (1980). *Long Waves of Capitalist Development.* Cambridge: Cambridge University Press.

McDonough, T. (1994a). "The Construction of Social Structures of Accumulation in US History." In *Social Structures of Accumulation: The Political Economy of Growth and Crisis.* Eds. David M. Kotz, Terrence McDonough, and Michael Reich. Cambridge: Cambridge University Press.

——. (1994b). "Social Structures of Accumulation, Contingent History, and Stages of Capitalism." In *Social Structures of Accumulation: The Political Economy of Growth and Crisis.* Eds. David M. Kotz, Terrence McDonough, and Michael Reich, pp. 101–132. Cambridge: Cambridge University Press.

——. (2000). "Who Blushes at the Name: John Kells Ingram and Minor Literature." In *The Canon in the History of Economic Thought: Critical Essays.* Ed. Michaelis Psalidopoulos, pp. 146–155. London: Routledge.

McDonough, T., M. Reich, and D. M. Kotz. (2010). *Contemporary Capitalism and Its Crises*, pp. 168–194. Cambridge: Cambridge University Press.

Nardone, E., and T. McDonough. (2010). "Global Neoliberalism and the Possibility of Transnational State Structures." In *Contemporary Capitalism and Its Crises.* Eds. Terrence McDonough, Michael Reich, and David M. Kotz. Cambridge: Cambridge University Press.

Reich, M., D. M. Gordon, and R. C. Edwards. (1973). "A Theory of Labor Market Segmentation," *American Economic Review* 63(May): 359–365.

Sweezy, P. M. [1942] (1968). *The Theory of Capitalist Development.* New York: Monthly Review Press.

Wolff, R. D., and S. A. Resnick. (1987). *Economics: Marxian Versus Neoclassical.* Baltimore: Johns Hopkins University Press.

Comparing Pension Systems in the Circular Flow of Income

By Andrew B. Trigg* and Jonquil T. Lowe*

Abstract. The neoliberal consensus is that state funded pensions are not sustainable in the long term, due to declining fertility and longevity. In response, policymakers have pointed to the advantages of privately funded pension systems. This article compares the social provisioning of these two systems using the circular flow of income as an organizing framework. A series of pitfalls in the private model are examined, including inequality of provision, mis-selling of investment products, and punitive charges.

Introduction

Under the Washington consensus, market-based solutions have been sought in areas as diverse as education, health, and social care. Individuals are encouraged to take responsibility for their own standard of living, health, and financial security, and the main function of the state is to ensure that the right incentives are established in efficient markets. A key area of neoliberal dominance, which affects us all, is in the area of retirement planning. Individuals are encouraged to make private plans for their retirement, investing their savings, either directly or via their employer, into pension funds.

The critical thrust of this consensus is that state funded Pay-as-You-Go pensions are not sustainable in the long term, due to declining fertility and increasing longevity. Policymakers have argued, for example, that the pension age should increase since more retirees will be increasingly dependent on a smaller workforce, and this workforce will not be able to afford, or will be unwilling, to pay taxes to finance the pensions of the swollen cohorts of older population. It is also argued in the neoliberal approach that collecting less tax to pay for

*A.B.Trigg@open.ac.uk, J.T.Lowe@open.ac.uk, Department of Economics, The Open University, UK.

American Journal of Economics and Sociology, Vol. 70, No. 5 (November, 2011).

state pensions would create room for more individual savings, with the dual benefits of giving individuals a share in the means of production and generating more private investment and, therefore, growth.

In this article we compare state and private pension systems using the circular flow of income as an organizing framework. As Toporowski (2000) has argued, this provides a way of examining the financial structures associated with phenomena such as pensions in a way that reflects reality: focusing on the key institutions that characterize mature capitalism. Instead of the neoclassical theoretical ideal of a rational agent, smoothing consumption over the life cycle, a systemic approach can be developed that focuses on the actual structure and interconnections between institutions. Developing the theme of this special issue, we examine the social provisioning of pensions: how pensions are organized by society, and in particular by key institutions such as the state and pension fund providers. The contribution of this article is to explore how the circular flow of income can be used to provide an overview of how pension systems work, and draw together some of the key issues. By looking at the circular flow as a whole, this approach generalizes, for example, from insights into the relationship between pension funds and finance (Toporowski 2000), the way in which savers are mistreated (Sullivan 2004), the inequalities associated with funded systems (Ginn and Arber 1999), and the relationship between savings and demand (Cesaratto 2006).

The first part of the article will show how the circular flow can be used to compare state and funded pensions systems, with the UK as an exemplar, setting out the key neoliberal case for funded pensions. In the second part, we explore how the circular flow can be used to draw together important elements of a critique of funded pensions. A concluding part summarizes the key issues suggested by this approach, and provides some suggestions for future empirical research.

Comparing State and Private Pension Systems

Common to all pension systems is the premise that most people retire after a substantial adult working life. The circular flow of income provides a way of capturing the importance of work by modeling the flow of wages from firms to households, and the flow of consumption from households to firms. The key problem at the heart of any nation's pension system is how a flow of consumption, at or above subsistence, can be maintained when adults no longer work, and no longer receive wages from work.

To explore how pensions can be modeled using the circular flow of income, we have made the simplifying assumption that there are two types of household: worker households and retired households.

Pay-as-You-Go Pension Systems in the Circular Flow

Figure 1 shows how the circular flow can be used for the case of the state Pay-as-You-Go (PAYG) pension system. This has three main elements. First, wages flow from firms to working households, and return back to firms in the form of consumption payments. Second, government receives taxes and pension contributions (national insurance in the UK) from working households and firms. Finally, retired households receive their state pension payment from government, and this is used as a basis for consumption payments to firms. This is a state-run tax-based system, of the type introduced by Bismarck in Germany in 1889 and, as implemented in the UK following the 1942 Beveridge report, still providing the core of social policy in the UK today.

Figure 1

Pay-as-You-Go Pension System

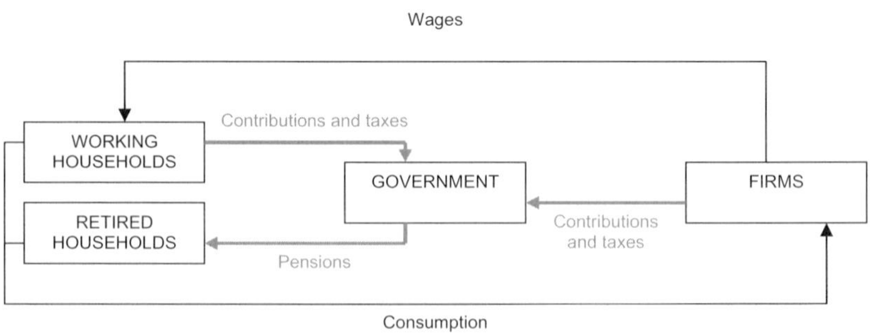

Sources: Adapted from Trigg (2010).

In 2008, UK state PAYG pensions paid out to retired households amounted to 4.7 percent of GDP, while national insurance contributions paid in by firms (employers) and working households (employees and the self-employed) totalled 7.6 percent of GDP (Office for National Statistics 2010d). National insurance contributions go into a fund used to finance a range of state benefits covering not just retirement but also bereavement, incapacity to work, and unemployment. While all these benefits are funded on a PAYG basis, the national insurance fund does not necessarily pay out exactly the amount gathered in during any one year, so it may carry forward a surplus (or deficit). In 2008–2009, retirement pensions accounted for 83 percent of the money paid out of the national insurance fund (Government Actuary's Department 2010: 100).

State pension systems have come under increasing pressure in recent years. Most important has been the claim that demographic change, caused by households having fewer children and people living longer, is challenging the future viability of this classic PAYG model. As shown in Figure 2, across the world countries are facing declining support ratios (number of workers per retired person). For the world as a whole, the support ratio is set to decline from 9 today to 4 by 2050. In the developed nations the ratio is already low and set to decline further—for example, in Europe from 4 today to 2 by 2050.

It is argued that declining support ratios put pressure on PAYG pension provision—where current pensions are funded directly by current contributions and taxes from the current generation of workers and employers, or through government borrowing (which shifts costs to future generations). Fewer workers are available to support pensioners, and, unless government borrowing is increased, it follows from this perspective that PAYG pensions will become unaffordable and unsustainable.

Hence, the neoliberal stance has been to criticize state pension schemes. The World Bank, for example, while recognizing that there is a place for PAYG in a "multipillared" approach to retirement provision, has been a particularly strident and influential critic of PAYG schemes (see, for example,World Bank 1994: 334). In addition to being unsustainable in the face of falling support ratios, creating rising

Figure 2

Support Ratios for Selected Countries and Regions

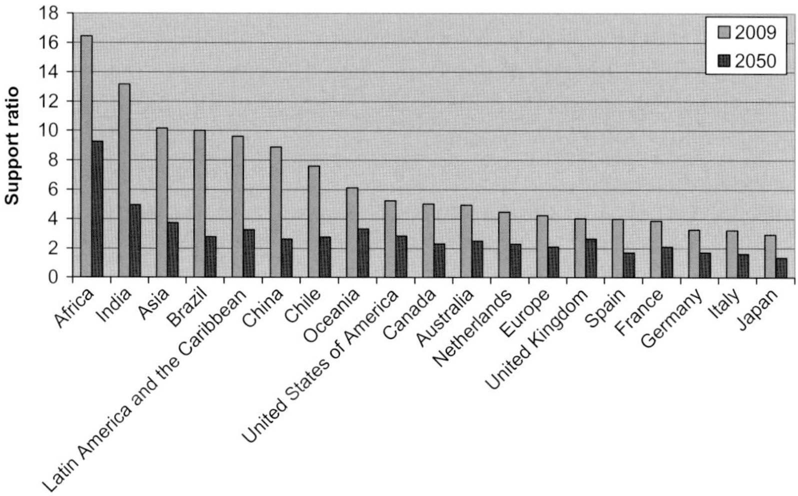

Data source: United Nations (2009).

government deficits and unacceptable cost burdens for future generations, it is claimed that state schemes distort the labor market by creating a tax on jobs and so reduce output (Holzmann and Hinz 2005: 24–34). From a neoliberal perspective the price mechanism should be allowed to function in efficient markets. Since wages are the price of labor, it follows that the labor market should be freed from the distortions generated by high taxes. Once wages are allowed to fluctuate free of tax distortions, demand and supply for labor can be brought into balance, ensuring low unemployment. The neoliberal view is that the environment for a healthy private market economy is the best solution to providing sufficient private resources for pension provision.

A further claim is that through the social legacy of their historical development, state schemes distort choices between work, lifelong education, and retirement (Holzman and Hinz 2005: 24–34). In a free market, individuals would choose to work and retrain to maintain the marketability of their labor and make rational decisions about how much to save in order to smooth consumption and about when to retire. In the absence of any moral hazard, whereby the state bails out the non-savers, the incentive would be there for individuals to take responsibility for their retirements. And, crucial to the neoliberal proposition, a higher rate of saving would lead to more finance available for the private sector to carry out real investment. This is a supply-side approach in which investment is determined by savings. A rolling back of the state frees up resources for a potentially dynamic private sector and creates the extra growth needed to support the increasing demographic bulge in pensioners.

This neoliberal approach has been enthusiastically adopted throughout the world, with the most radical response in parts of Latin America. The state pension system in Chile, for example, has been radically overhauled by introducing individual funded pension accounts. In place of the state system, individuals were offered a selection of five portfolio accounts (Barr and Diamond 2008: 228). In the UK it has been a stated government aim to change the balance between state and private pensions. The UK Labour government's 1998 Green Paper stated:

> Public spending on pensions will decline as a share of GDP, from 5.4 percent to 4.5 percent in 2050. By 2050, the proportion of pensioner incomes coming from the State, now 60 percent, will have fallen to 40 percent, and the proportion coming from private pension provision will have increased from 40 to 60 percent. This will ensure that the pension system remains both fair and affordable. (Department of Social Security 1998: 8)

The UK government is in the process of implementing changes to contain the cost of state pensions, in particular raising first women's state pension age to align it with that of men and then raising the state pension age for all in stages to at least age 68. Some of the savings will be offset by recent improvements to state pensions, but it is salient to note that, as shown above, state retirement pensions accounted for only 4.7 percent of GDP by 2008. This is already a significant drop from the 5.4 percent mentioned in the quote above, achieved largely through a policy (now partially changed) of increasing state pensions in line with prices rather than earnings.

Funded Pension Systems in the Circular Flow

As shown in Figure 3, the private funded pension system is a seemingly diametric alternative to the state PAYG system. In this system, working households are free to choose whether to save their wages in pension funds for later use in retirement, or to spend them on current consumption. The pensions that retired households receive are determined in part by the size of their pension pots, determined by earlier individual saving decisions. Firms also contribute to pension funds, for example, in the form of employer contributions to work-based schemes (which may, however, be thought of either as a subsidy from the employer or as deferred pay from the working household) and dividends paid on shares that are held by pension funds. Though the neoliberal rhetoric calls for a purely market-based system, the state may play a role in encouraging private saving through tax reliefs, as shown in Figure 3.

In 2008, contributions by working households to UK work-related pension schemes, together with the investment returns, amounted to

Figure 3

Privately Funded Pension System

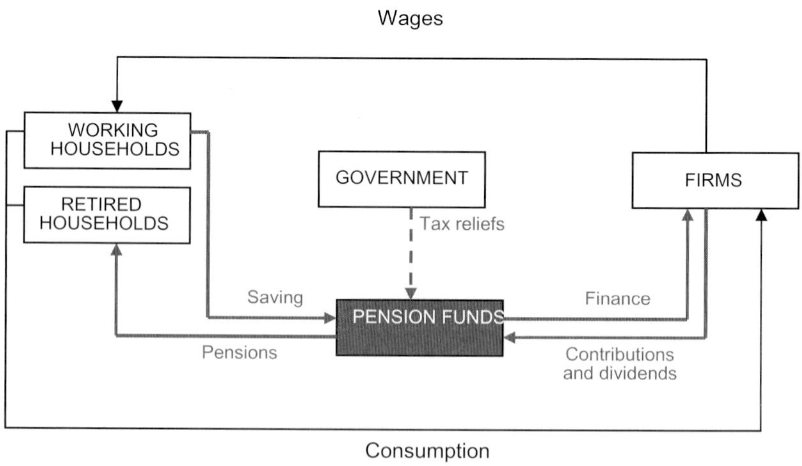

Sources: Adapted from Trigg (2010).

3.6 percent of GDP, contributions from firms were equal to 3.8 percent of GDP, and benefits paid out amounted to 4.2 percent of GDP (Office for National Statistics 2010d, 2010e). It is estimated that the net cost of tax reliefs (which is tax relief on contributions and pension fund investment returns less tax on pensions in payment) on all private pensions (work-related and individual personal pensions) came to around £27 billion or some 2.0 percent of GDP (Office for National Statistics 2010e).

At first sight a funded pension system does not have any advantage over PAYG in terms of dealing with declining support ratios. The relative decline in the number of working households leads either to lower contributions and taxes (Figure 1) or lower saving (Figure 3). Both systems require an inter-generational distribution from working to retired households. However, it is argued that the shift from a PAYG to a funded system does create a one-off step up in saving that promotes additional economic growth. Moreover, there are claimed advantages of the funded system, which are based on the more efficient functioning of a market economy. Less tax reduces labor market distortions, more choice provides flexibility in the balance between working, lifelong education, and retirement, and higher long-term saving during the phase when funded pension savings are accumulating can promote deeper and more innovative securities markets that provide a boost to private sector investment (Holzman and Hinz 2005: 45–52). These claims of the economic benefits from funding are founded on the neoclassical concept that, in a full-employment economy, additional saving will translate into increased (real) investment, expanding the capital stock, increasing the capital-labor ratio and thus labor productivity and so fueling economic growth.

Towards a Critique of Funded Pensions

Once we step away from the neoclassical lens, there are a host of arguments that can be leveled against funded pensions, including: their failure to channel savings into investment; their mistreatment of consumers; and their failure to prevent poverty in old age. Some of these arguments are brought together here using the circular flow of income as an organizing framework.

Figure 4

Risk Factors for Individual Outcomes in a Funded Pension Scheme

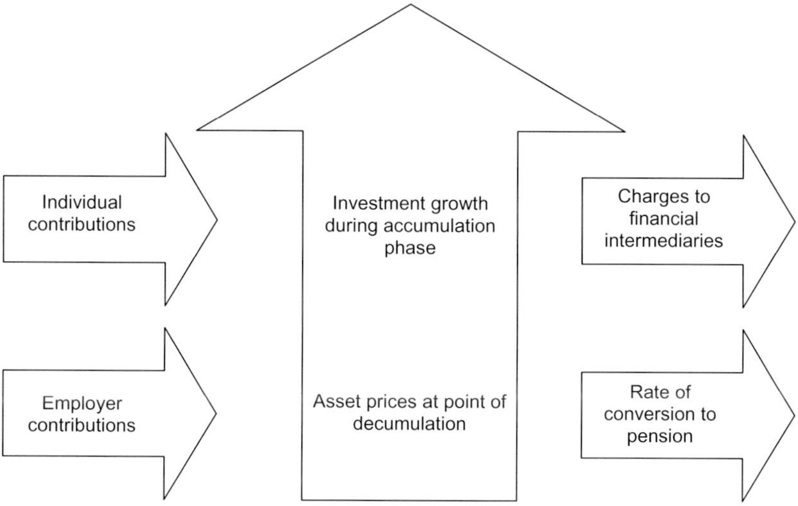

The Pensions Context

However, as a first step, it is useful to consider how a funded system delivers a pension to the individual and thus identify the stages at which matters can potentially go awry. From the individual perspective, the success of a defined-contribution funded pension depends on the six risk factors summarized in Figure 4 and discussed below (adjusted for tax relief, as applicable). The additional issue of the security of savings institutions is then considered before we make use of the circular flow approach.

Individual Contributions

The amount an individual voluntarily contributes towards his or her pension depends on both willingness to save and ability to save. There is a substantial and growing literature on the behavioral factors, such as myopia and hyperbolic discounting, that may inhibit

Figure 5

Pension Contributions by Gross Income Decile

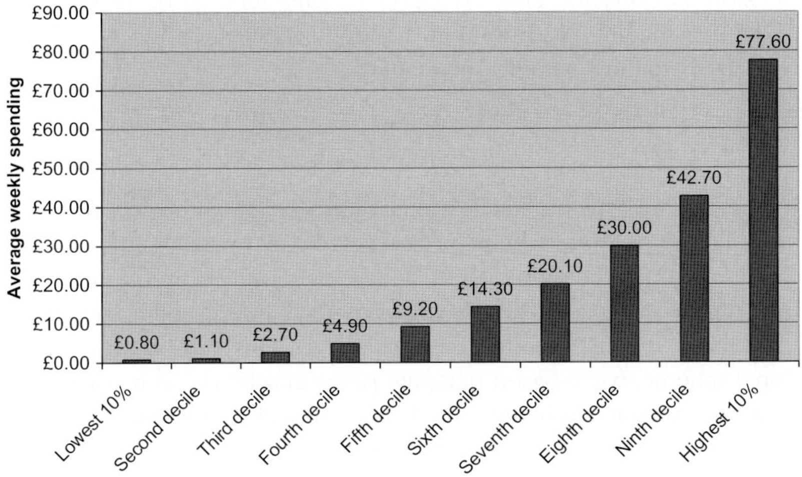

Source: Office for National Statistics (2009a: Table A8).

an individual's willingness to save (see, for example, Department of Work and Pensions 2009; Thaler and Sunstein 2008), and a range of policy initiatives are being adopted in an attempt to address these, such as the Save More Tomorrow scheme in the US (Thaler and Benartzi 2001) and automatic enrollment into pension schemes that is shortly to be introduced in the UK (Department of Work and Pensions 2011).

Less tractable are households that spend their working life close to subsistence, have very low ability to save, and may see very poor returns from any saving. Figure 5 displays average weekly household spending for the UK, in 2008, on life assurance and contributions to pension funds by gross income decile. The difference in the amount saved by the richest and the poorest households is nearly a hundred-fold and is a key reason why funded pension schemes contribute to inequality. Broadly, those who can afford to save more, do so and will tend to reap larger pensions as a result. By contrast, in a Beveridge-style PAYG system (with an emphasis on flat-rate rather than earnings-related pensions), those who can afford to pay in more do so, but receive broadly the same amount of pension as everyone else. So PAYG systems tend to be progressive and foster income redistribution. Funded schemes tend to be regressive, perpetuating income inequalities.

Employer Contributions

In the UK, all but the smallest employers are required to provide a work-based pension scheme. However, in many cases, there is no requirement for the employer to make contributions on the behalf of the employee. By 2016, all UK employers will have to offer some type of pension scheme through the workplace. This can be an occupational scheme, work-based personal pension scheme, or membership in a new national scheme called the National Employment Savings Trust (NEST). Employers will have to auto-enroll eligible employees and make mandatory employer contributions unless the employee opts out.

The UK is experiencing a marked shift from defined-benefit pension provision (where pension payouts are calculated according to a pre-set formula) to defined-contribution provision (where returns are determined by a private fund's investment return and other factors). It is salient that, whereas employers contribute on average around 16 percent of an employee's pay to defined-benefit occupational schemes, they contribute only an average 6 percent to defined-contribution schemes (Office of National Statistics 2010a). Moreover, the recommended employer contribution to the proposed new UK national scheme is just 3 percent (National Employment Trust 2010). It should also be borne in mind that a significant proportion of the working population is self-employed (around one in eight workers in the UK) and so cannot benefit from any employer contributions (Office for National Statistics 2010b). There will, therefore, be widely divergent pension outcomes for individuals, depending on their employment status and the generosity of any work-based pension arrangement to which they have access.

Investment Growth During the Accumulation Phase

While investment growth will normally have the greatest impact of all the factors on an individual's pension outcome, it is also (along with annuity rates—see below) the most unpredictable part of the process. In a defined-benefit scheme, the employer shoulders these risks; in a defined-contribution scheme, they are borne by each individual member. In the UK, pension fund projections are typically based on a 7 percent a year average growth, which is the UK regulator's central recommended rate for tax-free projections as at 2011, and 2.5 percent inflation (a real return of 4.39 percent a year). However, the actual experience of individual defined-contribution pension scheme members will be very different depending in part on the types of assets and investments they choose, but moreover on the external factors that shape stock-market performance over the period of their own particular investment.

An often recommended approach to pension accumulation is to invest largely in equities for the earlier years with a gradual shift to bonds in the last 10 years or so before the chosen vesting date (a process called lifestyling). Table 1 shows how, following this strategy, the size of pension fund would have varied for five hypothetical individuals retiring in 2001, 2003, 2005, 2007, and 2009, respectively, given actual stock-market performance in real terms. In other respects, the scenarios are the same, with individuals having identical contribution patterns, charges experience, and investment strategy. The difference is pronounced, with the 2005 retiree securing the largest pension fund. The 2007 retiree accumulates nearly one-fifth less and the 2009 retiree over a quarter less.

Asset Prices at Point of Decumulation

In the scenario above, the individual pension savers are assumed to have adopted a lifestyling strategy in order to protect themselves from any fall in equity prices close to retirement. If the intention is to secure a pension by purchasing a lifetime annuity (see below), since annuity rates are closely linked to the return on bonds, a lifestyling strategy of shifting to bonds will largely remove this risk. However, there still remains the possibility of an adverse affect from asset price changes at

Table 1

Variation in Pension Fund by Year of Investing

The table shows resulting pension fund for individuals saving £100 a month, increasing once a year in line with earnings, to which is added tax relief at the basic rate. [1] Individuals save for 40 years, retiring in different years between 2001 and 2009 inclusive. The fund shown is based on actual stock-market performance in real terms. [2] It is assumed that individuals invested 100% in equities for 30 years, then shifted 10% of their fund each year to bonds during the final 10 years. Charges are assumed to be as for stakeholder schemes [3] (even though these would not have been available for the whole term).

Retiring in:	Real value of fund	as % of highest valued fund
2001	£112,846	98.58%
2003	£112,384	98.17%
2005	£114,476	100.00%
2007	£94,958	82.95%
2009	£82,752	72.29%

[1] Earnings are assumed to grow by 4% a year. Basic rate tax is assumed to be 20%. Net contribution is assumed to have reached a real value of £100 by the year in which the pension is to vest.
[2] Based on data from Barclays (2010: 71–72).
[3] No initial charge; AMC 1.5% for 10 years, 1% thereafter.
Source: Authors' calculations.

the point at which the fund is being shifted from equities into bonds. This is mitigated to some extent by spreading the shift over a period of several years (10 years in the examples above).

Without lifestyling or a similar strategy, individuals would be fully exposed to the movements in the stock market. As Toporowski (2000) points out, asset prices do not necessarily reflect the intrinsic value of underlying assets but are influenced by asset inflation and deflation. This can make asset prices extremely volatile in the short run. For example, between December 2007 and 2008, the real return on equities in the UK was −30.4 percent (Barclays 2010). Such a large fall in an accumulated pension fund could have a devastating effect on an individual's retirement planning.

Charges to Financial Intermediaries

Prior to the introduction of stakeholder pension schemes in 2001, personal pension schemes in the UK were typically characterized by complex charging structures, making it difficult for individuals to assess the overall level of charges for any scheme they took out. Stakeholder pensions were a UK government initiative to ensure the availability of straightforward, good-value schemes that have to conform to a set of minimum terms and conditions. These include that the only form of direct charges is an annual management charge (AMC) set as a percentage of the fund and that this AMC will be no more than 1.5 percent a year in the first 10 years and 1 percent a year thereafter (originally, the maximum AMC was set at 1 percent a year throughout even including the early years, but was increased due to industry resistance to marketing stakeholder schemes with such low revenues). Stakeholder pension schemes have had some effect on the rest of the UK personal pension scheme market because their introduction was accompanied by a rule (RU64) imposed by the then financial regulator, the Personal Investment Authority (PIA), that required advisers to justify putting customers into personal pensions that were less attractive than stakeholder schemes if a stakeholder scheme would be suitable (PIA 1999). As a result, the charging structure for personal pensions has tended to become simpler and more transparent. The impact of stakeholder charging for an example individual earning £30,000 (roughly UK average earnings in 2011) is shown in Table 2.

Occupational schemes typically have lower charges (and these are sometimes borne by the employer rather than directly reducing the funds available to provide pensions). The proposed charging level for the UK's new national scheme, NEST, is considered to be close to the minimum possible and will comprise mainly an AMC of 0.3 percent. However, there will also be a 1.8 percent contribution charge (deduction from each contribution paid) in order to recoup the start-up costs of the scheme and it is anticipated that this charge will continue for the

Table 2

Impact of Charges in Government-Initiated Schemes

The table shows the value of pension fund after charges for an individual contributing £100 a month, increasing once a year in line with earnings, to which is added tax relief at the basic rate. [1] The pension fund is assumed to grow at an average rate of 7 percent a year. No employer contributions have been included (even though these would apply in the case of NEST and could apply to the stakeholder scheme).

	10 years		20 years		30 years		40 years	
	Value of fund [2]	% lost in charges	Value of fund [2]	% lost in charges	Value of fund [2]	% lost in charges	Value of fund [2]	% lost in charges
No charges	£19,732		£53,141		£108,049		£196,554	
NEST charges [3]	£19,075	−3.33%	£50,511	−4.95%	£100,850	−6.66%	£179,926	−8.46%
Stakeholder charges [4]	£18,349	−7.01%	£47,203	−11.17%	£90,751	−16.01%	£155,280	−21.00%

[1] Earnings are assumed to grow by 4% a year. Basic rate tax is assumed to be 20%.
[2] Real value, assuming price inflation averages 2.5% a year.
[3] Initial contribution charge 1.8%; AMC 0.3%.
[4] No initial charge; AMC 1.5% for 10 years, 1% thereafter.
Source: Authors' calculations.

first 20 years of the scheme. The impact of this level of charging is also illustrated in Table 2.

An AMC is an annual charge on the total value of the fund (not just on any growth in the fund). Therefore, the total impact of the charge increases the longer the term of the investment. Table 2 shows that, after 40 years, NEST charges have absorbed just under 9 percent of the final value of the fund. The stakeholder charges have a much greater impact and, even though these schemes are supposed to represent good value, over one-fifth of the final fund has been taken in charges by the end of 40 years. While this may represent a fair costing of the administration involved plus a reasonable profit margin, the individual pension saver would not necessarily agree that this is good value. For the impact of other levels of charging, see Table 4.

Rate of Conversion of Saving into Pension Payments

For many individuals, the conversion of saving into pension payments will depend on annuity rates, which are driven in particular by average longevity and the yield on long-term bonds. Figure 6 charts the path of annuity rates in the UK over the last 20 years, during which time the amount of income that can be purchased has halved. This does not, of course, imply an equivalent halving of pension income, since a fall in bond rates that cuts the annuity rate may coincide with a rise in equity returns that boosts the final value of the pension fund. However, the correlation between bond and equity returns is not always negative and the effect is not usually a 100 percent offset. Applying the annuity rates from Figure 6 to the lifestyled scenarios in Table 2, the 2001 retiree would have achieved the highest pension income (a level income of around £10,100). Retirees in the later years would have received progressively less: 85 percent of the 2001 amount for the 2003 retiree; 79 percent for 2005; 68 percent for 2007; and 52 percent for 2009.

The alternative to annuity purchase is to draw retirement income directly from the pension fund, in which case the individual continues to be exposed to variable investment returns, including asset price risk.

Figure 6

Annuity Rates in the UK [1]

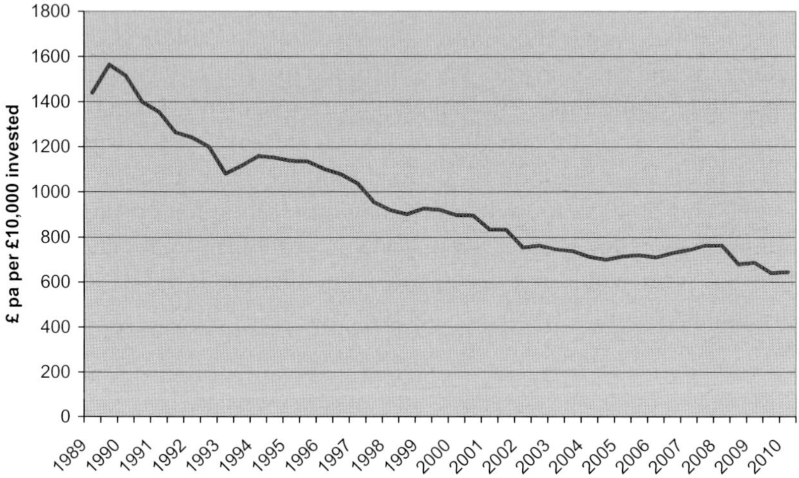

[1] Single-life compulsory purchase annuity rate for a man aged 65, non-smoker. Level annuity without guarantee.
Data source: FTBI (1990–2011).

Security of Savings Institutions

An additional factor that needs to be mentioned is the possibility of default on the part of the pension provider. In the case of occupational schemes, in the extreme the employer may become insolvent leaving a defined-benefit pension scheme underfunded and unable to meet the promised pension payments. In the UK, some protection is provided by the Pension Protection Fund and, where theft is involved, the Fraud Compensation Scheme. A lesser type of "default" is where a solvent employer with an ongoing business renegotiates the terms of the pension arrangements so that, without reneging on pensions already accumulated, promises of future benefits are less generous than scheme members had anticipated and perhaps planned for. This is evident in the UK with the shift of private sector schemes from defined-benefit to defined-contribution schemes and, increasingly in the public sector, with a shift from defined-benefit final salary to defined-benefit career average salary arrangements accompanied by increased employee contribution rates.

In personal pensions, the main risk of this type is that the financial institution with responsibility for the pension fund or pensions in payment is unable to meet its obligations. In the UK, Equitable Life, the oldest mutual life assurer in the world, failed to fund adequately for annuity guarantees attached to its pension schemes, creating losses for its customers. To address this type of scenario, the UK's Financial Services Compensation Scheme provides some protection where customers have a claim against a provider that has become insolvent.

Applying a Circular Flow Approach

Given the number and diversity of the risk factors embedded in the conversion of savings into pension, it is no surprise that defined-contribution funded systems deliver uncertain and highly unequal outcomes both within any cohort of pensioners and across different cohorts. Defined-benefit funding can address some of these inequalities, but are being affected by many of the same factors that are making governments shy away from defined-benefit PAYG schemes. Increasingly, funded systems are adopting the defined-contribution model. This is the context within which we must apply our circular flow approach.

The discussion that now follows will examine key parts of the circular flow diagram (Figure 3). Using the circular flow as an organizing framework will also highlight some questions for future empirical exploration.

The Flow of Saving: Employees

The main thrust of recent economic analysis of pensions has been on developing policies to encourage people to save. In a survey, 42 percent said that they agreed with the statement: "I would rather have a good standard of living today than plan for retirement" (Atkinson et al. 2006: 70). Behavioral economists attribute this attitude to myopia and excessive (hyperbolic) discounting, where little weight is attached to events in the future. And in this spirit, a financial education industry has developed in which web sites, financial literacy materials, and workplace seminars are made available to try to educate and change the public view. Consistent with a social provisioning approach, this can be viewed as an attempt to influence individual agency in order to reshape the culture of saving so that it conforms with the pension philosophy of the neoliberal state.

The circular flow of income can provide a context for assessing policy initiatives that promote saving. Figure 3 shows that decisions by working households are indeed critical to the flow of saving. But, quite apart from doubts about whether financial education can alter behavioral traits (see, for example, Willis 2008) and so influence *willingness* to save, there remains the question of *ability* to save. As noted in Figure 5, the level of pension contributions by individuals correlates strongly to household income. This is borne out by other data too. For example, a survey found that directors of the UK's top 103 companies had pensions 30 times larger than the average workplace pension (TUC 2009). The problem is critical for women, tending to have lower wages and interrupted pension contributions due to child-rearing responsibilities. Ginn and Arber (1999) found that women make up two-thirds of pensioners living in poverty.

The recently established British Wealth and Asset Survey (ONS 2010c) underlines the extent of inequality in pensions wealth between men and women and different socio-economic groups (see Table 3). For example, while over the survey period 2006–2008, 13 percent of individuals working for large employers have no private pension wealth, the proportion rises to 62 percent for workers in routine occupations. The median pension wealth for women is just £800 compared with £15,000 for men. The same survey shows that median pension wealth for men compares with a mean of nearly £115,000, demonstrating the marked skew in the wealth distribution.

The circular flow of income can also be used to monitor imperfections in funded pension provision. First, pension products are mis-sold on a regular basis. Concerted sales drives on the part of the financial services industry have in recent years not been con-

Table 3

Wealth Held by Individuals in Private Pensions 2006–2008

	Men		*Women*		*All*	
Socio-economic classification	Median pension wealth £	% with any pension wealth	Median pension wealth £	% with any pension wealth	Median pension wealth £	% with any pension wealth
Large employers and higher managerial	132,200	90	48,500	83	97,800	87
Higher professional	69,300	83	36,700	79	57,900	82
Lower managerial and professional	50,100	79	30,000	73	38,300	76
Intermediate occupations	23,300	68	6,000	61	8,500	63
Small employers and own account workers	5,000	60	0	42	2,200	54
Lower supervisory and technical	12,100	66	0	46	6,000	60
Semi-routine occupations	500	51	0	39	0	43
Routine occupations	0	47	0	27	0	38
Never worked/ long-term unemployed	0	11	0	8	0	9
All	15,000	65	800	52	6,000	58

Source: Office for National Statistics (2010c: Table 6.14).

Table 4

Theoretical Impact of Charges on Pension Fund Outcomes

The table shows the percentage of the final pension fund lost in charges where they are levied in the form of a fixed percentage annual management charge. [1]

	Investment term (years)				
Charges % pa	10	20	30	40	50
0	0.0%	0.0%	0.0%	0.0%	0.0%
0.3	−1.6%	−3.2%	−5.0%	−6.8%	−8.7%
0.5	−2.6%	−5.3%	−8.1%	−11.0%	−14.0%
1	−5.1%	−10.2%	−15.3%	−20.5%	−25.6%
1.5	−7.4%	−14.7%	−21.8%	−28.7%	−35.3%
2	−9.7%	−19.0%	−27.7%	−35.8%	−43.4%
2.5	−12.0%	−22.9%	−33.0%	−42.0%	−50.2%

[1] Assumes gross investment growth of 7% pa, charges are deducted monthly, net contribution of £100 per month, increasing once a year in line with earnings inflation of 4% pa.
Source: Authors' calculations.

fined to sub-prime mortgage products. In the 1980s, UK neoliberal policies encouraged the opting out from work-based into personal pensions; Sullivan (2004: 93) estimates that around a million pension products were mis-sold as a result. Cases also abound, such as Enron in the US, where fraudulent behavior has led to a collapse in pension provision. Second, in order to market pension products, the financial services industry has to make a profit, by making charges. These can be shocking high, as highlighted by a headline in the *Sunday Times* newspaper, "Hidden fees may halve pensions" (Montagu-Smith 2010). Theoretical calculations show that even relatively modest levels of charges result in a large loss of final pension fund—see Table 4. Moreover, experiments such as the introduction of stakeholder pensions in the UK show how the financial industry can resist policy moves to reduce charges.

Key questions for future analysis using the circular flow of income approach include not just how large is the impact of charges in total but also their impact across different types of pension scheme and different levels of contribution.

The Flow of Saving: Employers

The UK is unusual in having a public-private partnership in pension provision through a system known as "contracting out." This stems back to the introduction of the state additional pension in 1978, then in the form of the state earnings-related pension (SERPS). The Labour government of the day had noted that a key component in the inequality in the income of pensions was a lack of good occupational pensions. Pensioners without access to this source of income tended to have much lower incomes. The solution was seen to be some kind of state earnings-related pension that mimicked the best occupational schemes, but the cost could be prohibitive, depending on factors such as future wage inflation. The solution was to share the risks of the scheme between the state and employers through the system of contracting out. In return for a known cost to the state in terms of a reduction in national insurance contributions, employers could take on the responsibility of providing a defined-benefit substitute for the SERPS pension that would otherwise have built up. In this form, contracting out shared costs and risks between state and employer, but individuals bore no risk of lower pensions.

The Thatcher administration in 1988 substantially reformed contracting out and, for the first time, enabled individuals (rather than employers) to make the contracting out decision but, most significantly, enabled contracting out on a defined-contribution basis. Contracting out could now be a route to transferring substantial risks from the state direct to the individual.

In the buoyant climate of the 1970s and most of the 1980s, large employers signed up for contracting out and pension provision generally, confident they could deliver on their pension promises. As the 1990s progressed, with increasing legislation to secure employees' pension rights, changing accounting rules that matched the measurement of pension scheme assets to volatile stock markets, and mounting evidence of increasing longevity, it was no longer just the state that was concerned about the costs and risks of pension provision. Employers began to take flight as well, choosing to set up less generous types of pension arrangement and closing their earlier defined-benefit schemes. By 2007, nearly three-fifths of defined-benefit schemes dated from before 1980 and, of these, 56 percent had closed. Nearly all occupational defined-contribution schemes have been founded since 1984, with nearly half (48 percent) started since 2000. In 1997, 46 percent of employees belonged to an occupational defined-benefit scheme; by 2008, the proportion had fallen to 33 percent (Office for National Statistics 2009b).

These shifts in the costs and/or risks of pension provision from the state to employers and individuals, and from employers to individuals, are often presented as necessary to ensure the sustainability of the remaining state and employer-sponsored schemes. What is lost in the rhetoric is that the individual is the least able to bear these costs and risks. Aside from the problem of income inequality there is also a problem of inequality of power. The TUC (2009) survey found that 61 percent of top directors continued to enjoy defined benefit pensions in 2009, compared to only 13.5 percent of employees. As discussed above, the pension payments earned by those demoted to defined contribution pensions are dependent on a range of highly uncertain factors, including investment returns and annuity rates. Employees are vulnerable to macroeconomic trends, such as low interest rates (for annuities) and stagnant stock markets (for investment returns). Moreover, there is a variance in the performance of investment funds, with only some providing alpha returns, and many underperforming the market benchmarks.

What is significant here is not whether pensions are financed on a PAYG or funded basis, but whether they are provided on a defined-benefit or defined-contribution basis. Defined-benefit schemes, whether state PAYG or occupational schemes, allow for cross subsidies so that the better-off, better-able to pay contributors help to provide pensions of at least enough to take pensioners out of poverty. In other words, defined-benefit schemes enable a progressive pension system, while defined-contribution schemes perpetuate inequalities. Therefore, an analysis based around the circular flow of income should distinguish at the aggregate level between defined-benefit and defined-contribution provision.

The Flow of Tax Relief

Moving to the middle of Figure 3, the next flow to question is that of tax relief from government to pension funds. Tax relief on private pensions is skewed towards higher income groups: in the UK, up to 2010–2011, as much as £255,000 in contributions (and other annual increases in pension rights) each year could be eligible for tax relief (HM Treasury 2010a). As shown in Table 5, the net cost of pension tax reliefs in the UK was around £19 billion a year in 2008–2009 or £27.1 billion including relief from national insurance on employers' contributions (HM Revenue & Customs 2010).

A report by the Pensions Policy Institute (2004) estimating the net cost of pensions tax reliefs in 2004 at around £19 billion (1.8 percent of GDP and equivalent to about a quarter of the cost of state PAYG pensions) provides insights into the distribution of these reliefs. Around 55 percent of the tax relief benefited some 2.5 million higher-rate taxpayers, with 13 million basic-rate and non-taxpayers sharing the remainder. Around 9 million taxpayers were making no pension saving and so did not share in the tax relief at all—many of these will be the low income households who cannot afford retirement savings. Since only 20 percent of higher-rate taxpayers were women, the tax reliefs are not only biased towards higher earners but also towards men.

The UK limit on contributions (and other increases in pension rights) that can be eligible for tax relief is being reduced to £50,000 a year from 2011–2012, which together with other changes affecting larger pension savings is expected to reduce the net cost of pension reliefs by £4 billion a year (HM Treasury 2010b). This limit still marks a significant additional advantage for those households able to make larger contributions. In fact, it has been estimated that the reduction to £50,000 a year affects only some 100,000 individuals, four-fifths of whom have incomes over £100,000 and so are comfortably within the highest decile of gross income (HM Treasury 2010b).

Table 5

Pension Tax Reliefs in the UK, 2008–2009

Tax relief for/ tax on:	*2008* *£ million*	% GDP
Tax reliefs		
Occupational scheme contributions		
by employers	11,600	0.90%
by employees	4,200	0.32%
Personal pension scheme contributions		
by employers	2,529	0.20%
by employees	1,650	0.13%
Personal scheme contributions by the self-employed	1,250	0.10%
National insurance rebates to contracted-out personal schemes	120	0.01%
Investment income of funds	6,700	0.52%
Lump sum payments from unfunded schemes	450	0.03%
Total		2.20%
Less tax paid on		
Pensions in payment	9,500	0.73%
Refunds by funds to employers related to pension fund surpluses	1	0.00%
Total		0.73%
Net reliefs	**18,900**	**1.46%**
National insurance relief on employer contributions	8,200	0.63%

Source: HM Revenue & Customs (2010).

The Balance Between Contributions and Payments

Once tax relief is taken into account, the health and sustainability of pension funds, in particular work-based schemes, depends on the balance between flows of saving and pension payments, as displayed in Figure 3. The problem, as raised by Toporowski (2000), is that each pension fund goes through an immature accumulation phase, when there are more contributing employees than retirees, and a mature phase when retirees draw more than contributing employees. With pension funds first set up in the period following the Second World War, in an initial accumulation phase of high employee contributions, the argument is that eventually pension funds must start to be run down.

In the neoliberal world of the Washington consensus, this net dis-saving would depress investment and thus economic growth. From a demand-side perspective the outcomes are less certain. Investment—being exogenous—might be buoyant and funded from other sources (such as bank finance). Indeed, Toporowski (2000) argues that the abundance of pension fund savings does not necessarily create investment funding but may just produce asset price inflation. Therefore, a reversal of this abundance may manifest as asset price deflation rather than any reduction on capital investment. The outcome at the aggregate level, therefore, might not be a reduction in economic growth. However, it should be borne in mind that asset price inflation and deflation would drive unequal outcomes at the individual level for those approaching retirement with defined-contribution pension pots. In other words, the viability of funded schemes in terms of meeting pension expectations relies on the willingness and ability of working households to take up the assets that retired households no longer wish to hold. The ability of working households as a group to absorb this dis-saving depends not just on the demographics that determine the size of this sector of the economy but also incomes that determine the ability to save. Incomes in turn will be influenced by factors, such as the capital-to-labor ratio, including investment in human capital.

The running down of pension funds also implies an increased boost to consumption as pensioners spend their previous savings. As MacKellar (2000) has suggested, the composition of investment rather than the level may be affected as production shifts to the goods and services preferred by older households.

If we accept the neoclassical view that declining pension funds will depress economic growth, the main way in which the run down in pension funds can be avoided is if there is sufficient growth in wages (which means that working households would then have the means to purchase the assets being sold by pensioner households). Even though demographic support ratios are falling, with fewer people paying in than drawing out of pension funds, higher wages can keep funds buoyant, if only capitalism could deliver higher wages. Unfortunately, in recent years, despite a pronounced period of economic growth, wage growth has been stagnant. The problem is most stark in the US, as lucidly put by David Harvey:

> For the first time in US history, working people have failed to share in any of the gains from rising productivity. We have experienced thirty years of wage repression. (Harvey 2010: 12).

The counterpart to wage repression has been an increase in profits. Moreover, financial profits as a percentage of total profits have increased from just over 15 percent in 1965 to 40 percent in 2005 (Foster 2008). A question that could be posed in the circular flow of income is how much of these financial profits are attributed to funded pensions. As we have seen above, financial service providers set charges on sales of pension products that are met by individual savers; indeed, the selling of financial products is one of the main business activities of the sector. And although there is a literature on what type of pension product to choose—the choice between passive and active investing can result in charges varying from 0.5 to 2 percent a year or more, depending on the pension product—there has not been much attention paid to the aggregate size of charges and their contribution to financial profits.

Not much attention has been paid either to the arguments introduced above, and developed by Toporowski (2000), that pension funds lead to inflation in asset prices. He argues that pension funds have generated an inflow of money into stock markets. The consequent increase in asset prices has all the makings of an unsustainable bubble, and the threat of financial instability. Furthermore, it can be argued that the inflation in asset prices helps to further drive the increase in financial profits; and these profits are paid out in huge bonuses to the new financial class of super rich. And where do they tend to invest these bonuses?—in more financial assets, leading to even higher values.

The Flow of Finance to Firms

A fundamental issue is whether inflating asset prices lead to an increase in real investment. It would be hoped that firms are more able to have new share issues or to borrow from banks on the basis of these inflating assets. But one possible vehicle, as identified by Steindl (1952), is the use of inflated share prices for particular firms as a basis for mergers and takeover of other firms (Toporowski 2005). An additional question posed for the circular flow is to measure what proportion of financial surpluses is translated into real investment.

These questions about the neoliberal promotion of funded pensions point to a critique of Say's Law: the pre-Keynesian tenet of classical economics. According to Say's Law, at least as it was defined by the classical economist Ricardo, supply creates its own demand. So if an increased supply of private saving into funded pensions is encouraged, this should result in an increase in real investment. By suggesting, as an alternative, that finance has an autonomous role, in which inflows lead to the inflation of asset prices that do not automatically translate into the real economy, a critique of Say's Law is put forward. Related to this perspective, Cesaratto (2006) provides a detailed critique of funded pensions by invoking Keynes's paradox of saving, in which individual saving leads to lower aggregate demand and lower investment in capital stock.

This critique is further developed by looking at the implications of financialization on aggregate demand as a whole. As we have seen, the super rich in the financial sector have in large part invested their bonuses in financial assets, but this means that they are not contributing to aggregate demand. Although they may engage in conspicuous consumption (as argued by Thorstein Velben), the question has to be posed whether they can generate sufficient consumer expenditure in order to complete the circular flow of income. From a demand-side perspective, the combination of wage repression and huge financial profits generates a shortfall in aggregate demand for the circular flow of income. A key question is the extent to which pension funds, which we have seen can generate inequality in pension income, can contribute to this effective demand problem.

State Pensions as an Alternative

This set of issues with private pension systems raises a set of questions about the state PAYG system. Firstly, is the rhetoric of unsustainable state pensions that has been promulgated since the 1980s, and more recently the issues over sustainability of occupational defined-benefit schemes, focusing on the key question? Or is it side-stepping the more awkward question of whether the level of pensions expectations can be met at all whether through state PAYG schemes or funded alternatives? If the more valid question is the general level of affordability, this opens the debate to consideration of a more complete range of social provisioning questions, such as: Which types of pension system can best meet at least a minimum level of provision? Which can provide greater equality of outcome between individuals within a cohort and across different cohorts? Which types of system can be delivered with the lowest administrative costs? Which systems can channel resources into real investment? As argued above, at the level of the circular flow of income, there is less distinction between PAYG and funding than appears at first sight. As a result, the answers to the questions posed are more likely to lie in the distinction between defined-benefit (which can be provided on a PAYG or funded basis) and defined-contribution (which can only be funded)—although there are some possibilities of risk-sharing within defined-contribution schemes through, for example, collective defined-contribution schemes (see, for example, Hewitt Associates 2009).

If the circular flow approach suggests that a PAYG defined-benefit approach can achieve the same aggregate economic outcomes as a funded defined-benefit approach, the rationale for cutting back on PAYG pension systems is reduced to an ideological rather than economic position. It is salient to compare the distribution of public spending on pensions in different countries. Whereas the US spends only 6 percent of its GDP on pubic pensions, and the UK only 5.7 percent, other countries such as France and Germany allocate over 10 percent to state pension systems (see Figure 7). Furthermore, to illustrate the importance of this allocation of resources, the European Commission reports for the UK that 30 percent of its pensioner age population lives in relative poverty (income less than 60 percent of

Figure 7

Public Pension Spending in OECD Countries

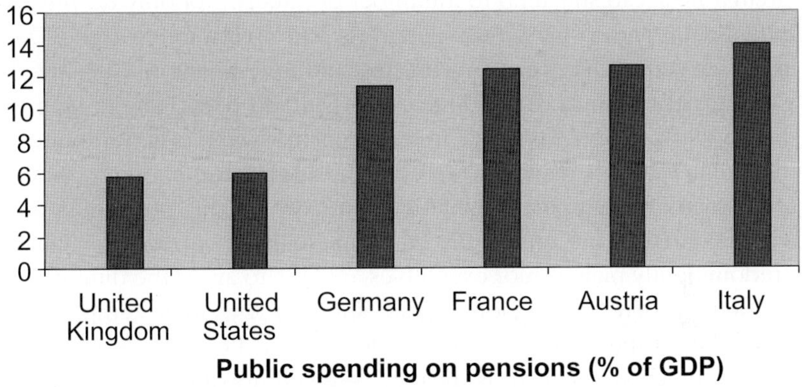

Source: OECD (2005).

median income), whereas in France pensioner poverty is only 13 percent and Germany only 17 percent (Eurostat 2009). The key question is how such countries feel able to afford to allocate more public resources to pensions. Is this at the expense of profits, or real investment, due to lower public expenditure on say military expenditure, or because of a willingness to tolerate higher taxes as the price of social benefits? A comparison of pension systems between countries suggests an investigation into the wider circular flow of income. The overall operation of Say's Law, under which saving automatically leads to investment, is brought into question by this circular flow perspective.

Conclusions

By using the circular flow of income as an organizing framework, an overview is provided of some key issues in retirement planning. Private and public pension systems are shown to have a comparable structure, each dependent on income from employment. This comparison provides the basis for a critique of private pension systems, as promoted in the neoliberal/Washington consensus, from a social provisioning perspective. Whereas in a state system taxation out of wages is for the most part mandatory, the flow of private saving in the circular flow can succumb to a number of pitfalls. Not only do private individuals tend to lack the willingness and ability to save, they are also exposed to the prevalence of mis-sold investment products, with varying performance and punitive charges and fees. Examination of the flow of pension payments in the circular flow reveals pronounced inequalities between income groups and between men and women. Low wages for women provide a key driver for this inequality, and such imbalances are further driven by inequalities of power, in which predominantly male senior executives are able to avoid the diminution of defined-benefit pension rights suffered by most employees. Inequality is then further compounded by the flow of tax relief for private pensions, which is heavily skewed towards high income earners. Far from being a neutral administrator, the state has a clear role to play in the social provisioning of pension resources.

The circular flow approach can also be used to examine the neoliberal argument that private pension systems promote economic growth. Issues are raised about whether increased pension savings lead to asset price inflation that, via charges and bonuses, further compounds income inequalities. Instead of a focus purely on demographics (declining support ratios), which are shown to affect funded as well as PAYG systems, the circular flow approach highlights the dangers for private pension systems of wage stagnation, which restricts savings, alongside higher profits, speculation, and financial activities such as merger acquisition on the part of firms.

This article provides some empirical evidence about the issues involved in designing pension systems, gathered together from disparate sources. What we are not able to offer as yet is a systematic analysis of how money flows in and out of the pension system as a whole—for either private or public systems. There is insufficient information to make any judgment as to where private pension systems are at their most disadvantageous. Is it, for example, the distribution of tax relief or problems of investment performance or charges that is the most important issue for private pension systems? And in which part of the circular flow of income might a comparable state pension system be more equitable. Why specifically might German and French state pension systems be preferable to a private pension system approach?

In future work a social accounts approach, following the principles developed by Stone (1986), will be considered as a possible vehicle for modeling pensions in the circular flow of income. In this approach, instead of focusing on Leontief input-output linkages between industries, of key interest will be the household and accumulation accounts. These would have to be disaggregated to take into account the employed and the retired, and the financial and real sectors of the economy. But this is the great advantage of a social accounting matrix: that the distribution of income between different groups and parts of the economy can be potentially examined in a disaggregated but consistent framework for society as a whole. The social accounting approach can potentially model the social provisioning of pensions, as a possible alternative to the emphasis on the private accounting of individuals and pension funds associated with pension economics.

References

Atkinson, A., S. MacKay, E. Kempson, and S. Collard. (2006). *Levels of Financial Capability in the UK: Results of a Baseline Survey.* London: Financial Services Authority.

Barclays. (2010). *Equity Gilt Study.* London: Barclays.

Barr, N., and P. Diamond. (2008). *Reforming Pensions.* Oxford: Oxford University Press.

Cesaratto, S. (2006). "Transition to Fully Funded Pension Schemes: A Non-Orthodox Criticism." *Cambridge Journal of Economics* 30: 33–48.

Department for Work and Pensions (DWP). (2009). *Saving for Retirement: Implications of Pension Reforms on Financial Incentives to Save for Retirement.* London: DWP.

——. (2011). *Pensions Bill 2011. Summary of Impacts.* London: DWP.

Department of Social Security. (1998). *A New Contract for Welfare: Partnership in Pensions*, Cmnd 4179. London: Stationary Office.

Eurostat. (2009). *Community Statistics on Income and Living Conditions.* Available at: www.epp.eurostat.eu (accessed 6 November 2009).

Financial Times Business Information. (1990–2011). *Pensions Management.* London: Financial Times.

Foster, J. B. (2008). "The Financialization of Capital and the Crisis." *Monthly Review* April.

Ginn, J., and S. Arber. (1999). "Changing Patterns in Pension Inequality." *Ageing and Society* 19(3): 319–342.

Government Actuary's Department. (2010). *Government Actuary's Quinquennial Review of the National Insurance Fund as at April 2005.* London: GAD.

Harvey, D. (2010). *The Enigma of Capital.* London: Profile Books.

Hewitt Associates Ltd. (2009). "Collective DC/Target Pensions." Conference presentation at University of Exeter, Risk-Sharing in Defined-Contribution Schemes, 7–8 January 2010.

HM Revenue & Customs. (2010). "Table 7.9 Registered Pension Schemes." Available at: http://www.hmrc.gov.uk/stats/pensions/table7-9.pdf (accessed 30 January 2011).

HM Treasury. (2010a). "Rates and Allowances in 2010–2011." Budget press notice PN02, 24 March. London: HMT.

——. (2010b). "Consultation on Finance Bill 2011: Restricting Pensions Tax Relief." Available at: http://www.hm-treasury.gov.uk/finance_bill_2011.htm (accessed 9 December 2010).

Holzmann, R., and R. Hinz. (2005). *Old-Age Income Support in the 21st Century. An International Perspective on Pension Systems and Reform,* Policy report. Washington: World Bank.

MacKellar, F. L. (2000). "The Predicament of Population Ageing: A Review Essay." *Population and Development Review* 26(2): 365–404.

Montagu-Smith, N. (2010). "Hidden Fees May Halve Pensions" *Sunday Times,* Money Section, p. 1, 12th December.

National Employment Trust. (2010). *NEST. Key Facts and Myths Buster.* Available at: http://www.nestpensions.org.uk. (accessed 19 September 2010).

Office for National Statistics. (2009a). *Family Spending.* London: Palgrave Macmillan.

——. (2009b). *Pension Trends,* Chapter 6. London: ONS.

——. (2010a). *Pension Trends,* Chapter 8. London: ONS.

——. (2010b). *Labour Market Statistics,* September 2010. London: ONS.

——. (2010c). *Wealth in Great Britain. Main Results from the Wealth and Assets Survey 2006/08.* London: ONS.

——. (2010d). *United Kingdom National Accounts. The Blue Book.* Basingstoke: Palgrave Macmillan.

——. (2010e). *Pension Trends,* Chapter 14. London: ONS.

Pensions Policy Institute. (2004). *Tax Relief and Incentives for Pension Saving.* London: PPI/Age Concern.

Personal Investment Authority (PIA). (1999). "Advice on Personal Pensions in Advance of the Introduction of Stakeholders Pensions." *Regulatory Update 64.* London: PIA.

Steindl, J. (1952). Maturity and Stagnation in American Capitalism. Institute of Statistics Monograph No. 4. Oxford: Basil Blackwell.

Stone, J. R. N. (1986). "Social Accounting: The State of Play." *Scandinavian Journal of Economics* 88(3): 453–472.

Sullivan, M. (2004). *Understanding Pensions.* Abingdon: Routledge.

Thaler, R., and S. Benartzi. (2001). *Save More Tomorrow: Using Behavioral Economics to Increase Employee Saving,* Los Angeles. Andersen School at UCLA. Available at: http://www.anderson.ucla.edu/faculty/shlomo.benartzi/savemore.htm. (accessed 26 January 2011).

Thaler, R., and C. Sunstein. (2008). *Nudge.* London: Penguin Books.

Toporowski, J. (2000). *The End of Finance.* London: Routledge.

——. (2005). *Theories of Financial Disturbance.* Cheltenham: Edward Elgar.

Trades Union Congress (TUC). (2009). PensionsWatch 2009. Available at: www.tuc.org.uk/extras/PensionWatch2009.pdf (accessed 6 November 2009).

Trigg, A. B. (2010). "Conclusion: Investing for the Long Term." In *Personal Investment: Financial Planning in an Uncertain World.* Eds. M. Mazzucato, J. Lowe, A. Shipman, and A. Trigg. pp. 361–388. London: Palgrave.

United Nations. (2009). *World Population Ageing 2009.* Available at: http://www.un.org/esa/population/publications/WPA2009/WPA2009_WorkingPaper.pdf (accessed 15 November 2010).

Willis, L. E. (2008). "Against Financial Literacy Education." Public Law and Legal Theory Research Paper Series Research Paper No. #08–10: Philadelphia: University of Pennsylvania Law School.

World Bank. (1994). *Averting the Old Age Crisis.* Washington: World Bank.

Modeling the Economy as a Whole: An Integrative Approach

By Frederic S. Lee*,†

Abstract. This article integrates the social surplus approach with input-output, stock-flow consistent, social accounting, and social fabric modeling with a structure-agency methodology to develop a historically grounded model of the economy. The first two sections develop a model of the monetary structure of the social provisioning process. The third section introduces agency into the model in the form of the acting organization. The fourth section uses the social fabric approach and historical context drawn from social structures of accumulation to develop a socially embedded, historically contextualized, structured-agency model of the economy as a whole. The final section discusses the importance of the model.

People have social, caring lives; they have households, parents, children, friends, colleagues, and a history; and they need to be fed, housed, clothed, married, schooled, and socially engaged. And the needed and desired goods and services are produced to sustain their socially constructed, caring lifestyle. Thus the social provisioning process is a continuous, non-accidental series of production-based, production-derived economic activities through historical time that provide "needy" individuals and households the private and state goods and services (that is, the social surplus) necessary to carry out their sequential, reoccurring, and changing social activities through time. As such then, a continuous provisioning process implies that it is something like a going concern whose core processes provide the material bases for social provisioning and are similar to a going plant and going business. This means, in part, that

*Department of Economics, 211 Haag Hall, University of Missouri–Kansas City, 5100 Rockhill Road, Kansas City, Missouri 64110, United States, E-mail: leefs@umkc.edu

†I would like to thank Tae-Hee Jo, Terry McDonough, and Erik Olsen for comments on earlier versions of the article.

American Journal of Economics and Sociology, Vol. 70, No. 5 (November, 2011).

the social provisioning process is embedded in the social surplus approach. It also suggests that social provisioning is affected by historically situated social norms and cultural values, by the social activities to be supported, and by the decisions of acting persons. Hence, modeling the social provisioning process or the economy as a whole involves, first, stock-flow, social accounting consistent modeling of its productive and monetary structures and the embedding of the acting person within them. This economic model of the provisioning process is in turn linked at one end to cultural values, norms, and societal institutions and at the other end by household social activities and government services. In addition, the concatenated model is "linked" to a historical context or stage of capitalist development. Consequently, the concatenated model of the provisioning process of the economy as a whole, which is predicated on the concept of a going economy, is an integration of the social surplus approach, of input-output, stock-flow, social fabric, and social accounting consistent modeling, of historical contextualization, and of structure-agency methodology (Jo 2011; Mongiovi 2011; McDonough 2011; Hayden 2011; Olsen 2011; Lee and Jo 2011).

As a theoretical concept and methodological approach, the economy as a going concern is abstracted from its historical origins and situated historically. That is, it represents a "currently" functioning working capitalist economy complete with structures, agency, social fabric, and social activities. Hence, the structures that give the economy its form, the organizations and institutions that structurally organize and coordinate economic activity, and the agency or acting person that initiates and directs economic activity operate interdependently, contemporarily, although not necessarily synchronically. So while the structures, organizations, and institutions provide the framework for the economy to be a going concern, to continuously generate economic activities, it is the acting person that makes it happen or not—the economy does nothing on its own accord.

Therefore, to construct qua delineate the model of the economy as a whole, the first step is to descriptively model the productive structure and the surplus, which involves articulating the nature of circular production, fixed investment goods, and scarcity, decomposing the surplus into government, consumption, and fixed investment goods and services, and linking the surplus to the provisioning of households, state, and the business enterprise. The next step involves "social accounting" modeling of these linkages in terms of money incomes vis-à-vis workers, capitalists, and the state. This requires the introduction of government expenditures, a chartalist theory of money, a banking sector, financial assets and liabilities, and finally the financial structure of the provisioning process. With this in place, the social accounting of the relationship between profits, incomes, and the surplus is delineated and then integrated with the models of the productive and financial structures to produce a descriptively consistent model of the monetary structure of the social provisioning process. This model of the provisioning process is comprised entirely of structures and hence lacks agency, lacks acting persons. Therefore, the third step is to introduce core organizations and institutions—the household, state, business enterprise, trade union, and market governance organizations—relevant to the social provisioning process and the acting persons whose agency or decisions, which take place through the organizations and institutions, direct, control, and sustain the social provisioning process. Combining these three steps creates the economic model of the provisioning process. In the penultimate section, the economic model is historically contextualized and linked to and situated in the social fabric of the society, hence creating a historically grounded, descriptively consistent model of the economy as a whole. The importance of the model for heterodox economics is discussed in the concluding section.

Modeling the Productive Structure of the Economy and the Surplus

The social provisioning process is founded on the social and interdependent production of goods and services; thus the structural framework of economic activity of a capitalist economy consists of its schema of production and the income flows relative to goods and services for social provisioning. The schema of production of the economy is represented in classical-Sraffian-Leontief terms as a circular production input-output matrix of material goods combined with different types of labor power skills to produce an array of goods and services as outputs (Lowe 1976; Gehrke and Kurz 2006; Kurz 2006; Kurz and Salvadori 2000, 2005, 2006). Many of the outputs replace the goods and services used up in production, and the rest constitutes the social surplus to be used for household consumption, private fixed investment, and government services.[1] More specifically, the production schema of the economy is empirically represented in terms of a product-by-product input-output table (or matrix). The table shows that *m* goods and services are produced, and that *n* goods and services and *z* labor power skills are used in their production, where the former constitute the *intermediate inputs* where $m > n$ and the latter constitute the labor power skills inputs where $z > m$. Thus, letting g_{ij} represent the amount of the *j*th product (good or service) and L_{iz} represent the amount of the *z*th labor power skill to produce Q_i amount of the *i*th product, the production schema of the *i*th good or service can be represented by

$$[g_{i1}, \ldots, g_{in}, L_{i1}, \ldots, L_{iz}] \rightarrow Q_i \text{ or } [\mathbf{G}_i, \mathbf{L}_i] \rightarrow Q_i \tag{1}$$

where $\mathbf{G}_i = (g_{i1}, \ldots, g_{in})$ is a row vector of *n* intermediate inputs; and $\mathbf{L}_i = (L_{i1}, \ldots, L_{iz})$ is a row vector of *z* labor power skills inputs.

Hence, the productive structure of the economy takes the following form:

$$\begin{array}{c} [\mathbf{G}_1, \mathbf{L}_1] \rightarrow Q_1 \\ \cdots\cdots\cdots\cdots \\ [\mathbf{G}_m, \mathbf{L}_m] \rightarrow Q_m \end{array} \tag{2}$$

Representing the array of $(\mathbf{G}_1, \ldots, \mathbf{G}_m)$ as G a product-by-product input-output table, the array of $(\mathbf{L}_1, \ldots, \mathbf{L}_m)$ as L a labor power skills-by-product table, and the total quantity produced of each product as **Q**, the production structure of the economy of Equation (2) is be depicted as

$$G \oplus L \rightarrow \mathbf{Q} \tag{3a}$$

or

$$\begin{bmatrix} G_{11} \\ G_{21} \end{bmatrix} \oplus \begin{bmatrix} L_{11} \\ L_{21} \end{bmatrix} \rightarrow \begin{bmatrix} Q_1 \\ Q_2 \end{bmatrix} \quad (3b)$$

where G is a $m \times n$ flow matrix of intermediate inputs consisting of produced goods and services;

L is a $m \times z$ flow matrix of labor power skills;

Q is a strictly positive $m \times 1$ column vector of output or the total social product;

G_{11} is a square $n \times n$ matrix of intermediate inputs used in the production of $\mathbf{Q}_1$ a strictly positive $n \times 1$ column vector of intermediate goods and services;

G_{21} is a $m - n \times n$ matrix of intermediate inputs used in the production of $\mathbf{Q}_2$ a strictly positive $m - n \times 1$ column vector of final goods and services for consumption, investment, and government use;

L_{11} is a $n \times z$ matrix of labor power skills used in the production of $\mathbf{Q}_1$;

L_{21} is a $m - n \times z$ matrix of labor power skills used in the production of $\mathbf{Q}_2$; and

$\oplus$ means both intermediate and labor power inputs are needed to produce the output.

One feature of the structure of production is that $G_{11} \rightarrow \mathbf{Q}_1$, meaning that all of $\mathbf{Q}_1$ are produced means of production. This implies that both inputs and outputs are tied to technically specified differentiated uses, production is a circular flow, all intermediate inputs are produced inputs, and the linear production schemas (Equation (1)) for each output are all linked together on the input side. Consequently, the production of intermediate inputs is a differentiated, indecomposable hence emergent system of production that cannot be segmented, aggregated, disaggregated, reduced, or increased. A second feature of the structure of production is that the production of any Q_i must directly involve at least one g_{ij} where $i \neq j$, which means that all of G_{11} is at least indirectly engaged in its production, making all intermediate inputs, $\mathbf{Q}_1$, Sraffian basic goods.

Circular Production, Labor Power, and Scarcity

Although labor power is not an intermediate produced good and service *per se*, neither is it a non-produced input with naturally given indestructible productive capabilities and talents that exist prior to production and externally to the structure of production as original factor input. Being producible within the structure of production, goods and services used as intermediate produced means of production are not original factors; and a similar argument can be used for labor power as well. Labor power is a socially produced input in that it is created or becomes. That is, humans are acting persons that have capabilities to learn particular skills. A particular state of technical knowledge will produce and reproduce those skills or specific forms of labor power while changes in it will render some skills obsolete and create new skills. In addition, any particular labor power skill or even the overall amount of labor power can vary as a result of changes in technical knowledge. Therefore, labor power is socially constructed hence similar to, but not the same as a good or service used as an intermediate input. Hence, while labor power is not produced within the system of production like a ton of steel, it is socially created in conjunction with technical knowledge and then enters the system of production as an "input."

With labor power, goods, and services being used as intermediate inputs co-created and co-existing internally within the structure of production, there do not exist original factors of production with naturally given indestructible capabilities and given unalterable endowments. Consequently, none of the inputs in G or L can be scarce factor inputs, as defined in mainstream economics, which implies that none of the outputs (**Q**) can be characterized as relatively scarce products. Therefore, production is not an activity to overcome scarcity, exchange does not arise from scarcity, and prices are not scarcity indexes. In short, under circular production, scarcity has no theoretical meaning and hence is not an organizing principle of economic inquiry in heterodox economics.[2] Finally, the absence of original factors of production and scarcity means that with circular production, the restraints on the social provisioning process are not a result of given quantities of scarce factor inputs located in production, but are located in the decisions and social values that affect the production of the surplus ($\mathbf{Q}_2$) and its distribution (McCormick 2002; De Gregori 1985, 1987; Zimmermann 1951; Levine 1977, 1978; Veblen 1908).

Fixed Investment Goods and the Surplus

Behind the usage of intermediate inputs and the employment of differentiated labor power skills for each product stands an array of differentiated fixed investment goods:

$$\mathbf{K}_{Si} = [k_{i1}, \ldots, k_{ik}] \tag{4}$$

where $\mathbf{K}_{Si}$ is a row vector of the stock of k_k fixed investment goods used in the production of Q_i.

The fixed investment goods are used in production, but they are not used up like intermediate inputs. Rather, they are separate from the intermediate and labor power inputs (hence the colon in Equation (5)) because they are repeatedly used in the repeated production of the output. Thus, the combined array of fixed investment goods ($\mathbf{K}_{Si}$), intermediate inputs ($\mathbf{G}_i$), and differentiated labor power ($\mathbf{L}_i$) used for the production of Q_i represents the complete stock-flow technology of the schema of production:

$$[\mathbf{K}_{Si} : \mathbf{G}_i \oplus \mathbf{L}_i] \rightarrow Q_i. \tag{5}$$

The technology of the schema embodies a specific set of socially created knowledge that is an emergent whole. In particular, the fixed investment goods, intermediate inputs, and the differentiated labor power inputs are the physical manifestations of the uniquely specific social knowledge or technology used in the production of Q_i. Being linked in an emergent technological arrangement for the production of Q_i, the schema of production cannot be separated into parts with each identified with a certain portion of the output; its fixed investment goods cannot be viewed as separate "dated output" to be hypothetically sold in the form of joint products; and the schema itself cannot be treated as joint outputs along with Q_i. Finally, from Equation (5), the entire structure of production can be represented as

$$\begin{bmatrix} K_{S1} : G_{11} \\ K_{S2} : G_{21} \end{bmatrix} \oplus \begin{bmatrix} L_{11} \\ L_{21} \end{bmatrix} \rightarrow \begin{bmatrix} \mathbf{Q}_1 \\ \mathbf{Q}_2 \end{bmatrix} \tag{6}$$

where K_{S1} is a $n \times k$ matrix of the basic sector stock of fixed investment goods used in the production of $\mathbf{Q}_1$; and
K_{S2} is a $m - n \times k$ matrix of the surplus sector stock of fixed investment goods used in the production of $\mathbf{Q}_2$.

The social surplus of the economy consists of the excess of total goods produced over what is used up in production:

$$(\mathbf{e}Q_d)^T - (\mathbf{e}G^*)^T = \mathbf{Q} - \mathbf{G}^* = \mathbf{S}^* \tag{7}$$

where $\mathbf{e}$ is a unit vector;
Q_d is $m \times m$ diagonal matrix of the total social product;
$(\mathbf{e}Q_d)^T = \mathbf{Q}$ the total social product and its composition;
G^* is an augmented G matrix with the $n+1$ to m columns consisting of zeros;
$(\mathbf{e}G^*)^T = \mathbf{G}^*$ is a semi-positive $m \times 1$ column vector of intermediate inputs; and
$\mathbf{S}^*$ is a semi-positive $m \times 1$ column vector of the goods and services that constitute the social surplus.

The social surplus includes "extra" intermediate inputs and final goods and services that go into inventory. However, since the inventory of goods and services constitutes less than plus or minus 1 percent of total economic activity, they will, for this article, be ignored by assuming that all of $\mathbf{Q}_1$ is used up in production or

$$(\mathbf{e}Q_{d1})^T - (\mathbf{e}G)^T = 0. \tag{8}$$

This means that the surplus of the economy is essentially technically defined and consists of Sraffian non-basic goods and services:

$$\mathbf{S} = \mathbf{Q}_2. \tag{9}$$

Being a surplus, the goods and services of $\mathbf{Q}_2$ have no technological links but rather social links. Thus, they are differentiated by their social destination or social accounts into which they flow—government goods ($\mathbf{Q}_{2G}$) for the state, consumption goods ($\mathbf{Q}_{2C}$) for the household, fixed investment goods ($\mathbf{Q}_{2I}$) for the business enterprise:

$$\mathbf{S} = \mathbf{Q}_2 = \mathbf{Q}_{2G} + \mathbf{Q}_{2C} + \mathbf{Q}_{2I} \qquad (10)$$

where $\mathbf{Q}_{2C}$, $\mathbf{Q}_{2I}$, and $\mathbf{Q}_{2G}$ are semi-positive $m-n \times 1$ column vectors of surplus goods and services.

Since the different destinations are engaged with broadly different economic and social activities, the array and composition of the three vectors differ. In particular, $\mathbf{Q}_{2I}$ not only differs in its array of goods from $\mathbf{Q}_{2G}$ and $\mathbf{Q}_{2C}$, it is also a differentiated array of goods and services due to the different technologies used to produce $\mathbf{Q}_{2G}$ and $\mathbf{Q}_{2C}$, which themselves are an array of differentiated goods and services. Moreover, $\mathbf{Q}_{2I}$ is connected as a flow of basic sector fixed investment goods K_{FI} to the stock of basic sector fixed investment goods K_{SI} and as a flow of surplus sector fixed investment goods K_{F2} to the stock of surplus sector fixed investment goods K_{SI}:

$$\mathbf{Q}_{2I}^{T} \rightarrow K_{FI-2} \rightarrow K_{S1-2} \qquad (11a)$$

Thus, the economy is productively linked together by the circular flow of the production of intermediate inputs and by a second circular flow via the surplus from the production of fixed investment goods to their final social destination as stocks and their subsequent use directly and/or indirectly in their own production as well as in the production of all intermediate inputs and final goods and services, which makes them "quasi-basic goods" in the Sraffian sense.

The array of differentiated goods in $\mathbf{Q}_{2G}$ indicates the range of social activities supported by the state and its composition indicates their relative social importance. Therefore, the state's contribution to social provisioning is affected by the cultural values, beliefs, and norms and by agency qua decisions that compel the production of $\mathbf{Q}_{2G}$. But to provide the desired government services (GS), the state's stock-flow "schema of production" draws upon government fixed investment goods and employs differently skilled workers, managers, and politicians, and combines them with $\mathbf{Q}_{2G}$ and government payments (GP):

$$\mathbf{K}_{S4} : \mathbf{Q}_{2G}^{T} \oplus \mathbf{L}_{41} \oplus \mathrm{GP} \rightarrow \mathrm{GS}, \mathbf{K}_{F4} \rightarrow \mathbf{K}_{S4} \qquad (11b)$$

where $\mathbf{K}_{S4}$ is a row vector of the stock of k government fixed investment goods used in providing of government services (obtained through past government purchases);
$\mathbf{Q}^{T}_{2G}$ is a $(1 \times m - n)$ row vector of surplus goods and services used in providing government services;
$\mathbf{L}_{41}$ is a $m + 2$ row vector of z labor power skills used in providing government services;
GP is the amount of dollars of government payments, such as unemployment or social welfare benefits, to dependent individuals and households that do not have current employment hence wage income or other forms of income, and interest payments to bank and non-bank enterprises and households that hold government bonds; and
$\mathbf{K}_{F4}$ is a row vector of the flow of k government fixed investment goods into $\mathbf{K}_{S4}$.[3]

Finally, the array of differentiated goods and services in $\mathbf{Q}_{2C}$ indicates the range of social activities undertaken by households, while its composition indicates their relative social importance:

$$\mathbf{Q}^{T}_{2C} \rightarrow \text{HSA} \tag{11c}$$

where $\mathbf{Q}^{T}_{2C}$ is a $(1 \times m - n)$ row vector of surplus goods and services that contribute to household social activities (HSA).

There are two further implications arising from $\mathbf{Q}_2$ being produced as Sraffian non-basic goods. The first is since consumption and investment are based on current production, the former is not constrained by the latter and the latter is not based on "savings." Secondly, as $\mathbf{Q}_2$ is produced for the purpose of maintaining an ongoing range of particular government services and household social activities, the overall array and composition of the social surplus is the physical component of the structure of the social provisioning process. But it also represents social relationships and decisions that produced it. This clearly makes the surplus socially (not naturally) constructed hence a *social* surplus; and the social determination of the volume and composition of the surplus also means the social determination of all means of production—goods, services, and labor power. Thus, all the actual economic activities that constitute the social provisioning process are manifestations of societal relations and decisions (Kurz and Salvadori 1995; Veblen 1908; Ranson 1987; Lower 1987; Lager 2006).

Social Provisioning as a Going Plant

What emerges from above is that the structure of the social provisioning process in terms of goods, services, and labor power consists, in part, of the structure of production required for the production of the social surplus (Equation (6)) and of the allocation qua contribution of the surplus to social provisioning through enabling government services and household social activities to occur and maintaining government and private sector productive capabilities (Equations (11a)–(11c)). This can be qualitatively represented in terms of a stock-flow, social accounting descriptively consistent model of the productive structure of the social provisioning process "producing" social activities (GS, HSA):

Stock-Flow, Social Accounting (SFSA) Model of the Productive Structure of the Social Provisioning Process

$$\begin{array}{lll}
\text{Basic Goods Sector} & K_{S1}: G_{11} \oplus L_{11} & \rightarrow \mathbf{Q}_1 \\
\text{Surplus Goods Sector} & K_{S2}: G_{21} \oplus L_{21} & \rightarrow \mathbf{Q}_2 = \mathbf{Q}_{2G} + \mathbf{Q}_{2C} + \mathbf{Q}_{2I} \\
 & & \\
\text{State} & \mathbf{K}_{S4}: \mathbf{Q}_{2G}^{T} \oplus \mathbf{L}_{41} \oplus GP \rightarrow GS,\ \mathbf{K}_{F4} \rightarrow \mathbf{K}_{S4} & \\
\text{Household} & \mathbf{Q}_{2C}^{T} \rightarrow HSA & \\
\text{Enterprise} & \mathbf{Q}_{2I}^{T} \rightarrow K_{F1-2} \rightarrow K_{S1-2} &
\end{array} \qquad (12)$$

As a whole, the social provisioning process acquires the structure of a going plant with unused capacity and fixed investment goods and the capability of producing additional capacity through producing fixed investment goods. So, as long as household social activities are ongoing and supported by government services, the structure of production ensures the continuous reproduction of the intermediate inputs and fixed investment goods. More specifically, the level of economic activity for the economy as a whole is determined by the decisions to produce consumption, investment, and government goods and services, that is, by effective demand. With the "input" requirements produced and reproducible simultaneously with the goods and services necessary for the household social activities and government services to take place, the social provisioning process is potentially sustainable, and thus has an expected future; and this is what makes the provisioning process a going plant.

Modeling the Relationship Between the Social Surplus and Income

The social provisioning process takes place through linkages between two broad social accounts: (1) the money incomes of workers, capitalists, politicians, and other members of society, profits of enterprises, and government spending and (2) the social surplus, that is, consumption, investment, and government goods and services (Miller and Blair 2009; Olsen 2011). They exist because the social surplus needs to be accessed qua distributed in a manner that maintains the economy as a going concern and particularly a capitalist going concern. Consequently, class and agency-linked incomes are associated with agent-created goods and services. Managers and owners of enterprises use their business income, that is, profits, to purchase fixed investment goods produced by other enterprises, while workers use their wage incomes to purchase consumption goods and the state uses its state money to purchase government goods, both of which are also produced by capitalists.

The particular forms that the linkages take involve exchange, markets, and state money, but they are based on a set of social relationships specific to capitalism. That is, under capitalism there exists a set of property rights that vest the ownership of the produced means of production and output in a group of acting persons, either business people or the corporate enterprise; and an associated set of legal rights that validate and "empower" a hierarchical organizational structure that enables the board of directors and senior management of business enterprises to unilaterally direct their activities. These two groups of acting persons—business people/corporate enterprise and members of boards of directors/senior management—constitute the *capitalist class*. In addition, the state, as opposed to the *political elite*, owns its activities and "property" while the elite, which also consist of acting persons, have the legal authority to direct its activities. Thus the combination of the capitalist class and the political elite constitutes the *ruling class* that owns the means of production, and output and directs the economic and political activities of enterprises and the state. In contrast, there is a second class of acting persons who engage in the production of the output but do not own it or the means of production by which it is produced and who engage in activities that provide government services; and neither can in any substantive sense direct, determine, or control the "working" activities in which they are engaged. These private and public sector employees constitute the *working class.* Finally there is a third class of acting persons who are not engaged in social provisioning activities, such as children, retirees, and others that constitutes the *dependent class.*

As noted above, it takes the entire going plant of the economy to provide for social provisioning and thus ensure the survival and continuation of households, business enterprises, and the state. This combined with the dominance of the ruling class means that the social provisioning process involves market exchange, which has four implications. First, all goods and services, **Q**, are produced for exchange, but once they are brought for their usefulness, they cease for the most part to be commodities, that is, to be offered for further exchange. Secondly, exchange is carried out in markets and involves prices hence the only analytical-theoretical starting point is a system of systematic, coordinated, and unending multiple exchanges involving state money. The third implication is that prices are state money prices denominated in the state monetary unit and hence are abstract indexes of credit qua debt obligations that are not grounded intrinsically in the commodities themselves. Finally, the last implication is that exchange, whether money for goods, services, or labor power or vice versa, arises from the need of households to gain access to a state-money monetized social provisioning process. The social relationship between the ruling class and the working and dependent classes combined with the former's control and use of state money produces a particular symbiotic relationship that defines capitalism. That is, the social relationship between the ruling class and the working and dependent classes is that the former owns the productive and administrative capabilities underpinning social provisioning, has the social power to direct it, and controls the access to state money that is necessary for access to social provisioning, while the latter have none of the above. This tripartite social relationship defines what is meant as *capitalism* as a social, political, and economic system embedding the provisioning process; and in doing so, it determines the particular structural form of the linkages between the money incomes of workers, managers, and other members of society, profits of enterprises, and state "money income" and expenditures on the social surplus (Wray 1998, 2003; Bell 2001).

Government Expenditures, State Money, and the Banking Sector

Since all outputs are commodities that are exchanged in markets, they have prices in terms of state money. Hence, letting $\mathbf{p} = (p_1, \ldots, p_m)$ be a column vector of state money prices of all *m* goods and services produced in the economy, $\mathbf{p_1} = (p_1, \ldots, p_n)$ be a column vector of prices of intermediate inputs, and $\mathbf{p_2} = (p_{n+1}, \ldots, p_m)$ be a column vector of all surplus goods and services, then the total value of the total social product is $\mathbf{Q}^T\mathbf{p}$, $\mathbf{Q}^T{}_1\mathbf{p_1}$ is the total value of the intermediate inputs, $\mathbf{Q}^T{}_{21}\mathbf{p_2}$ is the total value of investment goods, $\mathbf{Q}^T{}_{2G}\mathbf{p_2}$ is the total value of goods and services purchased by government, $\mathbf{Q}^T{}_{2C}\mathbf{p_2}$ is the total value of consumption goods and services, and the total value of the social surplus is

$$\mathbf{Q}_2^T\mathbf{p_2} = \mathbf{Q}_{2G}^T\mathbf{p_2} + \mathbf{Q}_{2C}^T\mathbf{p_2} + \mathbf{Q}_{21}^T\mathbf{p_2}. \tag{13}$$

Consequently, to gain access to social provisioning, it is necessary that all household incomes, enterprise revenues, and government expenditures be denominated in state money.

In terms of state money, government expenditures are equal to its purchases of final goods and services, to the wages and salaries of government employees and politicians, to government payments that are politically qua administratively determined income payments to the dependent class (GP_d), and to government interest payments to business enterprises (GP_{ib}), banks (GP_{iB}), and households (GP_{ih}) for holding state financial assets, that is, government bonds:

$$\begin{aligned} GOV_E &= \mathbf{Q}^T_{2G}\mathbf{p_2} + \mathbf{L}_{41}\mathbf{w} + GP_d + GP_{ib} + GP_{iB} + GP_{ih} \\ &= \mathbf{Q}^T_{2G}\mathbf{p_2} + \mathbf{L}_{41}\mathbf{w} + GP_4 \end{aligned} \tag{14}$$

where GOV_E is total government expenditures;
$\mathbf{Q}^T_{2G}\mathbf{p_2}$ is government expenditures on goods and services;
$\mathbf{w} = (w_1, \ldots, w_z)$ is a column vector of state money wage rates;
$\mathbf{L}_{41}\mathbf{w}$ is the government's wage bill; and

$$GP_4 = GP_d + GP_{ib} + GP_{iB} + GP_{ih}.$$

Because government expenditures are credited to bank accounts in the banking system, enterprises, individuals, and households must use state money for provisioning and reproduction purposes and all enterprises must accept it and utilize the banking system for making payments and receiving revenues. In addition, since the government does not actually produce $\mathbf{Q}_{2G}$ or the consumption goods and services purchased by government employees, politicians, and the dependent class, government expenditures are directly and indirectly spent on outputs owned by business enterprises and show up as a component of their profits and hence in the total profits for the economy—so the more the state spends, the more profits (given tax rates) the capitalist class receives. Because profits are also generated by expenditures on fixed investment goods, total profits are equal to investment and government expenditures after taxes. This means government-generated profits are converted into financial assets through the purchase of government bonds by non-bank and bank corporate enterprises, and by households via the distribution of dividends out of profits.[4]

The symbiotic relationship of the state and its governing activities and the capitalist class regarding state money creates banking activities distinct from the productive activities in the basic and surplus goods sectors that are managed by capitalists, which entails the existence of a separate banking sector. So the banking sector's stock-flow "schema of production" draws upon a stock of fixed investment goods ($\mathbf{K}_{S3}$), financial assets—government bonds (FA_{SGB3}) and bank loans (FA_{SBL3}), and financial liabilities—deposit accounts of business enterprises and households (LB_{S3}), utilizes intermediate inputs and labor power, income from the government bonds and loans minus the costs of demand deposits to produce qua create bank loans that are purchased by enterprises and households at the current bank interest rate:[5]

$$\mathbf{K}_{S3}, FA_{S3}, LB_{S3}: \mathbf{G}_{31} \oplus \mathbf{L}_{31} \rightarrow Q_{3L} \tag{15}$$

where $\mathbf{K}_{S3}$ is a row vector of k_k fixed investment goods and used in the production of bank loans;

$FA_{S3} = FA_{SGB3} + FA_{SBL3}$ is the total stock of financial assets of the banking sector and is a scalar;[6]

$\mathbf{G}_{31}$ is a $m+1$ row vector of n intermediate inputs used in the production of bank loans;

$\mathbf{L}_{31}$ is a $m+1$ row vector of z labor power skills used in the production of bank loans; and

Q_{3L} is a scalar and the amount of bank loans made to enterprises and households.

Since enterprises require bank loans for working capital on a continuous basis and for, at times, long term investment projects, they have a stock of financial liabilities. Similarly, households take out bank loans to purchase various goods and services needed for household social activities and so have a stock of financial activities. Finally, the state carries out government expenditures that are not completely compensated by taxes and so has a stock of financial liabilities called the national debt that is represented by the outstanding government bonds owned by non-bank and bank enterprises and by households. Combining this with Equations (14) and (15), the model of the productive structure of the social provisioning process (Equation (12)) is broadened to include a qualitative-descriptive model of the financial structure of the economy with stock-flow, social accounting consistent relationships of financial assets, and liabilities that produces social activities:

SFSA Model of the Productive and Financial Structure of the Social Provisioning Process

$$
\begin{array}{llll}
\text{Basic Goods Sector} & K_{S1}, FA_{S1}, LB_{S1}: & G_{11} \oplus L_{11} & \rightarrow \mathbf{Q}_1 \\
\text{Surplus Goods Sector} & K_{S2}, FA_{S2}, LB_{S2}: & G_{21} \oplus L_{21} & \rightarrow \mathbf{Q}_2 = \mathbf{Q}_{2G} + \mathbf{Q}_{2C} + \mathbf{Q}_{2I} \\
\text{Banking Sector} & \mathbf{K}_{S3}, FA_{S3}, LB_{S3}: & \mathbf{G}_{31} \oplus \mathbf{L}_{31} & \rightarrow Q_{3L} \rightarrow FA_{S3} \\
 & & & \qquad\quad \rightarrow LB_{1,2,5} \\
\text{State} & \mathbf{K}_{S4}, \qquad LB_{S4}: & \mathbf{Q}_{2G}^{T} \oplus \mathbf{L}_{41} \oplus GP_4 & \rightarrow GS, \mathbf{K}_{F4} \rightarrow \mathbf{K}_{S4}, \\
\text{Household} & FA_{S5}, LB_{S5}: & \mathbf{Q}_{2C}^{T} & \rightarrow HSA \\
\text{Enterprise} & & \mathbf{Q}_{2I}^{T} & \rightarrow K_{F1-3} \rightarrow K_{S1-3}
\end{array} \tag{16}
$$

$$
\begin{array}{lll}
\text{Financial Structural Balances} & \text{National Debt:} & LB_{S4} = FA_{SGB1-3,5} \\
 & \text{Bank Loans:} & FA_{SBL3} = LB_{1,2,5} \\
\text{Bank Demand Deposits:} \quad LB_{S3} = FA_{SDD1,2,5} & &
\end{array}
$$

where FA_{S1} and LB_{S1} are $n \times 1$ vectors of the stock of financial assets–government bonds (FA_{SGB1}) and demand deposits (FA_{SDD1})—and liabilities—bank loans (LB_{S1})—associated with the production of intermediate inputs or basic goods;

FA_{S2} and LB_{S2} are $m - n \times 1$ vectors of the stock of financial assets—government bonds (FA_{SGB2}) and demand deposits (FA_{SDD2})—and liabilities—bank loans (LB_{S2})—associated with the production of the social surplus;

FA_{S3} and LB_{S3} are scalars and the stock of financial assets—government bonds (FA_{SGB3}) and bank loans (FA_{SBL3})—and liabilities—demand deposits (LB_{S3})—associated with the production of bank loans;

LB_{S4} is a scalar and is the stock of financial liabilities (national debt) associated with providing government services; and

FA_{S5} and LB_{S5} are scalars and are the stock of financial assets—government bonds (FA_{SGB5}) and demand deposits (FA_{SDD5})—and liabilities—bank loans (LB_{S5})—associated household activities.

The model shows that the national debt consists of the government bonds are that held by bank and non-bank enterprises and by household; thus an increase in the national debt arising from government expenditures exceeding taxes increases private sector and household holdings of government bonds and hence their incomes and profits. Enterprises and households also take out bank loans (liabilities), which simultaneously create financial assets for the banking sector; but since bank loans are deposited in banks (thus creating financial assets), they also create banking sector liabilities. Therefore, an increase in bank loans increases at the same time banking sector financial assets and liabilities. In short, government decisions to spend (given tax rates) and enterprise and household decisions to take out bank loans create, drive, and change the economy's financial structure.

Profits, Incomes, and the Social Surplus

To simplify the analysis, gross profits are defined as the difference between intermediate and labor input costs and revenues; thus, it includes depreciation (which is an "income" stream to the enterprise) and interest income for the banking and non-banking enterprises. So, drawing on Equations (12)–(16), gross profits in a state money economy are:

$$\Pi_{GE} = (\mathbf{Q}^{T}\mathbf{p}) - \mathbf{e}[G\mathbf{p_1} + L\mathbf{w}] + TR_3 - i_D LB_{S3} - [\mathbf{G}_{31}\mathbf{p}_1 + \mathbf{L}_{31}\mathbf{w}] \quad (17a)$$

$$\Pi_{GE} = \Pi_{GNB} + \Pi_{GB} \quad (17b)$$

where Π_{GE} is a scalar and the total gross profits of the economy;
$\mathbf{Q}^{T}\mathbf{p}$ is the total value of the total social product;
$G\mathbf{p_1}$ is the value of the intermediate inputs by product used in the production of the social product;
$L\mathbf{w}$ is the wage bill by product incurred in the production of the social product;
TR_3 is the total interest income of the banking sector and is equal to interest income from government bonds ($i_G FA_{SGB3}$) plus interest income from bank loans ($i_{Bp} FA_{SBL3}$);
i_G is the rate of interest on government bonds;
i_{Bp} is the rate of interest on past bank loans;
$i_D LB_{S3}$ is the interest costs of demand deposits to the banking sector;

i_D is the rate of interest on demand deposits set by the banks;
$\mathbf{G}_{31}\mathbf{p}_1$ is the value of the intermediate inputs by product used in the production of the bank loans;
$\mathbf{L}_{31}\mathbf{w}$ is the wage bill by product incurred in the production of the bank loans;
Π_{GNB} is the total gross profits of the non-banking sector; and
Π_{GB} is the total gross profits of the banking sector.

Because demand deposits and interest payments on bank loans are a cost and income to the banking and non-banking sectors, gross profits of the economy reduces to net profits (Π_{NE}), depreciation (D_E), interest on government bonds (that is, government interest payments to banks and non-banks enterprises—Equation (14)), and household interest income (HII), which is the difference between the interest income made on loans to the household sector ($i_{Bp}FAH_{SBL3}$) minus the interest payments made on household demand deposits (i_DLBH_{S3}):

$$\Pi_{GE} = \Pi_{NE} + i_G FA_{SGB1-3} + D_E + HII = \Pi_{NE} + GP_E + D_E + HII \quad (18)$$

where $GP_E = GP_{iB} + GP_{ib}$ is government interest payments to enterprises; and

$$HII = i_{Bp} FAH_{SBL3} - i_D LBH_{S3}.$$

Profit and income taxes (as well as other payments to the state) are necessary to maintain the demand for state money; thus with regard to profits, there is a profit tax, t_p. In addition, the capitalist class allocates a percentage of its profits to dividends, and the rest is retained to purchase fixed investment goods, reduce liabilities, and acquire new government bonds. So net profits after taxes are distributed between dividends and retained earnings:

$$\Pi_{GE}(1 - t_p) = \Pi_{GRE}(1 - t_p) + \Pi_{GD}(1 - t_p) \quad (19a)$$

$$\Pi_{GEat} = \Pi_{GREat} + \Pi_{Gdat} \quad (19b)$$

where $\Pi_{GE}(1 - t_p) = \Pi_{GEat}$ is net profits after taxes;

$\Pi_{GRE}(1 - t_p) = \Pi_{GREat}$ is retained earnings after taxes used to purchase fixed investment goods and government bonds, and to make payments to retire their bank loans; and

$\Pi_{GD}(1 - t_p) = \Pi_{GDat}$ is dividends to be distributed to ruling class households.

From the above, the link between retained profits after taxes and fixed investment goods, assets, and liabilities is

$$\Pi_{GREat} = \mathbf{Q}_{21}^{T}\mathbf{p_2} + FA_{BE} + LB_{BE} \tag{20}$$

where FA_{BE} is the amount of government bonds purchased by bank and non-bank enterprises; and

LB_{BE} is the amount of liabilities ($LB_{S1,2}$) paid off by non-bank enterprises.

In addition, dividends are distributed to ruling class households, which use them to purchase government bonds (FA_{5RC}):

$$\Pi_{GDat} = FA_{5RC}. \tag{21}$$

Thus, total profits after taxes resolves into the purchase of investment goods and supporting production ($\mathbf{Q}^{T}_{21}\mathbf{p_2} + LB_{BE}$) and the purchase of government bonds (FA_{BE} + FA_{5RC}), which implies that decisions to produce investment goods, make government expenditures, and push workers into debt are the primary factors that determine profits (Erdos and Molnar 1990).

Finally, turning to households and their incomes, working class and dependent class households have bank loans and demand deposits, but do not own government bonds. Thus they spend their entire post-tax income (which consists of wages, government payments, and interest payments on demand deposits) on consumption goods and services and paying off bank loans (LB_{HWDC}) while maintaining their demand deposits. On the other hand, the ruling class spends only its post-tax salary and interest income on consumption goods and services, paying off bank loans (LB_{HRC}) and maintaining its demand deposits and utilizes its post-tax dividend income to purchase government bonds. Thus, drawing from Equations (14),

(15), and (21), the link between total income and consumption goods and services is

$$\begin{aligned}&\mathbf{e}(L^*\mathbf{w})(1-t_i)+GP_d(1-t_i)+i_D FA_{SDD5}(1-t_i)+GP_{ih}(1-t_i)\\&\quad+\Pi_{GD}(1-t_p)(1-t_i)=\mathbf{Q}_{2C}^T\mathbf{p_2}+FA_{5RC}+LB_5\\&\quad=(\alpha+\beta)\mathbf{Q}_{2C}^T\mathbf{p_2}+FA_{5RC}+LB_5\end{aligned} \tag{22}$$

where $\mathbf{e}(L^*\mathbf{w})$ is the total wage bill of the economy;
t_i is an income tax;
$i_D FA_{SDD5}$ is interest income from demand deposits;
FA_{5RC} is the amount of government bonds purchased by ruling class households;
LB_5 is the amount of banking sector liabilities paid off by the households (LB_{HRC} + LB_{HWDC});
and
α (β) is the percentage of consumption goods purchased by the working and dependent (ruling) classes where $\alpha + \beta = 1$.

The social accounting linkages between income-profit-government spending and the surplus delineated in Equations (13), (14), and (20)–(22) implies that incomes and profits before taxes equals the value of the social surplus; that the current government deficit is equal to the value of government bonds purchased by enterprises and the ruling elite; and that taxes represent the government's procurement of "free" labor power and goods and services for the benefit of society as a whole as interpreted by the ruling class.

Social Provisioning as a Going Business

Combining the models of the productive and financial structure of the social provisioning process (Equations (13) and (16)) and the above income-surplus linkages (Equations (18)–(22)), the stock-flow, social accounting descriptively consistent model of the monetary structure of the social provisioning process that produces social activities is the following:

SFSA Model of the Monetary Structure of the Social Provisioning Process

$$
\begin{array}{lll}
\text{Basic Goods Sector} & \mathrm{K_{S1}, FA_{S1}, LB_{S1}}: & \mathrm{G_{11}}\mathbf{p}_1 + \mathrm{L_{11}}\mathbf{w} + \mathbf{\Pi_1} = \mathrm{Q_{d1}}\mathbf{p}_1 \\
\text{Surplus Goods Sector} & \mathrm{K_{S2}, FA_{S2}, LB_{S2}}: & \mathrm{G_{21}}\mathbf{p}_1 + \mathrm{L_{21}}\mathbf{w} + \mathbf{\Pi_2} = \mathrm{Q_{d2}}\mathbf{p}_2 \rightarrow \mathbf{Q}_{2G}^{T}\mathbf{p}_2 + \mathbf{Q}_{2C}^{T}\mathbf{p}_2 + \mathbf{Q}_{2I}^{T}\mathbf{p}_2 \\
\text{Banking Sector} & \mathbf{K}_{S3}, \mathrm{FA_{S3}, LB_{S3}}: & \mathbf{G}_{31}\mathbf{p}_1 + \mathbf{L}_{31}\mathbf{w} + \Pi_{GB} = \mathrm{TR_3} \rightarrow \mathrm{Q_{3L}}(1 + \mathrm{i_B}) \rightarrow \mathrm{FA_{S3}} \\
 & & \qquad \rightarrow \mathrm{LB_{S1-3,5}} \\
\text{State} & \mathbf{K}_{S4}, \quad \mathrm{LB_{S4}}: & \mathbf{Q}_{2G}^{T}\mathbf{p}_2 + \mathbf{L}_{41}\mathbf{w} + \mathrm{GP_d} + \mathrm{GP_{ih}} + \mathrm{GP_E} \rightarrow \mathrm{GS}, \mathbf{K}_{F4} \rightarrow \mathbf{K}_{S4} \\
\text{Household} & \mathrm{FA_{S5}, LB_{S5}}: & \mathbf{e}(\mathrm{L}^{*}\mathbf{w})(1 - \mathrm{t_i}) + \mathrm{GD_d}(1 - \mathrm{t_i}) + \mathrm{i_D FA_{SDD5}}(1 - \mathrm{t_i}) + \mathrm{GP_{ih}}(1 - \mathrm{t_i}) + \\
 & & \Pi_{GD}(1 - \mathrm{t_p})(1 - \mathrm{t_i}) = (\alpha + \beta)\mathbf{Q}_{2C}^{T}\mathbf{p}_2 + \mathrm{FA_{5RC}} + \mathrm{LB_5} \rightarrow \mathrm{HSA, FA_{S5}}, \\
 & \mathrm{LB_{S5}} & \\
\text{Enterprise} & & \Pi_{GRE}(1 - \mathrm{t_p}) = \mathbf{Q}_{2I}^{T}\mathbf{p}_2 + \mathrm{FA_{BE}} + \mathrm{LB_{BE}} \rightarrow \mathrm{K_{S1-3}}, \rightarrow \mathrm{FA_{S1-3}, LB_{S1-3}} \\
 & & \\
\text{Financial Structural Balances} & \text{National Debt} & \mathrm{LB_{S4}} = \mathrm{FA_{SGB1-3,5}} \\
 & \text{Bank Loans:} & \mathrm{FA_{SBL3}} = \mathrm{LB_{1,2,5}} \\
 & \text{Bank Demand Deposits} & \mathrm{LB_{S3}} = \mathrm{FA_{SDD1,2,5}} \\
 & & \\
\text{Current Financial Balances} & \text{Government Deficit:} & \mathrm{GOV_E} - \text{Taxes} = \mathrm{FA_{BE}} + \mathrm{FA_{5RC}} \\
 & \text{Total Profits After Taxes:} & \Pi_{GEat} = \mathbf{Q}_{2I}^{T}\mathbf{p}_2 + \mathrm{LB_{BE}} + \mathrm{FA_{BE}} + \mathrm{FA_{5RC}}
\end{array}
\tag{23}
$$

where $\mathbf{\Pi_1}$ is a $n \times 1$ vector of profits for each intermediate input;
$\mathbf{\Pi_2}$ is a $m - n \times 1$ vector of profits for each surplus product; and
Π_3 is a scalar of profits for financial assets.

The model clearly distinguishes between stocks and flows and accounts for the social destinations of the various flows. For example, it shows the flows of intermediate inputs into the surplus goods sector, and the flows of the various surplus goods and services into their social accounts of households, enterprises, and the state. At the same time, the model mirrors this flow of goods and services with the flow of wage, profit, and state incomes required by households, the state, and enterprises to purchase them. In this manner, the monetized social provisioning process is stock-flow, social accounting consistent and hence acquires the structure of a going business. With the provisioning process as a going plant, the flow of state money ties together market transactions and non-market activities that ensure the continuation of household activities and government services through time. The model also implicitly identifies the central decisions that drive the provisioning process: the decisions that determine the social surplus, employment, prices, profits, household incomes, and interest rates. Because the ruling class (as opposed to the capitalist class by itself) through its acting persons has the productive and administrative capabilities and the legal rights to these decisions, it can direct the provisioning process in its own current and changing future interests. Therefore, the social provisioning process is a socially sustainable process in which each state money transaction is a manifestation and reproduction of the capitalist relationships and hence both sustains and promises a future for the ruling elite and their dependents (Bortis 1997, 2003; Lee 1998; Levine 1978; Kregel 1975).

Agency, Organizations, and Social Provisioning

As it is, the monetary structure model lacks agency that is acting persons. Consequently, the key variables that "drive" the provisioning process, from the social surplus and prices to interest rates and government payments, lack determination. Agency is vested in the acting person (O'Boyle 2010, 2011), which in turn is embedded in various social relationships that give meaning, direction to his/her decisions and acts. That is, the acting person has an ongoing, repeated pattern of culturally particular, ethically informed social relationships. Moreover, in a transmutable world where certain ends are not known, trust, fairness, and inter-personal comparisons along with social relationships affect every decision made by an acting person. Finally, the acting person makes decisions and takes actions to achieve something that is relationally social. Taken together, all decisions regarding prices, social surplus, interest rates, and other key variables are social, non-optimal acts taken to achieve outcomes that affect the social provisioning process and have an impact on government services and household social activities. Thus, the acting person is not a neutered individual, isolated agent, or a representative agent for the entire economy; and neither is the acting person passive, simply reactive, and unwilling to make decisions and intentionally act to change the structures of the provisioning process and the acting person itself. Rather, the acting person has the remarkable property of making the social provisioning process non-self-regulating.

For acting persons to act they need to be located in organizations and institutions, thus analytically transforming the latter into acting persons as well that make decisions and carry out intentional activities. Under capitalism, the social provisioning process has two central "acting" organizations, the state and the business enterprise, and one central "acting" institution, the household. There are additional acting organizations that, through their actions on specific variables, assist in governing economic activity and access to social provisioning, such as market governance organizations (for example, cartels, price leaders, and government regulatory commissions) and class-based organizations (for example, trade unions).[7] Specifically, the key decisions emanating from business enterprises set prices and private sector interest rates, demand investment goods and bank loans, determine the production of consumption goods, employment, profit mark ups, and dividends and retained earnings, affect if not determine wage rates and salaries, and influence taxes on profits; decisions emanating from the state set state interest rates on government bonds and tax rates on incomes and profits, demand government goods and services, determine government payments, employment, and wages and salaries, and influence private sector interest rates; decisions emanating from households allocate their income to purchase the various consumption goods and services produced by enterprises, demand bank loans, and influence wages and salaries; decisions emanating from market governance organizations affect if not determine prices, private sector interest rates, wages and salaries, and profit mark ups; and decisions emanating from trade unions influence if not determine working conditions hence employment and wages and salaries—see Table 1.

Modeling the Economy as a Whole

Combining the monetary structure of the social provisioning process (Equation (23)) with acting organizations and institutions (Table 1) creates the economic model of the social provisioning process that produces social activities:

Table 1

Agency and Key Decisions

Key Decision Variables	Organizations and Institutions with Agency: Business Enterprise	State	Household	Market Governance Organizations	Class-Based Organization—Trade Union
Social Surplus	Demand—$\mathbf{Q}_{2I}$ Determine—$\mathbf{Q}_{2C}$	Demand—$\mathbf{Q}_{2G}$	Choose among—$\mathbf{Q}_{2C}$		
Bank Loans	Demand—$LB_{1,2}$ Determine—Q_{3L}		Demand—LB_5		
Employment	Determine—L_{11}, L_{21}, $\mathbf{L}_{31}$	Determine—$\mathbf{L}_{41}$			Determine/Influence—L_{11}, L_{21}, $\mathbf{L}_{31}$, $\mathbf{L}_{41}$
Prices	Set—$\mathbf{p}$			Set/Affect—$\mathbf{p}$	
Wages/Salaries	Determine/Affect—$\mathbf{w}$	Determine—$\mathbf{w}$	Influence—$\mathbf{w}$	Affect—$\mathbf{w}$	Determine/Influence—$\mathbf{w}$
Profit Mark-Ups (pmu)	Determine—pmu			Determine/Affect—pmu	
Dividends/Retained Earnings	Determine—Π_{GRE}, Π_{GD}				
Interest Rates	Set—i_B, i_D	Set—i_G Influence—i_B		Set/Influence—i_B, i_D	
Government Payments		Determine—GP_4			Influence—GP_d
Taxes	Influence—t_p	Determine—t_i, t_p			

Economic Model of the Social Provisioning Process

Structures

Basic Goods Sector	K_{S1}, FA_{S1}, LB_{S1}:	$G_{11}\mathbf{p}_1 + L_{11}\mathbf{w} + \mathbf{\Pi_1} = Q_{d1}\mathbf{p}_1$
Surplus Goods Sector	K_{S2}, FA_{S2}, LB_{S2}:	$G_{21}\mathbf{p}_1 + L_{21}\mathbf{w} + \mathbf{\Pi_2} = Q_{d2}\mathbf{p}_2 \rightarrow \mathbf{Q}^T_{2G}\mathbf{p}_2 + \mathbf{Q}^T_{2C}\mathbf{p}_2 + \mathbf{Q}^T_{2I}\mathbf{p}_2$
Banking Sector	$\mathbf{K}_{S3}, FA_{S3}, LB_{S3}$:	$\mathbf{G}_{31}\mathbf{p}_1 + \mathbf{L}_{31}\mathbf{w} + \Pi_{GB} = TR_3 \rightarrow Q_{3L}(1 + i_B) \rightarrow FA_{S3} \rightarrow LB_{S1-3,5}$
State	$\mathbf{K}_{S4}, LB_{S4}$:	$\mathbf{Q}^T_{2G}\mathbf{p}_2 + \mathbf{L}_{41}\mathbf{w} + GP_d + GP_{ih} + GP_E \rightarrow GS, \mathbf{K}_{F4} \rightarrow \mathbf{K}_{S4}$
Household	FA_{S5}, LB_{S5}:	$\mathbf{e}(L^*\mathbf{w})(1 - t_i) + GD_d(1 - t_i) + i_D FA_{SDD5}(1 - t_i) + GP_{ih}(1 - t_i) + \Pi_{GD}(1 - t_p)(1 - t_i) = (\alpha + \beta)\mathbf{Q}^T_{2C}\mathbf{p_2} + FA_{5RC} + LB_5 \rightarrow HSA, FA_{S5}, LB_{S5}$
Enterprise		$\Pi_{GRE}(1 - t_p) = \mathbf{Q}^T_{2I}\mathbf{p_2} + FA_{BE} + LB_{BE} \rightarrow K_{S1-3}, \rightarrow FA_{S1-3}, LB_{S1-3}$

Financial Structural Balances	National Debt	$LB_{S4} = FA_{SGB1-3,5}$	
	Bank Loans:	$FA_{SBL3} = LB_{1,2,5}$	(24)
	Bank Demand Deposits	$LB_{S3} = FA_{SDD1,2,5}$	
Current Financial Balances	Government Deficit:	$GOV_E - \text{Taxes} = FA_{BE} + FA_{5RC}$	
	Total Profits after Taxes:	$\Pi_{GEat} = \mathbf{Q}^T_{2I}\mathbf{p_2} + LB_{BE} + FA_{BE} + FA_{5RC}$.	

Agency

Acting Organizations	Key Decision Variables
Business Enterprise	$\mathbf{Q}_{2I}, \mathbf{Q}_{2C}, \mathbf{Q}_{3L}, LB_{1,2}, L_{11}, L_{21}, \mathbf{L}_{31}, \mathbf{p}, \mathbf{w}$, pmu, $\Pi_{GRE}, \Pi_{GD}, i_B, i_D, t_p$
State	$\mathbf{Q}_{2G}, \mathbf{L}_{41}, \mathbf{w}, i_G, i_B, GP_4, t_i, t_p$
Household	$\mathbf{Q}_{2C}, LB_5, \mathbf{w}$
Market Governance	$\mathbf{p}, \mathbf{w}$, pmu, i_B, i_D
Trade Union	$L_{11}, L_{21}, \mathbf{L}_{31}, \mathbf{L}_{41}, \mathbf{w}, GP_d$

The model descriptively links agency with key decisions qua economic variables embedded in the economic structures, thus linking agency with structures. Decisions about any economic variable, given structures, pushes the provisioning process in a particular direction and doing so generates transfactual outcomes. But those same decisions may also transform the structures (and the economic variables and acting organizations as well)—slowly most of the time but rather quickly at other times. This suggests that both structures and acting organizations are historically contingent, that is, vary as capitalism changes. Moreover, given the social nature of the acting person, the acting organization is not separable from society. As a result, the economy and its economic activities are interlinked with various cultural values (such as individualism and egalitarianism) that are evaluative criteria for establishing which social activities are worthwhile and desirable; with norms and beliefs (such as property rights and the work ethic) that explain or justify particular social activities; with societal institutions (such as the legal system and specifically competition and labor laws, state money, and markets); and with technology (such as technical and social knowledge necessary for producing goods and services). These components of the *social fabric* affect the acting organizations and hence the pattern and organization of economic activities delivering the goods and services that make government services and household social activities possible: they give this delivery mechanism or the social provisioning process its meaning, its value (Hayden 1982, 1986, 2006, 2011).

The penultimate step to descriptively model the economy as a whole is to connect the social fabric to acting organizations—see Figure 1. The social fabric, as noted above, consists of cultural values, norms and beliefs, societal institutions, and technology; and they influence the actions of the acting organizations and institutions. In turn, the acting organizations and institutions act on the social provisioning process and social activities, and the latter has an impact on the provisioning process. Thus, in Figure 1 the model of the economy as a whole consists of the economic model of the social provisioning process (acting organizations and the provisioning mechanism) being bracketed at one end by the social fabric and at the other end by government services and household social activities. Hence, not only is the model of the economy socially encased, so is, quite clearly, the economic model of the social provisioning process. Therefore, all social provisioning qua economic activity and decisions are socially embedded, impregnated.

Since agency and structures change, capitalism and its social provisioning process change as well. In particular, the structures and agency that constitute capitalism can be relatively stable for a period of time, followed by a much shorter period of time in which they change more quickly, therefore giving rise to an ongoing stage-crisis-stage-crisis conceptual history of capitalism. Hence, the last step to descriptively model the economy as a whole is to historically contex-

Figure 1

Historically Grounded Model of the Economy as a Whole

Historical Stage of Capitalist Development	Ideology ↓	Capital-Capital Harmony, Capital-Labor Differences, State's Role ↓					↓	Ideology ↓	
Economy as a Whole	Social Fabric	Acting Organizations and Institutions					Provisioning Mechanism	Social Activities	
Column Delivering, Rows Receiving	Cultural Values, Norms, Institutions, Technology	Business Enterprise	State	Household	Market Governance	Trade Union	Social Provisioning Process	Government Services	Household Social Activities
Cultural Values, Norms, Institutions, Technology									
Business Enterprise	Influence								
State	Influence								
Household	Influence								
Market Governance	Influence								
Trade Union	Influence								
Social Provisioning Process		Agency	Agency	Agency	Agency	Agency		Structural Impact	Structural Impact
Government Services		Demand/ Influence	Demand/ Influence	Demand/ Influence	Demand/ Influence	Demand/ Influence	Influence/ Impact		
Household Social Activities		Influence	Influence	Demand/ Influence			Influence/ Impact		

tualize it (McDonough 2010, 2011). Each historical stage of capitalism is distinguished by its ideology, by capital-capital harmony or competitive relationships between business enterprises, by its class-based capital-labor differences or nature of workplace control, and by the state's role in the economy.[8] These features establish the concrete historical form of the model of the economy as a whole and hence of the social provisioning process. In particular, for a given stage of capitalism, ideology informs both the social fabric and social activities; while the capital-capital harmony specifically informs market governance, the capital-labor differences specifically informs trade unions, the state's role specifically informs the state, and all three generally inform all acting organizations and institutions and the provisioning mechanism as well. With this last step, the historically grounded, descriptively consistent model of the economy as a whole can be represented (see Figure 1) as a series of linked components: history linked to the model of the economy, social fabric linked to the economic model of the social provisioning process, agency linked to structures, and social provisioning linked to social activities.

Conclusion

The implications of the model for heterodox economics are visible on a number of different levels. First, it is clear from the way the model of the economy was constructed that it draws upon different modeling approaches and melds them into a coherent whole. In particular, it shows that it is possible to integrate the Sraffian social surplus approach, with the post-Keynesian emphasis on state money, finance, and uncertainty, with the Marxist concern with classes, with the institutionalist social fabric matrix approach, with the acting person of social (and feminist) economics, and with the critical realist methodology of structures, agency, and transmutable reality and still produce a coherent model. Thus, there is little substance to the often voiced view that heterodox economics consists of a disparate group of theories and approaches that cannot be brought together and integrated into a single theoretical approach. Secondly, the model is empirically grounded and draws upon modeling and data found in flow of funds data (http://www.federalreserve.gov/apps/fof/

Default.aspx) and in input-output analysis and GNP data that is generated by governments around the world—for example, see Miller and Blair (2009) and the U.S. Department of Commerce, Bureau of Economic Analysis: http://www.bea.gov/index.htm. Moreover, the social fabric approach has been used for empirical research (Natarajan, Elsner, and Fullwiler 2009). These two points together lead to the conclusion that this model of the economy is well-grounded and almost theoretically unremarkable, which suggests that it should be widely used by heterodox economists.

While the various components of the model are familiar to heterodox economists and empirically well-grounded, the way it is theoretically constructed makes it quite different. For example, the model makes it quite clear, with, for example, its prices as credit-debt indexes, circular production and the absence of scarcity, and the acting person, that heterodox economics is theoretically distinct from mainstream economic theory. Moreover, with agency and the provisioning process bracketed by the social fabric and social activities, the going economy as a whole cannot be reduced to simply a circuit of capital where the only interest of business enterprises and the capitalist class is to make more money. Finally, the model rejects the microeconomics-macroeconomics divide; rather, there is the economy as a whole, which has emergent interconnected components that can be studied. Because this model of the economy is empirically well-grounded, theoretically coherent, includes components well-known to heterodox economists, and rejects mainstream economic theory, it should be, in spite of its theoretical novelties, the model of choice for heterodox economists. In fact, it should be the only model of the economy as a whole that heterodox economist use.

Notes

1. To simplify the analysis, resources are omitted. However, this is not a real shortcoming since following institutional analysis, resources are a produced means of production just like other intermediate inputs. Non-produced relatively scarce inputs or factors of production simply do not exist (De Gregori 1985, 1987; Zimmermann 1951).

2. While scarcity is an organizing principle in mainstream economics, it is also a theoretically incoherent concept—see Levine (1977: 180–186). The

problem with scarcity is that it is an asocial or pre-social concept being used to organize explanations of what are inescapably social activities.

3. The banking sector and $\mathbf{G}_{31}$ and $\mathbf{L}_{31}$ will be introduced below.

4. Beginning with Kalecki (1954: 242–243), this point is frequently argued in post-Keynesian literature: see, for example, Erdos and Molnar (1980, 1983, 1990), Molnar (1981).

5. In a chartalist monetary system where the state has a national debt and runs a current account deficit, banking system reserve requirements have no analytical relevance.

6. It is assumed that the government backs all demand deposits at par, thus making demand deposits equivalent to state money.

7. There are also institutions within the business enterprise and the state, such as working rules, that help facilitate the articulating and defining of objectives and goals and the making of decisions to attain them.

8. In addition, there is an international dimension to capitalism, but because of space constraints, it will not be dealt with.

References

Bell, S. (2001). "The Role of the State and the Hierarchy of Money." *Cambridge Journal of Economics* 25(2): 149–163.

Bortis, H. (1997). *Institutions, Behaviour and Economics Theory: A Contribution to Classical-Keynesian Political Economy.* Cambridge: Cambridge University Press.

——. (2003). "Keynes and the Classics: Notes on the Monetary Theory of Production." In *Modern Theories of Money: The Nature and Role of Money in Capitalist Economies.* Eds. L.-P. Rochon and S. Rossi. pp. 411–474. Cheltenham: Edward Elgar.

DeGregori, T. R. (1985). *A Theory of Technology: Continuity and Changes in Human Development.* Ames: Iowa State University Press.

——. (1987). "Resources Are Not: They Become: An Institutional Theory." *Journal of Economic Issues* 21(3): 1241–1263.

Erdos, P., and F. Molnar. (1980). "Profit and Paper Profit: Some Kaleckian Evolution." *Journal of Post Keynesian Economics* 3(1): 3–18.

——. (1983). "An Answer to Asimakopulos's Comment." *Journal of Post Keynesian Economics* 6(1): 133–139.

——. (1990). *Inflation and Recessions in the U.S. Economy in the 1970s: Price, Profit, and Business Cycles in Theory and Practice.* Budapest: Akademiai.

Gehrke, C., and H. D. Kurz. (2006). "Sraffa on von Borkiewicz: Reconstructing the Classical Theory of Value and Distribution." *History of Political Economy* 38(1): 91–149.

Hayden, F. G. (1982). "Social Fabric Matrix: From Perspective to Analytical Tool." *Journal of Economic Issues* 16(3): 637–662.

——. (1986). "Values, Beliefs, and Attitudes in a Sociotechnical Setting." *Journal of Economic Issues* 22(2): 415–426.

——. (2006). *Policymaking for a Good Society: The Social Fabric Matrix Approach to Policy Analysis and Program Evaluation.* New York: Springer.

——. (2011). "Assessment of the Possibility of Integrating the Social Structure of Accumulation and Social Accounting Matrix with the Social Fabric Matrix Approach." *American Journal of Economics and Sociology* 70(5): 1208–1233.

Jo, T.-H. (2011). "Social Provisioning Process and Socio-Economic Modeling." *American Journal of Economics and Sociology* 70(5): 1094–1116.

Kalecki, M. (1954/1990). *Theory of Economic Dynamics.* In *Collected Works of Michal Kalecki*, vol. II, *Capitalism: Economic Dynamics.* Ed. J. Osiatynski. pp. 205–348. Oxford: Clarendon Press.

Kregel, J. A. (1975). *The Reconstruction of Political Economy: An Introduction to Post-Keynesian Economics.* 2nd ed. London: Macmillan Press.

Kurz, H. D. (2006). "The Agents of Production are the Commodities Themselves: On the Classical Theory of Production, Distribution and Value." *Structural Change and Economic Dynamics* 17: 1–26.

Kurz, H. D., and N. Salvadori. (1995). *Theory of Production: A Long-Period Analysis.* Cambridge: Cambridge University Press.

——. (2000). "Classical Roots of Input-Output Analysis: A Short Account of its Long Prehistory." *Economic Systems Research* 12(2): 153–179.

——. (2005). "Representing the Production and Circulation of Commodities in Material Terms: On Sraffa's Objectivism." *Review of Political Economy* 17(3): 413–441.

——. (2006). "Input-Output Analysis from a Wider Perspective: A Comparison of the Early Works of Leontief and Sraffa." *Economic Systems Research*, 18(4): 373–390.

Lager, C. (2006). "The Treatment of Fixed Capital in the Long Period." *Economic Systems Research* 18(4): 411–426.

Lee, F. S. (1998). *Post Keynesian Price Theory.* Cambridge: Cambridge University Press.

Lee, F. S., and T.-H. Jo. (2011). "Social Surplus Approach and Heterodox Economics." *Journal of Economic Issues* 45(4): forthcoming.

Levine, D. P. (1977). *Economic Studies: Contributions to the Critique of Economic Theory.* London: Routledge and Kegan Paul.

——. (1978). *Economic Theory: The Elementary Relations of Economic Life.* London: Routledge and Kegan Paul.

Lowe, A. (1976). *The Path of Economic Growth.* Cambridge: Cambridge University Press.

Lower, M. D. (1987). "The Concept of Technology Within the Institutionalist Perspective." *Journal of Economic Issues* 21(3): 1147–1176.

McCormick, K. (2002). "Veblen and the New Growth Theory: Community as the Source of Capital's Productivity." *Review of Social Economy* 60(2): 263–277.

McDonough, T. (2010). "The State of the Art of the Social Structure of Accumulation Theory." In *Contemporary Capitalism and its Crisis.* Eds. T. McDonough, M. Reich, and D. M. Kotz. pp. 23–44. Cambridge: Cambridge University Press.

——. (2011). "Social Structures of Accumulation: A 'Punctuated' View of Embeddedness." *American Journal of Economics and Sociology* 70(5): 1234–1247.

Molnar, F. (1981). "Consumers' Investment Versus Capital Investment: A Contribution to Contemporary Business Fluctuations." *Acta Oeconomica* 26(1–2): 133–155.

Mongiovi, G. (2011). "Demand, Structural Interdependence, and Economic Provisioning." *American Journal of Economics and Sociology* 70(5): 1147–1174.

Miller, R. E., and P. D. Blair. (2009). *Input-Output Analysis: Foundations and Extensions.* 2nd ed. Cambridge: Cambridge University Press.

Natarajan, T., W. Elsner, and S. Fullwiler. (2009). *Institutional Analysis and Praxis: The Social Fabric Matrix Approach.* New York: Springer.

O'Boyle, E. J. (2010). "From Individual to Person: An Evolutionary Process Grounded in Human Communication." In *Looking Beyond the Individualism and Homo Economicus of Neoclassical Economics.* Ed. E. J. O'Boyle. pp. 91–118. Milwaukee: Marquette University Press.

——. (2011). "The *Acting* Person: Social Capital and Sustainable Development." *Forum for Social Economics* 40(1): 79–98.

Olsen, E. K. (2011). "Modeling the Economic Surplus in a SAM Framework." *American Journal of Economics and Sociology* 70(5): 1175–1207.

Ranson, B. (1987). "The Institutionalist Theory of Capital Formation." *Journal of Economic Issues* 21(3): 1265–1278.

Veblen, T. (1908). "On the Nature of Capital." *Quarterly Journal of Economics* 22(4): 517–542.

Wray, L. R. (1998). *Understanding Modern Money: The Key to Full Employment and Price Stability.* Cheltenham: Edward Elgar.

——. (2003). "Seigniorage or Sovereignty?" In *Modern Theories of Money: The Nature and Role of Money in Capitalist Economies.* Eds. L.-P. Rochon and S. Rossi. pp. 84–102. Cheltenham: Edward Elgar.

Zimmermann, E. W. (1951). *World Resources and Industries: A Functional Appraisal of the Availability of Agricultural and Industrial Materials.* Revised ed. New York: Harper and Brothers, Publishers.

Index

for

Studies in Economic Reform and Social Justice: Social Provisioning, Embeddedness, and Modeling the Economy